Peter, Bogey, Mike

PETER, BOGEY, MIKE

A Love Story, a War Story, 1942–1945

Irvin S. Cooper

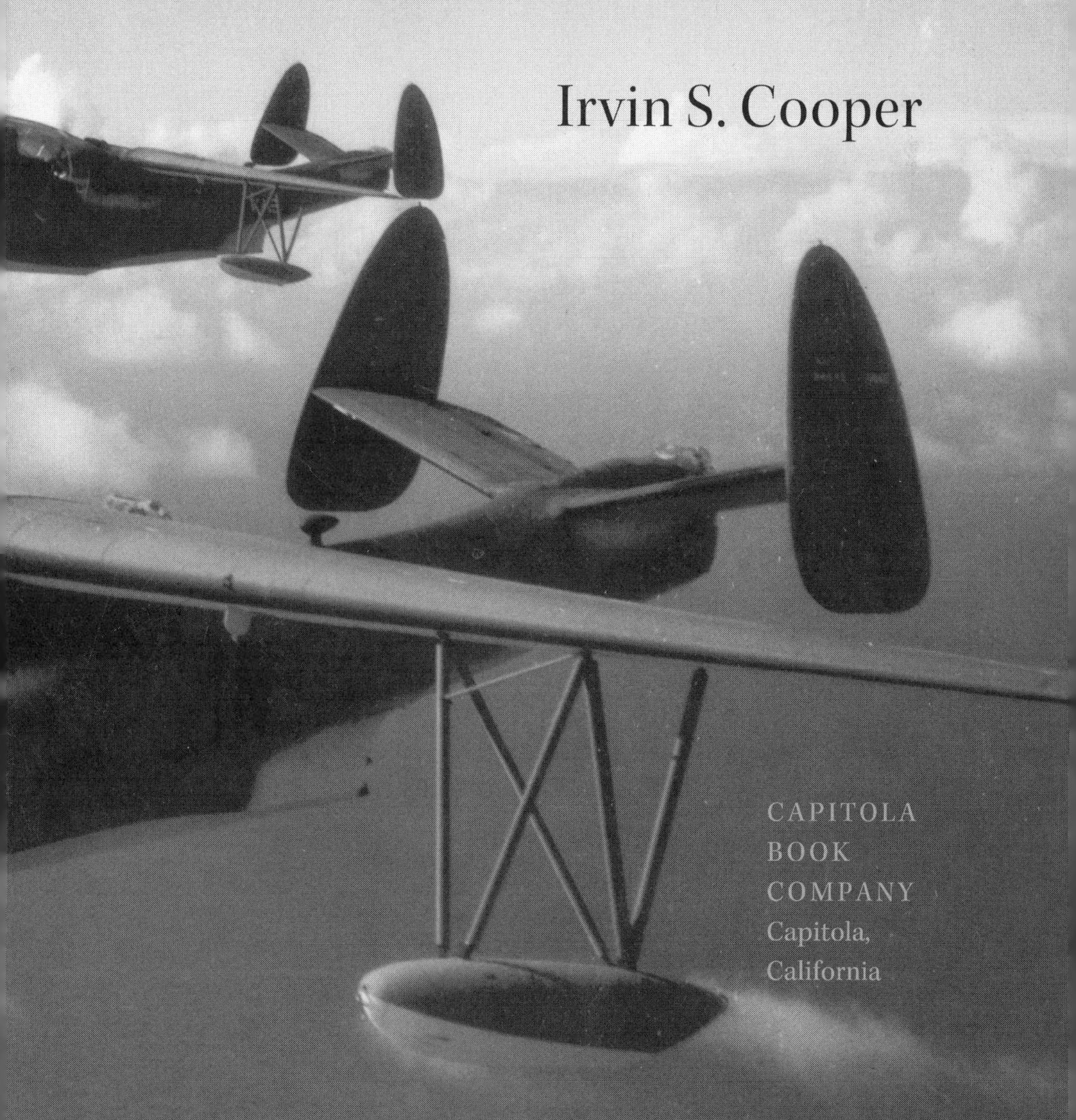

CAPITOLA BOOK COMPANY
Capitola, California

Capitola Book Company
1601 41st Avenue
Capitola, CA 95010
www.capitolabook.com

Designed and produced at Side By Side Studios, San Francisco, CA
sidebysidestudios.net

Hardcover:
13 digit: 978-0-932319-16-6
10 digit: 0-932319-16-5

Softcover:
13 digit: 978-0-932319-17-3
10 digit: 0-932319-17-3

First edition 2014

Printed in the United States of America

14 15 16 17 18 5 4 3 2 1

To Elaine,
to my plane,
to those who didn't get a chance to tell their stories

Contents

Acknowledgements

This started as an odd group of short stories of incidents during WWII that affected my determination and thoughts, and reflected my memories as the years have passed. George Ow, the patriarch of our Santa Cruz family, seemed intrigued and suggested putting them into a single narrative of my enlisted years. He took over the role as patron in getting this story published, and solicited a top designer in Mark Ong to expedite its publishing. My wife, Elaine, who along with the aircraft I flew, is really the heroine of the story. Her recollections and help are part of the narrative as it came together. From handwritten sheets to an old IBM typewriter, I found Doris Goldman Horning, who enthusiastically recorded them on her computer and helped getting me started on my own.

Since I was a pilot of the Navy's largest twin engine seaplane, the PBM Martin Mariner, I read a book, *For a Bag of Rice,* as told by a PBM pilot named William Quinn, recalling his horrific experiences in a forced landing and capture by the Japanese. I was influenced by another book, *Twice Surreal,* by Stuart Gardner Hunt, a Canadian pilot shot down over Europe in his Halifax Mark III, who became a German prisoner in the infamous Stalag Luft III barracks. I contacted him by e-mail and we became friends through the process.

With his wife, Bridget, and my wife, Elaine, we broke bread together in Rancho Bernardo, California, and I thank him for his friendship, encouragement, and guidance. My fellow pilot, Austin Puvogel, wrestling with his own story, kept pushing me on my own.

My brother-in-law, Dr. Ernest Shaw, his son, Dr. Dan Shaw, and the rest of my San Diego family seemed overly enthusiastic about my story and kept prodding for continuous chapters. Their support was most encouraging. My son, Robert, was invaluable in the computer transmissions, and along with his sister, Kitty, contributed as comma critics and paragraph paragons. Second daughter Peggy, and her husband, Bob Waters, were most verbal in pushing the story forward, along with the support of my four grown grandkids, Kelsey, Merrick, Tori, and Greg. Not limited to family, Rudy Saltzer, Connie Bartosh, Cathy Strull, Eva Elkins, and DFC compatriot, Captain Tim Hays, USN, retired, all kept urging me on. The Zimmerman family, Derk, Susan, and Luke, were a constant rooting support. A little help from Google didn't hurt. It was my good friend, Jerry Fox, who seemed most practical. His suggestion was, "Write fast, time is running out." I was most fortunate in being able to heed his advice.

Introduction

It all started while I was walking under the pier at Venice Beach, California. I stumbled upon a rather smooth object and picked it up out of curiosity. It was a worn bottle smoothed by what I discovered were thousands of years of tumbling seas and surfs. As I manipulated the cap, an odd-shaped genie suddenly flitted out of the bottle and hovered above me. I was startled and excited because I thought all genies were capable of producing whatever the finder wished. However, this genie explained that I had discovered it eons before its maturity, and therefore it was limited in its powers. The genie was quite apologetic about its abilities to produce miracles for its finder. However, it did claim to have the ability to help me recollect things past. I apologized for releasing it prematurely, and in contrast to our understanding of genies, I asked what help I could be? Since I could not get the genie back in its bottle, it insisted on being as helpful as its powers would allow.

Through a telecommunication system far more sophisticated than our advances of the science, the genie was aware of the powers that genies generally provided in the event of their release from confinement. It even recalled the story of the drunk who had discovered a genie that could provide him with any two wishes in the world. The drunk asked for a bottle of beer that would never empty.

The genie immediately produced the requested bottle. The drunk was so thrilled that for his second request, he asked for another bottle just like the first.

To get back to our business at hand, the genie said, due to its lack of maturity, it could not give me any wish I wanted as a genie normally would. However, it could give me a limited review of any three years of my life that I would like to relive. This, of course, was done with due apologies for the limitations of its abilities at this time of its release. I guess it wasn't too difficult a choice for me, but in a quick analysis of my life so far, I selected the years 1942 through 1945. It was during these years that I fell in love, joined the Naval Air Corps, and went off to World War II. The timeframe thus established, with a click and a *Poof!* the genie was gone.

I suddenly reflected on the written contents of this book: my life as a Navy pilot, flying the largest twin-engine seaplane of its time, the PBM Martin Mariner. As much as my tale is about the airplane, it is also a love story of my pursuit of Elaine, the girl I met and loved. But the hero is the Mariner that brought me home to my wife, a war marriage that has lasted sixty-nine years so far. This is my true story of the woman and the airplane I loved, and the PBM's contribution in WWII.

As I started to recall the events between '42 and '45, many memorable incidents came to light. However, the inadequacy of my genie's powers became evident as I recorded my memories for the years chosen. My genie gave me a great overview, but fell short on some finer details. With my straining memory and a sixty-year-old flight log book, some specific names of characters and dates are still not clear. Some names have been changed and some incidents may have been neglected or exaggerated, but the character of the recollections and experiences of the years recorded are as authentic as memories permit.

In hopes of clarifying any questions or doubts that I may have had, I keep shuffling and looking along the sand of Venice Beach for magic bottles. The only thing I've managed to encounter so far is a contemporary beer can half-filled with water and seaweed. No genie could have resided there, and I'm sure if it had, it would have been long gone. . . . *Poof!*

It is with my genie's help that I share with you my war years between 1942 and 1945, my bond with my Elaine, and the awareness and contributions of the seaplane and her crews in the war against Japan. Anywhere, anytime, the PBM Martin Mariner—whose call letters were "Peter, Bogey, Mike."

1

A Light in a Blackout

February 3, 1942. Searching for Japanese aircraft over Los Angeles

Sirens screeched through the air of Los Angeles. Wurlitzer and RCA Victor radios of the day blared broadcasts excitedly warning the public to turn off their house lights and draw all blinds and curtains. Electric signs and streetlights were turned off. Motorists were directed to dim their headlights if driving. A Japanese submarine with a catapult aircraft was sighted off the coast of Santa Barbara, preparing to bomb Los Angeles. It was February 3, 1942, less than two months after the Pearl Harbor attack.

The National Guard had installed a battery of guns and Hollywood klieg lights atop Baldwin Hills in the West Adams district of L.A. Their piercing shafts of light angled upward into the darkened sky. Our lack of proper military equipment was evident in the use of temporary paraphernalia to ward off possible attack of an enemy threatening our shores. Our newsreels at the time showed how unprepared America was as the war broke out with Japan. Our minimal deterrence showed new recruits feigning bayonet attacks with broom handles. Factory production was being converted from peacetime products to weapons of war. These movie preview search lights angled upward, searching for an enemy until the real lights could be produced.

I stepped out of my family duplex on Buckingham Road and looked up into the black night. With no streetlights or reflective lighting, you could clearly see stars and lights of the heavenly worlds blinking brightly as rarely seen in a city atmosphere. It was an enthralling sight, bringing to mind my Boy Scout campouts in the local mountains of Big Bear and Lake Arrowhead.

As I got into my maroon '41 Chevy Club Coupe, I dimmed my lights and backed smartly out of my driveway. I had paid $900 cash for the car, brand new, from my Lockheed paychecks of $50 per week. I crossed the sidewalk into the street and saw the reverse silhouette of a magnificent feminine figure standing on the sidewalk two doors north of my house. I moved my car slowly along the same curb side of the street and stopped. I saw her looking upward at the sparkling scene. "Isn't that something?" I called out. She looked at me, surprised, and responded "I've never seen the stars so bright."

I recognized her. Her parents ran a little delicatessen store on West Adams, where my folks frequently shopped. I had seen her on occasion helping out behind the counter. She was two years behind me in Dorsey High School, and I certainly didn't know she lived there.

"I remember you," I said. "I'm Irv Cooper, and I live two doors down. What's your name?"

"Elaine," she volunteered. "I know who you are. You were a senior when I was a freshman. You were a cheerleader, and you were on the, what's it called, the track team, and the editor of the school newspaper."

That was my full high school resume and the highlight of my high school years. I was flustered and flattered. I turned off the ignition and looked directly at her.

Dorsey High opened in 1938 as the newest and most modern school in Los Angeles. I was the first editor of the school newspaper and my name appeared in the headline on the first page, so I was pretty well known on campus.

Although I remembered seeing her behind the counter in her parents' store, I certainly didn't recall how pretty she was. Of course she was much younger then, and now I thought, what a difference.

I tried to pick up where she left off. "Yeah, we called the new school paper the Dorseygram, after the popularity of the telegram."

"Who came up with that name?" she asked.

I opened the door to my car, got out, and stood next to her on the walkway between the curb and the sidewalk.

"It was chosen by the newspaper staff in journalism. I thought it was right for the time." I went on to explain. "Private telephones were rather expensive and most lines were shared with unknown neighbors. Telegrams were fairly cheap and a lot more private." I paused and then thought I'd try a touch of humor.

"Do you know the fastest ways of communication?" I asked.

She looked at me oddly as I answered before she could respond. "Telegraph, telegram, or tell a woman."

That joke went nowhere, and I suddenly found myself without words. I was so surprised to be suddenly talking to someone so attractive. I pretended to look skyward, but my peripheral vision delivered a view far more appealing. Still looking up, with an eye on her, I blurted out "Beautiful."

The word was directed to the stars, but my feelings were earth-bound for the profile next to me. Her head was tilted upward as she nodded and continued admiring nature's lights. This whole episode was so spontaneous, I was completely caught off guard. I didn't want this moment to pass. A searchlight cast a momentary arc across the sky, while my mind kept groping for something to say. In that pause she asked me, "What are you doing now? Are you in college?"

I was able to gather my thoughts quickly. "Well, I'm working the graveyard shift at Lockheed Aircraft in Burbank, and then I go to L.A. City College on Vermont Avenue in the morning."

I thought I detected a touch of smugness when she responded. "I'm going to U.C.L.A."

"Yeah, Vermont is where U.C.L.A. was located before they moved to Westwood," was the only thing I could come up with.

I tried another tack. "Did you hear about the Japanese submarine?" I glanced skyward and continued. "It has a catapult plane that's supposed to bomb L.A."

"I heard it on the radio before I came out," she said.

I stood next to her and saw no fear in her face. What I did see were her beautiful green eyes, brunette hair with an amber clip, an athletic figure, and a perky nose. With her bobby socks and penny loafers, she wore a light beige pullover, filled to perfection. I was smitten and encouraged. I pursued the action.

"Would you like to sit on the lawn? I have a cover in the seat of my car."

Before she could answer I pulled out a red plaid blanket from the backseat and set it on the grass behind the sidewalk. I sat down and suspected a touch of hesitancy as she came forward. I offered my hand, but she proved herself quite capable of getting comfortable on her own.

We sat quietly with a mutual moment of appraisal. We talked, or should I say, I talked. I told her that several nights a week, I would go to the Palladium in Hollywood and stand around the bandstand and watch Tommy or Jimmy Dorsey, or Benny Goodman, or Glenn Miller, or any of the big-name bands that came into town. I would listen to live music until I had to leave for Lockheed. My favorite performer, I continued, was Frank Sinatra. I would stand under his mike and look up at him as he sang, looking at a thin scar on his neck, and even catching his spittle as he crooned out his songs. Couples would be hugging and dancing, and I would have to leave for work.

She nodded as I went along, and she told me she liked swing music. Then she asked me about the Service. Since every young man was being called to serve unless they planned to finish college, she asked me my plans. I told her I had not received a draft notice but was wondering in what branch I wanted to enlist. I told her I had been a pacifist, and whenever I passed the Veterans Hospital on the corner of Wilshire and San Vicente I would see several hundred World War I veterans sitting in wheelchairs, staring out at the traffic. I was told they were victims of mustard gas and not capable of taking care of themselves. At that point, I decided I was against war and that I would get an important job in civilian defense. While working at Lockheed, the Japanese attacked Pearl Harbor and my attitude changed, quickly. I wanted to fight for my country.

I noticed someone, whom I suspected was a brother, occasionally looking out a window to check on his baby sister. She told me her brother Harry was an engineer and was just commissioned an officer in the Navy. I knew her other brother, Ernie, from Boy Scouts and school classes, and he was now in med school and was going to be commissioned in the Army as a doctor. Whatever thoughts I may have had about joining the Navy as a sailor immediately left my mind. I felt I was already competing with Elaine's brothers. If they were officers, I had to become an officer. With a couple years of junior college, how could I qualify? If you had a high school diploma and could pass an entry test, you could qualify for Army flight training. If you succeeded in earning your wings, you would become an Army pilot and be commissioned a second lieutenant. The Navy Air Corps required a college degree to apply.

The sirens went off. People emerged from their homes to announce the air raid was over. A gas storage tank had actually been bombed in the Santa Barbara area, and the bombing threat to L.A. was over. The streetlights went on. People emerged from their homes as the klieg lights stopped flashing across the sky; motorists on the street turned on their full headlights. It was getting late for work, so I thanked Elaine for her company and tossed the blanket in the backseat of my car. I did not stop at the Palladium that night, but went to work riveting P-38 fighter planes at Lockheed Aircraft. I don't know how many rivets I bucked, or missed; my mind was completely on the girl in the beige pullover sweater.

Truly, a light in a blackout!

2

Pursuing Elaine and the Naval Air Corps

My '41 Chevy Club Coupe

You never met my best friend. His name was Bud Plone and had you ever met him, you would have really liked him. Everyone did. He and I were inseparable starting from the eighth grade in junior high until long after we graduated from Dorsey High School. We became Eagle Scouts together, shared classes, played sports, rode the waves at Venice Beach, and, naturally, wanted to join the Service together. We both wanted the Navy. Bud was fascinated by the blimps and wanted to get into Lighter than Air. We had spent too many days ditching school to qualify for a college entry, so we were trying to make it up at junior college while working at Lockheed. I could hardly wait to tell him about Elaine.

Whenever I was leaving or returning to my home, I would slowly drive by her home hoping to catch her outside. She lived in a nice white Spanish-style house with a red tile roof. I became more familiar with her home as I made numerous efforts to casually walk by and hope for a chance meeting. I finally realized her lack of exposure must be due to her dedication to study or to helping her folks in the family store. My walking seemed a repetitious step in futility. Eventually, I decided that going to her parent's store for an unnecessary loaf of bread seemed like a good idea.

It was a late Friday afternoon when I meandered into Warshawky's Delicatessen, and pretended surprise at seeing her behind the counter. As she rang up the sale on an antique cash register, I tried not to stare. I had memorized the look of her hazel eyes in the blackout, but under the open bulb overhead, and the light through the glass storefront, the passion of my memory was amplified. She had high cheek bones and a perfectly formed nose to veil a look of sweet aloofness. I casually asked her if she would like to go to the movies Saturday night. She told me she had to study after work and that she had a date that night. A jealous pang hit me in the chest, but I kept trying. I told her I had a pickup softball game every Saturday morning, but my best friend and I were going to Ocean Park in the afternoon, and asked if she would like to join us. As casual as I tried to appear on the outside, my heart was pounding on the inside. She mentioned something about studying, or working, then cleared the time with her mother, and agreed, if we could be back within four hours.

Bud had made a full-size drawing of a cartoon cowboy on my bedroom wall, waving his hand goodbye. He had drawn the same cowboy on his bedroom wall, waving hello. I had cut an old western hat in two, and pinned one half on the head on my wall and the other half on the head in Bud's bedroom. We had appliquéd a checkered cowboy shirt cut to fit the torso of the drawings on both walls. A cartoon balloon was drawn where mine said, "I'm going to Bud's," and on his wall the balloon said, "I just came from Cooper's." We used to wear matching cowboy shirts and boots from

Two buddies: me (left) and Bud Plone (right)

Sears, Roebuck. On Saturday, after softball, Bud came to my house and we went to get Elaine, two doors away.

I rang her doorbell and before a series of chimes completed their musical entrance, she stepped out on the porch. She wore a skirt and sweater with bobby socks in penny loafer shoes. She seemed very nonchalant and I introduced her to Bud when we walked to the car. She acknowledged that she knew of him when she was a freshman at Dorsey and voted for him when he had run for school president against our best friend, George Woodford. Bud's ego was comforted, and he graciously climbed into the backseat while Elaine joined me in the front. She brought three sandwiches made from the store and looked for an open bench when we arrived at the beach. Bud suggested we walk to Venice, a short distance from Santa Monica, and watch the athletes at Muscle Beach. We found a bench and observed a few stalwarts working out on the rings, the bars, and the weights as we ate a delicious deli lunch. Bud told Elaine that he and I occasionally took advantage of the Muscle Beach facilities. A quiet spell passed as we overlooked the sand and the ocean beyond.

Bud and me on Muscle Beach

I tried to be clever. A couple walked by trying to bribe their child with some form of cookie. Bud set up a line from a series of jokes we had used in the past, "Look, they're trying to give him cookies for being good."

I immediately responded by saying, "Hey, when I was his age, I was good for nothing."

A very thin lady passed by and I flippantly said, "My God,

that gal is so thin that if she drank tomato juice, she would look like a thermometer."

Elaine was reserved and I couldn't tell if I was making points or just being an idiot.

It was a little cool for the beach, but we toured the pier and threw pennies in some open jars and darts at balloons and threw baseballs at wooden bottles. In spite of our athletic prowess, we won no teddy bears or furry stuffed animal. We talked about school, and Elaine told us that she was majoring in sociology but was heavily into French. We told her our concerns about the Service and our hopes of getting into the Naval Air Corps. She was warm with a feeling of reserve that hyped my desire to know her better than just in the thoughts of my fantasy.

The time melted away, but we returned Elaine home within the prescribed hour, and I walked her to the door as Bud waited in the car. I tried hinting about her date, but she laughed and said it was an old school friend and that she was not involved with anyone nor had the time. She thanked me for a fun break from the store and gave me her phone number to call. I bounded off her front porch steps, energized with hope. Bud enjoyed our four-hour threesome and heartily approved of my enchantment. And so the pursuit and courtship of Elaine began.

Somewhere along the third or fourth date, our lips touched. It happened in my Chevy Club Coupe, saying goodnight after going to the movies. She quickly disappeared into the house as soon as I got her to the door. I figured she didn't want to take a chance on either of her brothers catching her in any compromised position. But, in my case, it was my affirmation of love at every sight.

Night work at Lockheed and Los Angeles Junior College in the morning proved a rather tight schedule. The War was escalating, and Bud and I still hadn't received our draft notices. Was our job of building airplanes going to keep us out of the Service? People were already staring at us and wondering why two healthy young men like us weren't in uniform.

As each week passed, hundreds of Army Air Corps cadets were assigned to preflight school in Santa Ana. Weekends were a mass migration to Hollywood. Young men from all over the country, in California for the first time, were free to realize their fantasy world of Hollywood and the beaches of the Pacific Ocean. Sunset Boulevard was closed to traffic for the hub of weekend leaves for the thousands of Service people training within its proximity. The Hollywood Canteen was set up and movie stars showed their support by attending dances, distributing doughnuts, and posing for photographs to a most appreciative fan base. Celebrities were on a constant move, selling War Bonds to the public. Action, promotion, support, everywhere.

Two of our closest friends in high school joined the Army Air Corps. Jerry Foreman was Dorsey's quarterback on the football team and the catcher in baseball. He was an A student and wanted to become a doctor so he could cure an infirmed sister. George Woodford, who beat Bud by a dozen votes for student body president, followed Jerry into the Army Air Corps shortly after.

My twenty-first birthday was about to show up on the 6th of June. I asked Elaine to celebrate it with me by inviting her to the Palladium for dinner and dancing. Upon her acceptance, I bought a sports jacket at Desmond's and new slacks at Silverwood's, two men's clothing stores in what was the beginning of the Miracle Mile on Wilshire Boulevard. Why I purchased new clothes when I expected to be in a military uniform shortly, is hard to explain because it was an extravagant expenditure. But that was the date that pretty well secured our relationship. It was the first time I held her in my arms, dancing and trying to coordinate a smooth two-step to the music. I actually laid out $3.00 for a snapshot at our table, framed in a Pal-

Elaine and me on my twenty-first birthday date at the Hollywood Palladium, 1942

ladium folder from a scantily dressed photographer. That moment still smiles out at me in the bookcase of our home.

Our patience bore fruit. As the Army Air Corps continued to sign up high school graduates into their flight training program, the pool of eligible college graduates became more limited. The Navy's college graduate requirement became a concern in their enlistment program. In order to compete for more enlistees, it opened a window for application. If you had two years of college and could pass a strict entry and physical test, you could apply for the Navy's V-12 program as a naval air cadet. Bud and I finished our semester and applied to the Naval Air Corps.

I was terrified of failing. I had not been one to study and, to me, the thought of not qualifying would have devastated my ego in

Elaine's eyes. To bolster my spirits, I said to myself, "If they don't take me, it is their loss."

I have tried to carry that creed through all applications of my life.

Bud and I took the test with a dozen other applicants and went through a roundhouse of questions, covering varied topics. It seemed that the test was also searching for reaction, stability, and adjustment to situations rather than specifics. We also had to respond within a specified time period. Bud and I passed, congratulated by an officer in charge, and were told we would be notified where and when to take our "physical."

It was 3rd and Broadway in an older brick office building in downtown Los Angeles, where we were subjected to a thorough physical examination by Dr. Joel Pressman. He wore the insignias of a lieutenant commander, and was the husband of Claudette Colbert, the actress who starred with Clark Gable in *It Happened One Night*. We sailed through the exam and were told to report to the adjacent recruitment office for further instruction, information, and the swearing-in process.

We met the lieutenant in charge with several naval personnel sitting at desks surrounded by posters of naval aircraft, "Buy Bonds," and "We Want You!" We were excited but had one reservation. Before signing our commitment to the Navy, we broached our greatest concern. With pen in hand, I asked, "Will the Navy be able to keep friends together?"

Without hesitation, the officer placed a hand on each of our shoulders, almost shocked at the question, and responded, "Why of course, the Navy will do everything it can to keep buddies together." Naively, Bud and I couldn't have been more pleased.

With this assurance, we were eagerly sworn into the Navy's V-12 program and told we would be called upon as soon as facilities opened. We expressed our excitement by jumping into Bud's '39 convertible Buick, top down, and drove the length of Wilshire Bou-

Ensign Harry Warshawsky

Dr. Ernest Shaw

levard to the Santa Monica Pier. We headed to the roller coaster to challenge our bravery. It was in the front seat that I went through the twists and turns, climbs and dips, and experienced the most frightening moments of my life. In my whole Navy career, nothing was as gripping as that ride. What I realized was that I had no control over the maneuvers of the roller coaster, but the control of the aircraft was completely in my hands.

I called Elaine to tell her that Bud and I had passed the tests and were sworn into the Navy's V-12 program. We would soon be called to start training as U.S. naval aviators. For me, it was everything I had been hoping for: the chance to match the status of Elaine's brothers, with the title of Officer and Gentleman.

Elaine's oldest brother was commissioned as Ensign Harry Warshawsky. He liked his name because he claimed everyone always remembered him. Her other brother Ernie changed his name after graduating from high school when he enrolled at U.C.L.A. In spite of his Phi Beta Kappa credentials, he went through college and got into medical school, evading existing ethnic prejudices, with his name changed to Dr. Ernest Shaw. Elaine, who recalled people making fun of her name, followed Ernie through U.C.L.A. as Elaine Shaw.

Heck, my name was Irving Harold Cooper when I graduated high school. My step-dad, a great guy named Sam Shiell, wanted to officially adopt me and give me his name. I explained to him that for eighteen years I had gone with my name Cooper, and I didn't want to give it up. In order to honor him, I legally changed my name to Irvin Shiell Cooper, using his last name as my middle name. While I was at it, I dropped the "g" off Irving and made it Irvin. When I was a kid, I was sometimes teased as "Oyving," and I really got upset and didn't want that to happen once I joined the Service. I used to get so mad, I even developed a good left jab, and had an occasional black eye to prove it.

3

Lone Pine and Susanville

Lone Pine, California, 1943

Weeks passed with no call from the Navy. People continued to stare, wondering if we were draft dodgers. It was the middle of summer when we got our first notice. The preflight program was backed up and the Navy advised us that we would be sent to a civilian pilot training school until we could enter the V-12 program. We reported to the recruitment office to get our orders. I was assigned to Lone Pine, California, and Bud was assigned to Baker. Here the Navy had promised to keep us together and the first act was separation. We were crushed. We didn't know to whom to complain, so we launched our unhappiness at the yeoman, a Navy all-around secretary giving out the orders. We explained that the enlisting officer promised to keep us together. We emphasized his promise. With some amusement, the yeoman eyed the two of us, flipped some papers on his desk, and switched names from Baker to Lone Pine. Bud and I would be together and some other candidate would go to Baker. We expressed our gratitude and vowed to check with the yeoman on all future assignments.

The Navy asked us to provide our own khaki shirts, and pants, a black tie, a brown leather jacket, and hiking boot shoes. We were to bring a change of clothes and our own toiletries and to meet at the recruitment office on the appointed day. Two buses, one to Lone Pine, a 220-mile drive, and the other to Baker about 180 miles away, waited to take us to our destinations.

Through heat and dust, our bus stopped in front of Lone Pine High School at the edge of town. We were assigned to the football field behind the school. Paralleling the running track were ten canvas tents with wooden floors. A coach came forward and asked the group to line up for roll call. As each name was called out, we were to take our gear into a tent that contained four metal bed frames, a mattress, and a roll of linen on each. The coach turned out to be Glenn Ackerman, our coach at Los Angeles City College, hired by the Navy to conduct its civilian program. Apparently acting under

Navy orders, he was very brisk and did not respond to our greeting. Each student was asked to answer "Aye, aye," when their name was called. After the fortieth "Aye, aye," we were dismissed to our assigned tents and given thirty minutes to line up promptly for dinner.

Bud and I were assigned different tents. I met Milt Gibson, an athletic product from Pasadena, and Al Nadler, a Jewish kid from Boyle Heights. Bob Phillips, a handsome young man from Central California, was the fourth of our group. We selected our cots, stowed our belongings, and reported in line for dinner. From the field at Lone Pine High School, we marched in an orderly fashion two blocks into the heart of Lone Pine, where we filled the entire restaurant allocated by the Navy for our daily meals.

The Lone Pine camp was divided into two groups. Half of us were assigned to flight school in the morning and ground school in the afternoon, and the other half, the reverse. We ate in two shifts, thirty minutes apart. Reveille was at 6:00 a.m. and showers and bathroom facilities were in the adjacent gym. My tent was assigned the morning flight school, and Bud's tent as well.

We all became fast friends. Al, who was raised in Boyle Heights, had gone to the same schools as I until I moved to West Adams at the age of thirteen. He helped me with ground school, teaching me, instead of Bud, who tried telling me. Our only tie with Milt was that he lived near the Rose Bowl and Bud and I had sold Coca-Colas and hot dogs at many of the games. We discussed and studied our ground school, but in flight school we were on our own. We were all aware that failure in either section was cause for "washout" even before we started our V-12 program. This program was to keep us occupied until the real Navy facilities were ready.

Don't ask me how I graduated high school without taking a science, math, or foreign language course. I was good in journalism and English, and did very well in art, metal, print, and woodshop.

I loved phys ed. Somehow, without guidance, I had been academically deprived. Ground school was difficult. I found myself trying to catch up and keep up with everyone else. On one of the major math tests, I got stuck on a question whose answer was worth fifty percent of the score. Although we were closely monitored, out of panic, I caught Al's eye. He excused himself to the bathroom, and upon his return I was extended the same courtesy. In the bathroom, (or as we were instructed to use the Naval term, "head"), in the toilet paper holder between the roll and the clamp, Al had folded the answer on a small piece of paper. The angle of the eclipse was noted and I passed the test. I justified this potential "washout" offense in my mind. Sometimes it is more important to be creative and ingenious in a situation of concern than to be academically correct.

Part of our preliminary training was physical. Coach Ackerman acted as if we were his varsity football team. We learned to duck-walk, stretch, and run 440-yard laps around the track for any infraction. We were required to perform daily exercises and engage in assigned sporting activities, basketball, football, and track. I did pretty well and bettered my friend Al.

The town of Lone Pine had about ten girls in our age range and about forty young men seeking company. Bud spent free time drawing cartoons. Milt and I were always writing to our girlfriends, and Al, as we got to know, always got the local girl, and modestly bragged about it. But it was the civilian flight school that was most important.

The Lone Pine Airport was a block away from the high school. It consisted of a single dirt airstrip, an office shack, and a dozen-plus Cessnas and Cub airplanes to train in. My instructor was Norman Granger, a tall, amiable pilot, who showed great concern for his students. On my first flight, he helped strap me into his Cessna, and rolled down the runway and into the air. At about 2,000 feet, with dual controls in the aircraft, sitting side by side, he asked me to take the joystick and hold steady to get the feel of flying the plane. I guess I jostled the control up and down, and could feel the aircraft reacting in an undulating manner. It was not the response Mr. Granger was looking for. He then took over the controls, saying, "This plane can fly better than you can." He showed me how to trim the craft and rested his hand on the stick, and with practically no movement, it flew itself smoothly ahead. "You can't fly any better than that. Don't overdo the controls."

I was sitting on the right side when he said, "Open your door." At 2,000 feet up in the air, I was surprised, but being strapped in tightly, I pushed my door open as instructed and the air stream turned the plane immediately to the right. I closed the door and the Cessna flew straight ahead. Mr. Granger then opened his door, and the craft then turned easily to the left. Obviously, we don't open doors to turn, but he showed me the effect in making my turns. He showed me how to use the rudders, dip the nose, or raise it up. He demonstrated a stall, and cautioned me on the use of power and what to watch on the needle and ball on the limited dashboard. The hour went quickly, and we landed smoothly and taxied to the parking line and cut the engine. I successfully survived my first flight demonstration and looked forward to taking the controls.

In subsequent days, I imitated his actions. We practiced stalls, spins, and diving out of them. I did wingovers and flew figure eights, practiced landings and takeoffs in touch-and-go exercises, and learned to taxi with care. I wrote Elaine daily describing my flying progress.

After about ten hours of flight time, Mr. Granger climbed into the plane and sat with his arms folded without touching the joystick that controlled the plane. He had me take off and I circled the field and landed smoothly. "Try it again," he said. I took off on a touch-and-go and came back in a bounce landing that caused him to frown. "Again," he said, and I pushed the throttle forward.

The next landing was smooth as glass, and he pushed his hand forward for another go-around. Again, I bounced all over the place. He was exasperated. "Pull over," he growled. I taxied off to the side of the runway and braked to a stop. I was frustrated. He opened his door and turned back to me as he started out of the plane. "I'm trying to get you to make two smooth landings in a row. It's not safe in this damn plane. I'm getting the hell out."

As he hit the ground, he looked at me and winked. He put his thumb up and yelled "Good luck," and closed the door and walked away. I sat alone in the two-seat plane.

I checked for other aircraft, taxied to the end of the runway, and hit the throttle to take off on my first solo flight. As the Cessna left the ground and headed skyward, I let out a loud yelp that no one could hear but me. I think I screamed, "Yippee!"

It was a moment of realization that I was alone. I got myself up in the air, and the only one who could get me down safely was me. I had trained and been tested daily and felt perfectly confident. I followed the course that I had practiced each day, and after thirty minutes of flight headed back to the airstrip. I banked into a turn and eased back the throttle. As the wheels touched the runway, I coasted smoothly, braking enough to taxi back to the line. Mr. Granger had a grin on his face as I climbed out of the cabin. Following a Navy tradition for someone's first solo flight, those on the ground waiting for their turn heaved a bucket of water at me, but it missed its mark.

Our group completed our training, all with about fifty hours of flight time. We had flown over Manzanar, a Japanese internment camp, which was not too far from Lone Pine, with mixed feelings. We all had Japanese friends in school that we couldn't possibly suspect as spies. Disturbed, we looked down on the barrack-type buildings and the chain-link fencing around the enclosure. I wondered where my high school friend Jimmy Ishimoto had gone? We completed ground school and with a cross-country flight and a final test, were rewarded with private pilot licenses and little silver wings that had the letters C.P.T. on them, designating us as completing Civilian Pilot Training.

We arrived home, tan and accomplished. I met Elaine in my store-bought khaki outfit with my miniature silver wings proudly pinned to my chest. We were able to go out together that night, both of us realizing how much we missed each other in spite of the daily exchange of letters.

Bud and I wore our makeshift uniforms everywhere. People couldn't possibly guess what we were. I suppose we really didn't know ourselves. The Navy still didn't call and we still didn't feel part of the Service. Our next notice was a repeat of our initial assignment. There were not enough facilities to accommodate new recruits, so the Navy assigned us to a civilian intermediate flight school in Susanville, California. At least it would keep us active.

This trip was by train. Bud, Al, Milt, Bob, and I were still in the same group. Susanville was an agricultural lumber area just west of Reno, Nevada. Our quarters were in a storefront in the heart of the town. A restaurant was contracted for our meals and a jump bus took us to a private airstrip adjacent to the main highway, several miles away. We pursued the same program of ground school half the day, and flight school at the private airport the other half. The planes were all yellow Piper Cubs. Some of the instructors wore Army Air Corps uniforms with officer's bars on their shoulders. We addressed the head of the school as "Captain," and we were required to salute the flight instructors with their self-prescribed uniform and rank.

This was my first experience in the snow. The weather was freezing. When the snow hit the ground, I wrapped newspapers inside my boots to keep warm. We would march through the snow from our storefront quarters to the restaurant for meals and were often the target for snowballs thrown by the resident kids. The aircraft were colder, and skies were exchanged for wheels as we skidded forward and sideways learning to taxi and take off.

As we continued our program, Susanville brought me a vicarious Hollywood moment. I was flying solo and practicing my required exercises when a flurry of snow hit my windshield. I was a good ten miles northeast of the airstrip as the snow started falling harder. If I headed back to the field, I knew all the other aircraft would be doing the same. It was difficult seeing, and the prospect of running into other aircraft trying to land at the same time concerned me. Everything below me was agriculture with a few scattered houses and barns between long stretches of open fields. I dropped to about 500 feet and saw an open one-room school with a flagpole in front and plenty of smooth, snow-covered playground area. I checked for any obstacles and swung back away into a steady wind, lowered flaps, and landed with as little power as possible. I taxied close to a chain-link fence at the side of the school and tied the aircraft. Kid's faces were pressed against the window, fascinated by the airplane on their school ground. I pictured myself as the actor Robert Taylor, imagining a beautiful young schoolteacher coming out to comfort the young pilot in distress. For me it was truly a cinema moment. Unfortunately, the beautiful young teacher turned out to be a gray, weathered schoolmarm working past her retirement years, without a telephone and somewhat upset with my disturbing her class.

I kept the engine running and froze in the pilot's seat for well over an hour. There was no way to call when the snow stopped, and whatever ice had accumulated on my wing had been blown away by my propeller. With kids still ogling out the window, I untied the plane and taxied back to the far end of the playground and took off with as much power as I could muster. I arrived back at the flight strip just as several instructors were preparing for an air search on my behalf. My Hollywood moment had passed.

It may have been the weather, but our daily hour of flight training never lasted more than forty minutes. As it turned out, the flight school was charging the Navy for sixty minutes of flight time and only providing forty. The Navy sued for overcharging and may have closed the school after we left. Some instructors, none of whom were in the Service, were cited for wearing Service uniforms and impersonating officers.

Home again. Bud and I wore our Sears, Roebuck khaki outfits with our silver C.P.T. wings pinned above our breast pocket. We were proud of the 100 hours of flight time we had accumulated and felt ready to take on the fighters and dive bombers and seacraft the Navy had to offer. People still looked at us curiously in our makeshift uniforms, trying to figure out what we really were. What we were was anxious. We still didn't feel like we were in the real Navy. And we weren't.

Our civilian flight training had isolated us from the realities of the ongoing war. While we lived on our island of life, the war toll continued at an unimaginable pace. Millions of men were engaged in battles of conquest and resistance. America was producing weapons of war and the men to use them. Newsreels of the day showed the bombing of England and the retaliation of the Allies. The Wellington and Lancaster bombers of England and Canada and the massive strikes of America's B-17s produced losses beyond comprehension. Typically, 300 plane missions, night after night, bombed German and European targets. Sixty to ninety aircraft, each carrying a crew of ten or twelve men, more often failed to return from their missions. The dead, the wounded, the prisoners of war, all became numbers, except to the individual families grieving their loss.

The fighter pilots accompanying the missions paid a constant high price against the German Luftwaffe and the antiaircraft shells exploding at 20,000 feet into the sky. How many were lost because of minimal training, navigational errors, running out of gas, trying to get the needed aircraft in combat with minimum experience? They were sent into the air at any cost, learning on the job.

Our enthusiasm was tempered by the news that our close friend, Jerry Foreman, whose ambition was to become a medical doctor, was shot down in his P-38 fighter over England. The time from his early enlistment in the Army Air Corps to his participation in aerial combat was a little over nine months. His mother, whom we all called "Mom," told us Jerry was decorated for heroism and was buried in England. She proudly displayed her Gold Star flag in the window of her home. He was Dorsey High's first war fatality.

It was a sobering pause that personalized the war's reality. It made our free time more meaningful and valuable. Elaine and I spent as much time together as we could. I took great pride in visiting her in her classrooms at U.C.L.A. She made me promise her that when the war ended I would go back and finish college. I promised. I still had to try to keep up with her brothers.

LONE PINE, CALIFORNIA

Our tents on the Lone Pine High School field

Typical chow time

Bud Plone, left; Al Nadler, front, right; me in the back, studying

My flight instructor, Norman Granger

LONE PINE, CALIFORNIA

Attention! . . . at ease

My first solo flight:
November 21, 1942

Coach Glenn Ackerman

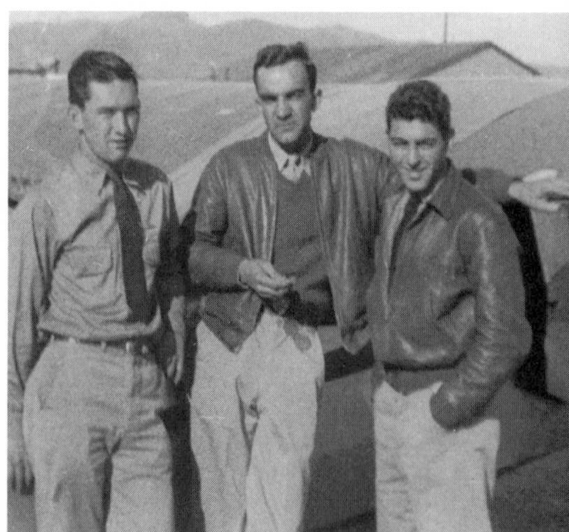

Student Howard Darrow,
Instructor Granger, and me

left Proudly in front of my Cessna

SUSANVILLE, CALIFORNIA

My flight instructor, "Lt." Harry Donaily, before assigning me "muskat duty" for missing a flight procedure

Susanville, California, 1943

Muskat duty

SUSANVILLE, CALIFORNIA

Bud Plone in a patriotic pose

I had to run around in circles as a reminder to dip my wings when flying

4

Del Monte Pre-Flight School

Monterey, California

NAVAL AVIATION CADET SELECTION BOARD
Fifth Floor, Metropolitan Water District Building
306 West 3rd St., Los Angeles, California

September 15, 1942

Mrs. Evelyn C. Shiell
2849 Buckingham Road
Los Angeles, California

Dear Mrs. Shiell:

Your son, Irvin Shiell Cooper, has been enlisted by this activity as an Aviation Cadet the U. S. Naval Reserve. Many boys aspire to be Naval Aviators. Unfortunately, not all can be accepted. Our tests must be stringent and exacting because the men accepted have a big job to do. Hence, we know that you feel a definite measure of justifiable pride in the fact that your boy has made the grade.

Boys don't just meet standards overnight. It takes a matter of years; years, in which their physical bodies are watched over carefully; years, in which their educational training is guided; years, in which they are inspired to become wholesome, genuine Americans.

We realize that much of the credit for your son should go back to the home and to the ideals that you have established. We are sincerely glad, therefore, to welcome you into the rapidly expanding circle of mothers whose sons are training for the great responsibility, the protection of the land we cherish.

Very truly yours,

F.A. Brossy

Lt-Comdr., A-V (G) USNR

At last, our Call to Arms.

I don't know what other Service sent mothers of their enlistees the kind of letter my mom received when I joined the Naval Air Corps, but the Navy credited her with raising a son who could meet the standards required to qualify for its program. My mom was awfully proud and had it printed in the local newspaper. That little gesture confirmed my feelings that the Naval Air Corps was something special, and that certainly made me proud.

It was March 1943 when the official notice finally came to Bud and me. We were to report to the new Los Angeles Train Depot, a beautiful Spanish-style structure built in 1939, and board a special train to Monterey Bay, California. We were to start our Navy V-12 flight training program at Del Monte Pre-Flight School. The terminal was the center of a constant point of arrivals and departures, clogged with men in uniform of all services. An overflow of family and friends, to see personnel arrive or depart, engulfed the massive marble rotunda in the center of the station. Bud and I maneuvered our way through the crowds and found our designated location, joining up with several Lone Pine, Baker, and Susanville alumni. We found Al and Milt and spotted Bob in the gathering of the potential Eagles. We were assigned a special Pullman car, directed by, according to the badge on his uniform, Ensign Quinn. He, along with several other Navy officers, barked authoritative commands at the group. We lined up as ordered. and boarded a special Pullman train reserved for our contingent. All of the other cars were jammed with a first-come, first-sit availability.

My proud mother with her son

Late in the afternoon, the train pulled into Monterey and sidetracked to a special rail behind a high restricted wall. Stern orders were shouted and we left the train, lined up, and marched through a gate onto the magnificent grounds of what once had been the exclusive Del Monte Hotel, now taken over by the United States Navy.

Ensign Quinn directed our group to the front steps of the Del Monte. He turned and saluted a full Lieutenant who immediately snapped at us to line up properly. Since we all carried a single bag of personal belongings, we set them down and had our first lesson in formation. "Stand straight, eyes forward, hands at your side, turn on your heels, spread your legs, at ease."

We were the third class of the Del Monte Pre-Flight School and were cautioned that any infraction of the rules, or failure in the courses, would be cause for washout. Names were called and rooms were assigned on the third floor. Each of the former bedroom suites was furnished with two or three beds and a private bath between. We were advised to "stow our gear" and wait for our dinner call. This turned out to be a cafeteria-style meal in a beautiful dining room shared by several hundred cadets in matching khaki uniforms.

The following morning would be our formal indoctrination. After breakfast, we lined up to receive our government issue. Each cadet received khaki uniforms, shoes, ties, caps, belt, and toiletries. The next line was the barber shop. It was here that we met another of our high school buddies. Les Silver was one of our group, called The Jesters, who, along with Jerry and George, had participated in all our activities. Les had played football, baseball, and track, and worked on the school paper along with Bud and me. He had left in the middle of college at U.C.L.A., but had failed an eye exam for Navy flight training. He came into the Navy as a sailor, with reasonably free reign as a base athlete. He worked out with the world record holder in the pole vault, Cornelius Warmerdam, the first man to clear fifteen feet with a bamboo pole, and represented Del Monte in competitive track meets with other Service teams. We were excited to meet but restricted from fraternizing. As an athlete, Les seemed to have a free run of Del Monte.

The barbers ran the cadets through like the shearing of sheep. When Bud and I came for our turn, Les asked the barber, in an exaggerated flourish, to give us special treatment. This consisted of skinning our heads to a far greater degree than the other cadets. Les was pleased with his influence, and we weren't particularly amused by our friend. We were aware we would not be seen in public for the first six weeks of our residency, but it was my first sensation of a naked head.

In keeping with Navy procedure, half the day was devoted to ground school and the other half to physical fitness. On our first math class, the instructor wrote 1 and 1 on the blackboard. He drew a line at the bottom and announced, "That equals two. We will all start at this same point."

He wanted everyone to start even. Most of the class were college graduates or had college experience. Some even majored in sciences and mathematics. Some may have been bored, but we all completed elementary math at the end of our first lesson. Before the week ended, we completed basic high school math. From there, we went into algebra, geometry, algebra 2, and somewhere into logarithms. My head spun, keeping up with the classes: weather, science, basic aerodynamics, and the identification of foreign ships and planes.

The Navy used a machine called a visual identification projector, which flashed the silhouettes of war planes and ships on a screen. We studied the subjects, and then the machine started flashing frames at one-tenth of a second. We learned to identify all the ships and aircraft building up to one-hundredth of a second. The equipment was later used for illiterate students to read words by sight instead of the phonetic method of learning.

I relieved my mental strain through wholehearted involvement in the physical activities. Three polo fields on the grounds were used for soccer. In 1943, soccer was a foreign game. We didn't play it as kids and didn't know anything about it. The purpose of soccer in our training program was to develop toughness and to teach us to win at any cost. No sportsmanship rules—our rules were to kick the hell out of anybody in our way. And we did. Shoving, elbowing, knocking your opponent down if necessary. This was not a game. This was teaching to win any way you can. When a soccer teammate was kicked and fell to the ground, unable to get up, they moved the game to the next field while waiting for the corpsmen (medics) to arrive. No time to pause. You will be fighting an enemy. Win, any way, at any cost. This is not a game. This is war!

We played football in pads. We boxed in mixed weights and heights and took our pounding. I had a pretty good flicking left and managed to dance away from stronger opponents. Bud had an arm of steel and I had to box against him. He blocked my punch, and I thought I had broken my arm! I hated wrestling, with my nose getting stuck in some guy's armpit. I did well in cross-country, once leading the pack and taking a wrong turn to a dead end. We were introduced to skeet shooting to test our coordination, eyes, and motor skills. I had never owned a gun, and only shot one at the Venice Beach gallery to earn a furry toy bear. On my second series, I hit twenty-four out of twenty-five clay targets. Maybe it was twenty-three, but I remember I was pleased with myself and so was my instructor.

Swimming was my strongest event. A burning oil slick was set on the pool and each cadet was dropped from a short parachute lift above the water and into the pool, each coming up with arms churning to open an air spot, take a breath, and swim under water away from the burning oil. This exercise was taught to avert future disaster. I loved the challenge and was quick and successful. Bud and I were partners in lifesaving, and I helped him save my life while he struggled in the water acting to save me. Next thing I knew, I was called by the administration as an honor to give up my Sunday free time and report on an afternoon shift as a lifeguard for the officers' wives and children at the Del Monte pool.

The only free time we had was after the dinner meal. We were somewhat confined to quarters but managed to congregate in different rooms for nightly bull sessions. Sometimes Les would sneak into our quarters and join in on our theories on the salvation of the world. Our group of cadets came from every part of our country. There was no such thing as television, so accents were easily discernible. It was easy to identify from what parts of the country people came. Hollywood was always big news. When they heard I lived

Training pool at Hotel Del Monte, California

near Hollywood, the questions of movie stars always took front and center. "Do you know Henry Fonda?" was a good start. My answer was, since I had never really met a movie star, "Well, I really didn't know him that well, but I was at a lot of parties with him. Yeah, he really is a nice guy." (So was Robert Taylor and Tyrone Power and anyone they asked about.)

My answer went home to the families and sweethearts, and the one relating the news became a celebrity by association. You can't believe how many parties with movie stars I hadn't gone to that I casually claimed, while becoming a celebrity in my own right. But that's what they wanted to hear, so I just made them happy.

One of the nightly subjects would generally come around to religion. It led me to think of a time when I was about ten or eleven years old living in Boyle Heights. I was accosted by a younger Mexican kid who demanded me to answer, "Are you a Jew?" Since I had never heard differently, I answered "Yes." "You killed Jesus," he blurted at me, but being smaller, decided against fighting me. I was surprised. "I never killed nobody," I said. "Who's Jesus?"

I think Bud, Al, and I were the only three cadets of the Jewish faith in our battalion. None of us formally practiced religion and certainly didn't have the appearance of the stereotyped Jew as sometimes depicted by our fellow cadets. How strange, to live in Los Angeles and meet up with mid-Americans who had never seen a Jew, but knew nothing of them except what they had learned in their Sunday schools and churches. It was almost frightening. I wasn't sure how they would react to my being Jewish, so I tried a different approach. I justified my attitude as not cowardly, but a thoughtful way of integrating and making a point. When asked my religious beliefs, I claimed to be "half-Jewish." What in the hell was that? But to meet someone between the ages of nineteen and twenty-four who had never seen a Jew was strange to me, having been raised in mixed ethnic neighborhoods. I explained that my dad was Jewish and my mother was English, or maybe the other way around, I can't remember. I claimed that I was raised in an open faith and my parents presented both sides. I was given my choice as a Protestant or Jew, and that I had selected Judaism. I told my fellow cadets, who were somewhat intrigued, that by comparison, the Jewish faith was more comfortable, and espoused the treating of your fellow man equally and respecting the Ten Commandments. "Frankly," I'd argue, "I just couldn't believe in the Virgin Mary or living in the hereafter."

"That's funny," I was challenged. "Cooper doesn't sound Jewish."

I explained that my family was born in America and dropped their original name of Cooperwasser, which in German meant water barrel maker. I summarized by saying that may be why I really didn't care for alcohol.

I was then subjected to some philosophical rebuttal, but I respectfully held my ground and never had a problem in my whole Navy career. In retrospect, I suppose I was a coward. In later years, I returned to being a full-time Jew in my own agnostic way.

We continued our regime of study and physical activities. The strain took a toll. Several cadets opted out of the program and several were "washed out." The V-12 program allowed individuals to transfer to different naval programs or to even enlist in a different Service if they failed or quit.

In the midst of the academic and athletic pressure, we were called to be measured for our cadet custom blue Navy suits. Surely, our first step toward being recognized as future naval officers. They were the same double-breasted suits officers wore, with six gold buttons and a single star on the sleeve, without the gold stripe or stripes designating rank. We formed our lines as directed, aware of the time and expense the Navy had now invested in us. First, we were fitted with an official overcoat, without insignia of rank, and an officer's cap that featured a naval anchor instead of the officer's crest and braid. An assembly line of tailors took an assembled line of cadets, one on one, measuring and recording each individual's shoulders, waist, and arms.

As my tailor measured my pants, he looked up at me and asked, "What side do you dress on?" That seemed like an odd question. I couldn't have been more startled. In trying to reconcile an answer, the tailor tried again, "What side do you hang on?" I would never have considered what side my genitals favored in wearing a pair of pants. But these were custom-tailored uniforms. I meekly suggested the left.

We took constant running and marching exercises along the sand and to the Monterey Pier. We would march through the streets of Monterey in precise order. A few days before our first six-hour Sunday leave, we stopped our jogging and marched in our sweats back to the hotel. We swung our arms in unison with our step. I was really excited because that Sunday Elaine would be coming to visit me, along with my mother, Bud's mother, Les's mother, and our adopted "Mom" Foreman. As a Navy cadet, it was prohibited to marry until you were commissioned. Getting engaged was permitted and I had asked my mother to bring a single-carat diamond she owned so that I could propose to Elaine. I marched with enthusiasm, anticipating Sunday's visit. The sweat was running off my forehead and along the top of my nose, dangling from the tip. As I swung my arms back and forth, with a little extra effort, I swung high enough for my thumb to flick the drip away without missing a beat. At the precise moment, Ensign Quinn, chanting our marching beat, bleated out, "Cooper, that will be one hour!"

Sunday, dressed in our new Navy blues, our group was free to meet family and friends for the first time since we had been at Del Monte. Elaine was free to sit along a walk on a decorative concrete bench and watch me march back and forth, shouldering an Army rifle, quietly completing my one-hour penalty for flicking sweat off my nose in public.

I met the entourage from home on the streets of Del Monte. We were cautioned not to take the hand of any female while walking together other than to offer support if needed. Within my allotted time period, I was able to get away with Elaine, alone, back to my marching bench, and proposed that we get married at an appropriate time. I kidded her by saying I had written so many letters to her, I was afraid she would run off with the postman. Then I offered her my mother's diamond ring in engagement. We were both excited at our future prospects. We were prohibited to kiss in public. As a future officer it was considered demeaning, and the penalty would be a heavy dose of shouldering a rifle in meaningless marching. Elaine looked beautiful and with all the time that had passed since we had last seen each other, it was difficult to seal our pact in as meaningful a way as we desired. Elaine's excitement, however, was tempered by my mother's concern. Elaine confessed that she was disturbed because my mother had inferred that in the event our marriage did not take place, she would like the ring back. The ring, incidentally, had a minor chip.

We exchanged stories about our activities since last meeting. I told Elaine the guys in this flight program were terrific. I expressed my fascination that I had friends who had never seen a Jew before

Elaine at Del Monte

and who only knew what their priests or ministers had told them. I assured her that Bud and Al and I had no problems, and everyone respected each other for their ability and their commitment to becoming naval aviators. Elaine followed with an experience of her own.

She told me she, along with several classmates, had been invited to attend a prominent sorority on Hilgard Avenue, adjacent to the U.C.L.A. campus. Since her normal routine was to fill in at her parents' store whenever she wasn't in class, she was still fascinated by sorority life, even though she could never have the time or money to join. Out of curiosity, she accepted the invitation just to see what a sorority looked like. She entered a lovely two-story Spanish home, with a tiled roof and high, pitched beam ceilings, and was shown a number of bedrooms, a modem kitchen, and study and entertainment areas. The sorority girls, gregarious and warm, mingled with their guests, and everyone left the gathering with friendly expectations.

The following week, Elaine was invited back for tea. She had felt too casually dressed on her first visit, so she upgraded her outfit by wearing a cashmere sweater with pleated skirt, and her best shoes. She was only one of two girls invited back and was surprised when she was asked into a separate room, where the sorority president and several other girls asked her to sit. They all smiled as their leader said, "Elaine Shaw, we have one vacancy in our group, and it would please us very much to have you join us."

"I guess I was a little shocked," Elaine told me. "I know my answer was more Warshawsky than Shaw. So I asked them, was this a non-

Al Nadler, Bud Plone, and me in cadet uniform, Del Monte Pre-Flight School

With my mom and dad, Sam and Evelyn Shiell, July 1943

denominational sorority? My goodness, the girls were flustered, and looked a little taken aback. They started to look at each other for support, and in response to their concern, I told them I was Jewish. This was followed by an awkward silence. I smiled, and thanked them for their invitation. I then explained that I had a heavy school load and a job that I had committed to, and would be unable to participate in sorority life at this time. You can't imagine how relieved they were."

On April 11, 1943, the Third Battalion of Del Monte Pre-Flight School graduated approximately 230 cadets. From preflight to real flight, we received assignments to primary Navy flight schools in different parts of the country. Bud and I were lucky to be assigned to Livermore, California. Al was being sent to Olathe, Kansas, with orders no yeoman could switch. The procedures of real Navy flight training would establish our capability.

Most importantly, we had seventy-two hours to report to the Livermore Naval Air Station, and with a less-than-eight-hour bus ride away, Los Angeles beckoned. Bud decided to hang out with Les, even though fraternizing was not tolerated. There were no rules against fraternizing with one's fiancée as long as it was in proper decorum. I headed for Los Angeles eager to challenge the rule.

5

Livermore and the Yellow Peril

The Stearman "Yellow Peril"

The time window was tempting. I said goodbye to Al and made arrangements to keep in touch. Bud agreed to take my new Navy-issued duffel bag, holding my current life's belongings with him when he checked in at Livermore just a few hours away. I took a quick change of shorts, socks, and T-shirts, and headed for the Greyhound Station to surprise Elaine. My official naval uniform was khaki pants, shirt, black tie, and a V-12 insignia patch. I was as exhilarated by my successful completion of pre-flight school as I was excited at the prospect of seeing Elaine.

My folks picked me up at the bus station, and without calling, I stood unannounced at Elaine's front door. When she answered the ringing chime, the happy surprise on her face rewarded my efforts. It was followed by a frown of concern, "Is everything all right?"

We spent two days together and two nights apart in our respective bedrooms. Our passion was limited to varying degrees of lip-to-lip pressure. In the terminology of the day this was called "necking," and the height was my touching a breast firmly cupped by a bra under a cashmere sweater. We talked and planned, and the time to leave came before we were ready. The few moments we shared were worth the anxiety of my efforts. Now my thoughts ranged from "heaven more" to Livermore.

I was fortunate to get a ticket on the last bus north in order to check in on time. The seats had been sold out and as the bus was about to leave, two frantic sailors who were denied transportation anxiously offered to sit in the aisles. Rules prohibited them, and they ran around the bus pleading for someone to give up their seats or they would be A.W.O.L., absent without leave, and in big trouble. The two sailors, in sheer panic, begged for help. As the bus driver prepared to pull out, an older couple stood up, carrying small carry-on bags, and relinquished their seats. As they stepped off the bus, the sailors were ecstatic, thanking and blessing the couple who were unsure whether they would get seats on the next departure.

The witnesses on the bus and in the adjacent lines applauded the pair as the bus blew a growl of blue smoke and revved its engine forward. In the midst of this drama, Elaine's eyes and mine were locked until the bus lurched out of the terminal and headed north to my next adventure.

The Greyhound rolled through the California countryside and finally through the town of Livermore, dropping passengers off at designated stops. My orders were to check in at 8:00 a.m., or 0800 Navy time. I had been fortunate getting my seat as the next arrival would have been at 1000 the following morning. It was dusk as the bus stopped at the entry road off the main highway, marked Livermore Naval Air Station.

Several naval personnel, including the two sailors, another cadet, and me, thanked the driver and walked the short block to the entry guardhouse where two marines waited for check-ins. The others passed through and proceeded to the chain-link compound where two other marines passed them through. The marine with a clipboard in hand checked our paper orders, confirmed our names with his list, and looked into our carry-on bags. "Are you carrying any liquor?" We both answered "Negative," and were instructed to enter the second gate and report to the office building on the left for further instructions.

A yeoman at the front desk reviewed our orders, assigned our barrack, and gave us a packet of rules, regulations, schedules, procedures to follow, and assignment for meals and quarters. After breakfast the next morning, we were to report to the base hospital for an extensive physical checkup, including eye and dental examinations. I passed without problems and was rewarded by having a corpsman give me several shots in each arm for a variety of unknown diseases.

I found Bud, who had checked in earlier in a different barrack, with cadets from preflight schools all over the country. Again our course of action was ground school and physical education in the morning and flight training in the afternoon. We now concentrated on courses in flight and safety rules, aeronautics and weather, elementary navigation, mapping, and instruments as related to flying. All our texts and preparation were now geared to the prime purpose of becoming a naval aviator.

I was still fascinated by how airplanes can fly. From the Wright brothers to now, passing the little, light aircraft, looking at the large bombers and transports and the loads they carried was beyond my comprehension. I had learned about the dynamics of "lift, thrust, and drag," but still reverted to the bumblebee classic. According to science, it was proven aerodynamically impossible for a bumblebee to fly. However, the bumblebee didn't know that, so it flew anyway.

It was the second or third day. I was issued a real Navy flight jacket, a flight suit, helmet, and goggles, and ordered to report to the flight line. A long three-block line of open-cockpit, bi-wing Stearman aircraft were poised wingtip to wingtip, randomly numbered on each side of the fuselage. I found the number of the aircraft assigned to me and met Lt.(jg) McCaslin, my instructor pilot, sitting on the inside wing of a shiny new yellow plane. I walked forward as he rose, and with a snappy salute, I introduced myself, "Cadet Cooper, reporting for flight instruction, Sir."

Officer McCaslin waved a casual salute and responded with, "Welcome to the Yellow Peril," which is what the Stearman aircraft were called. "I understand you have some flight experience?" referring to my civilian pilot training course.

"Yes, Sir," I answered.

"Good. Now, the first thing we do is check the aircraft before we take off."

We walked around the plane, first making sure the pitot tube was uncovered (which allows the wind to blow through and indicate the airspeed on the panel of the plane). We then checked the wingtips and lights, the tail and rudder for any defects. We visually checked the tires for unusual air pressure. We stopped at the propeller and discussed the proper way to start. I removed the chocks that blocked the wheels for takeoff. I was then instructed on how to enter the open cockpit, stepping on the interior portion of the wing, and respecting the vulnerable canvas fabric that covered the wings and fuselage.

I climbed into the front cockpit as Officer McCaslin showed me the throttle on the left side. He had me place my feet on the foot pedals and test the controls. He climbed into the rear cockpit, started the engine, and eased forward of the line of planes, taxiing to the start of the runway.

I pulled my goggles on as we rolled down a large concrete concourse with other planes on both wings, in a somewhat mass migration to the skies. I followed the throttle with my left hand as McCaslin eased it forward, and rested my feet on the pedals, feeling each move he made. The Stearman picked up speed and moved along the seemingly endless length of runway. Our tail raised quickly, and somewhere near forty knots, McCaslin lifted the plane off the concrete and into the air. The wind whipped over the plastic windshield, and with my seat belt tightened and my goggles and helmet secure to my face, I enjoyed the open view.

After clearing the airfield and away from the flock of aircraft that had taken to the skies in a simultaneous takeoff, he signaled me to reach under my seat and pantomimed the use of an intercom tube for further instruction. I pulled out a small rubber hose attached to a metal funnel and stopped before putting it to my mouth to speak. My suspicion was confirmed as Lt.(jg) McCaslin, watching my skepticism, burst into laughter. I shoved the pee tube back under my seat. He almost had me.

I did have an intercom ear-piece in my helmet and was motioned where to plug it in. He had purposely neglected to show me during my Stearman familiarization talk in order to pull off his prank. With that, he headed for a large cumulus cloud at about 3,500 feet. As he approached the whirling cotton fluff, he spoke into the mike, "As long as you are flying at this base, I don't want you flying through any of these clouds. There are too many planes and too many cadets that you can't see that could be inside."

With that, he dipped the plane on its wing and swung away into a clear blue sky. He banked the plane from left to right and removed his hands and feet from the controls. He asked me to repeat his moves. I did that to his satisfaction and then he took the controls back. He put the plane into a steep dive and pulled up into a loop. He followed with another loop and at the top, upside down, rolled the aircraft level into a maneuver known as an Immelmann. He pulled the joystick back without applying power, and the plane nosed up and stalled, and fell nose-first into a twisting, turning spin. He kicked the rudders and powered forward, and dove out of the spin and leveled off. These were all maneuvers I had experienced while obtaining my private pilot's license, but the rush of the air in the open cockpit was unique. I felt a little nausea and was relieved when we headed back to the base and landed with other planes on each wing. That flight lasted an hour and a half, and I felt I had successfully managed my familiarization as Instructor McCaslin gave me a thumbs-up sign.

It was the following day that I was hit with reservations. We took off, and once away from traffic, I was comfortable repeating my initial maneuvers. I was cautioned to make sure my seat belt was tight. McCaslin took over and put the aircraft through every gyration in its repertoire. Loops, dives, spins, and barrel rolls, one after the other as he tried to "wring me out." He was successful. I turned green. He leveled off and I felt my stomach coming to my mouth. I tried to rip my throat strap from my helmet. As I lay my head to the side of the open cockpit, McCaslin skidded the aircraft sideways through the air, and my upheaval followed the air current horizontally and harmlessly without touching the plane. The penalty for dirtying the Stearman aircraft was a complete wash job by the perpetrator, and being the butt of considerable chiding by one's peers. I was grateful for my instructor's technique in my saving face, but I worried about the notation in my log book, "Cadet has tendency for air sickness. McC."

I somewhat controlled my air sickness by carrying a large brown paper bag folded in my rear pocket. It served as my baby blanket and gave me a sense of security. After my fourth flight with Lt.(jg) McCaslin, I was assigned to Lt.(jg) Watson, who taught me basic Navy flight procedures. I learned to land with my tail touching first as if landing on an aircraft carrier. I mastered taxiing, touch-and-go takeoffs and landings, figure eights around pylons, and proper flight procedures. Precision and formation flying proved my strongest assets. The last half hour of each flight, which was reserved for acrobatics, exposed my weakness. I had no feel or reaction and pushed my training by rote moves that proved me rather dismal. On July 3, 1943, a Lt. Trindle gave me my first check flight and cleared me to solo. Starting on the 4th, we flew two 90-minute flights daily throughout our training at Livermore. The constant pressure of ground school, physical athletics, and flying demands took its toll. Wing-over crashes and academic and flight failures eliminated several friends along the way. Each day seemed to bring added pressure.

The versatility of the Yellow Peril was remarkable in its construction. To take the stress and pressure of all the aeronautical dives and twists and all-out power surges placed on its frame by a variety of pilots, and to return intact after each outing, was a tribute to American engineering. As each cadet received his O.K. to solo, the major flying objective was to perfect the control of every aspect of the procedures required. A majority of flights were solo, where we worked to raise our performance level for the check flights to come. Our familiarity and control of the Stearman became a part of our being. The open cockpit caused our faces to become deeply tanned. When our goggles and helmet were removed, the areas protected from the sun caused a sharp outline of white against the exposed tan of our faces. It identified our status as the aviators we were. It was a sign of distinction, and we reveled in its macho look. We even developed a cocky walk and attitude because of our self-proclaimed mastery of the Yellow Peril. That plane did everything we asked it to do.

I spent most of my time perfecting the required procedures. My fellow cadets used their last half hour practicing acrobatics. I generally limited my time to the last ten minutes or so, forcing my way through a sloppy acrobatic sequence, and then headed home. I knew I could pull out of an emergency situation if necessary, even though my technique was not very presentable. I just didn't enjoy being upside down and subject to nausea. Who ever heard of an airsick Navy pilot?

I passed all my check flights until I hit the overall flight review on August 1. Lt.(jg) Gates, according to my log book, gave me a thumbs-down in acrobatics, a failing grade. I now had to pass two check rides in order to continue my flight training. To offset the down check, I had to receive two "ups" to continue. Two thumbs down and I would be washed out, dismissed from the Navy V-12 program. I could apply for other naval specialties or be free to apply for any other military Service. On the following day, my second flight check, a Lt. Parker put me through the routine. Again, I performed my basic requirements very well, followed by a consistently sloppy exercise in acrobatics. Lt. Parker, on balance, gave me an adequate O.K., with one more chance for a final check ride. The thought of being washed out and returning home as a failure was a pressure too hard to bear. How would I face Elaine, my parents, my friends, my ego? If I couldn't be an officer, how could

I compete with Elaine's bothers, Harry and Ernie? The thought of turning in my Navy blues and the only overcoat I ever owned, my officer's cap, my flight jacket, was something I couldn't imagine. I had several days to fly solo and practice the required routine on my own. On August 5, an Ensign Edward was assigned to test my final review. He put me through a number of precision exercises and then stopped the engine, placing me in a series of emergency landings. My reaction and adeptness were quick and positive. I slipped and glided the powerless craft to land in the center of a designated white circle. As my tail touched down first, the instructor hit the power and pulled the plane up to find the most uncompromising elevation, and cut the power again. I hit the center of the circle six times in a row and was motioned to climb to 4,500 feet. For the next half hour, I went through my series of acrobatics. I pushed and kicked my way through loops and barrel roles without once ending in line of the point and elevation required.

Devastated, I headed back to the base. I made a smooth tail-first landing and taxied to my stop. Ensign Edward climbed out of the plane, perplexed, concerned, and groping for words. He eyed me and spoke. "That was probably one of the worst set of acrobatics I've had to check." He paused. He stood quietly, somewhat deep in thought. "On the other hand," another pause, then, "maybe you just had a bad acrobatic day. Your other procedures were practically perfect, and I just can't ignore that."

He gave me a thumbs-up and signed my sheet to continue my Navy flight training. I thanked him for his consideration and gave him a snappy parting salute. He waved me off, and I recalled that acrobatic "down check" as the only down check I received in my whole Navy career. As I reported to my fellow cadets, they needled me and assured me I had met Santa Claus well before the holidays.

I passed the next series of checks without problems. We started formation flying and worked with different cadets in our class. On one flight, Bud, who loved acrobatics, was assigned to fly formation with me and another friend, Gene Oster. We practiced various crossovers, changing positions and leads. We stretched the rules by showing our prowess in overly tight formations. By a series of hand signals, Bud and I pulled tight and tapped wing on wing in midair, careful not to damage the wingtip light. That would have been strictly a "washout" offense. Was that cockiness or stupidity? In hindsight, we agreed it was the latter, but we somehow relished a pride in our antic and a smugness in our skill. I think with the amount of time and money invested in our training so far, the Navy might have given us a severe reprimand. But let us continue.

On August 18, my check flight with Lt.(jg) Metcalf cleared me for night flying. This was truly a frightening experience because forty to sixty aircraft took to the night skies all at one time, flying at various designated elevations, trying not to run into each other. We landed en masse with planes above and below and wingtip to wingtip. It was a harrowing exercise, and the fact we all survived each other was a tribute to our training, survival skills, and good luck.

During the next dozen solo flights later, we were allowed to take eager enlisted personnel as passengers for joy rides. I'm sure I disappointed some of my mechanics and base sailors by not going through an acrobatic routine, but I did get compliments and thanks for a smooth ride. Our class concluded our last primary flight at the Livermore Naval Air Base on September 2, 1943. As we now eagerly awaited our orders to advanced flight training, we were so involved in our own progress that we hardly had time to think why we were here. The pause caused us to realize that there was a war going on.

The war continued in Europe and the Pacific. The Navy was involved in the battles of the Atlantic and fighting the Japanese in the Pacific. They attacked the enemy on land and sea and delivered, covered, and supported the Marines in island-to-island fighting. They resisted the Japanese, now taking back islands and fighting

The Stearman "Yellow Peril" flying in formation

to recapture strange places like New Guinea, New Georgia, and the Solomons. Carrier aircraft with battleships supported the bravest of American fighting men, charging through churning surfs, securing beaches with weapons in hand, facing unseen shells and man-to-man battle in jungle warfare.

While the Navy was primarily fighting the war in the Pacific, the Allies were making strides in Europe. The Germans had lost in Russia and were forced to give up in North Africa, and now were capitulating in Italy. But the Germans were still a deadly force. To hear and see on film the casualties and capture of thousands of military and civilian personnel, armies, navies, marines, and air forces of all countries was a shocking revelation of the magnitude of death and destruction of a world at war. And here I was, ready to take the next step in training, as so many of the men before me, not knowing what kind of action I would be called to perform. Of all the options, my destiny was a question mark in the hands of others.

We were so engrossed in our daily pattern, we hardly realized that no flights were scheduled this day. It was after a typical breakfast that a loud speaker startled us with, "Now hear this." It started with congratulating our class on successfully completing our primary flight training. We were to line up at alphabetized stations to pick up our primary orders. Bud and I were assigned to advanced training in Corpus Christi, Texas, with two weeks to report.

Of course, as excited as I was to have completed my relationship with the "Yellow Peril," I was overwhelmed with the excitement of heading home to see my Elaine.

6

Home on Leave

Home on leave with Elaine and my Chevy

It was an exuberant group of goggle-tanned cadets that boarded the Greyhound for Los Angeles. Bud, Al, and I, along with Milt Gibson and Bob Phillips and others from the original Lone Pine group, headed home. With our large Navy-issued canvas bags tucked into the side baggage panels of the bus, we found seats among the travelers, families, migrants, and other Service personnel en route. I sat smugly against a center window, feeling a great sense of accomplishment, equal to my peers who had achieved this status of flying proficiency. I savored seeing the two cadets in forward seats, their hands lifting into the air, turning their wrists, then diving down in an imaginary flight maneuver. Whenever pilots got together, their camaraderie inevitably brought their hands and arms into play. As one described a maneuver, there was always an exaggerated follow-up by the other.

Acres of beautiful farmland rolled past my window. I admired the bus driver speeding along the two-lane highway, on constant alert, with both hands negotiating each turn, and maintaining a prescribed time schedule. I wondered, when he got back to his terminal, did he share his actions with the other drivers? Did they have the sense of "belonging" that we had in the air? And then it struck me. How would this bus ride feel had I washed out? My insecurity, or ego, was pierced with the reaction of what Elaine would have really thought.

When I got to her home, Elaine's enthusiastic greeting eliminated any thoughts I may have harbored. Her hug and kiss turned me from an untested warrior to a conquering hero. Our excitement was tempered by the frustrating reality that she was studying for midterms the following day. U.C.L.A., like most colleges, was on a trimester schedule to accelerate the educational needs of the wartime demands. I made arrangements to meet Elaine after her last test on the morrow, and would spend some time with my parents. As I walked back to my house, two doors away, passing the plaster box duplex on a fifty-foot lot between our houses, I measured my steps at about ninety-eight feet separating the distance between her bed and mine.

The next day, late in the afternoon, I sat on a balustrade outside Royce Hall, a beautiful brick structure on the U.C.L.A. grounds. I waited for Elaine to emerge from French IV, her last test of the day. I kept looking at my watch between observing the beauty of the college campus. Graceful, angular brick walks meandered between the grass areas and a main walkway leading to a cast concrete bridge spanning a dry riverbed gully. The branches of trees lazily fanned the air on both sides, with several matching masonry buildings visible between them. The campus was wide and spacious, and students carrying books walked at varying paces along the brick pathways between the school structures.

It was hard to believe the world was engaged in a war until you realized most of the male students traversing the campus walks were in various uniforms representing different branches of the Services. I wore my khaki shirt with my Naval Air Cadet insignia sewn on my sleeve, with black tie, khaki pants, and cap. My muse was broken by a grinding bell, followed by a clatter of moving chairs and shuffling feet, as doors were thrown open and students emerged from the classroom. A dozen figures passed as Elaine cleared through the doorway, eyes searching, locking onto mine. We hugged between juggling books. Her sigh was one of relief and mine was one of passion. We walked and talked and had dinner in Westwood Village, the business area adjacent to the university. It was a quaint college town with the middle of the streets divided by a lengthy center planter trimmed with blue and gold tiles, U.C.L.A.'s colors. We talked and planned our future in hypothetical fantasies. We parted in front of her house, late and tired, with my plans set for the next day. We went to sleep in our own beds, approximately ninety-eight feet apart.

Whatever distance separated us, the same distance separated our families. Even though they were friendly with each other and discussed our engagement, there had never been a formal get-together acknowledging the joining of the family relationship. To culminate this important union, reservations were made for the Florentine Gardens, one of Hollywood's popular dinner clubs, the first weekend of my leave. It was a rare occasion that Elaine's parents ever went out in an evening, but cousin Martin volunteered to keep the family delicatessen open so they could go out for this special event.

Both dads were dressed in suits and ties and both mothers wore their best dresses and hats. I was proud in my Navy blues and Elaine was stunning in a dress that came with a pearl necklace. When I found out the pearls were decorative, I vowed to myself to buy her real ones.

Once the food was on the table and the exchange of casual conversation under way, you could feel the emotions shared by both parents. A daughter planning to marry in the midst of a war, and leaving the nest for the first time. A son, not knowing what demands would be made, committing to caring for a wife while barely conquering his responsibility to straighten his room at home. As an only child, I think my folks were secure in my independence. I fared well for myself. Bud and I were often away on Boy Scout outings and summer camps, and I spent many weekends on my own. Elaine's folks counted on their children working in the family store between shifts and classes. Now with Elaine's older brothers, Harry, a naval engineer in Washington, D.C., and Ernie in medical school in San Francisco, the family unity was physically bare.

Whatever trepidation or concern each side held, it was eased away in the celebratory ambiance and certainly in the happiness exhibited by their offspring this night. The evening continued with discussions about the war, the short supply of materials, the allocation of food rations and gas stamps, and the helpless feeling of the unknown. The evening ended with hugs and kisses and blessings to all. Elaine and I looked forward to the next day that I planned just for the two of us.

My folks on the left, Elaine's folks on the right, at the Florentine Gardens, Hollywood, California, 1943

We awoke to a Southern California morning in all its glory. The weather was beautiful, the temperature in the low eighties. I had told Elaine to dress in a light sunsuit. It was going to be hotter, and I wore a boxer bathing suit with a Navy sweat top. I picked up Elaine and we drove up Sepulveda Boulevard past Sunset heading toward the San Fernando Valley. Sepulveda was a two-lane road meandering through the hills to the top of Mulholland Drive, a dirt road along the top of the ridge, dividing Los Angeles and the Valley. Halfway up, I pulled my car off to the side between a recessed corner of an open hillside. Elaine was perplexed when I pulled a single-shot .22 Remington rifle from the back of my car. I had purchased the gun at Sears, Roebuck, having never owned a weapon of any kind before. After being introduced to target practice and skeet shooting, I was going to show off my prowess as an expert marksman.

I had scrounged around for a dozen empty cans or so, and had them packed into my Chevy's trunk. Few cars passed our way, and I brought out the cans and set them in the background of the slope away from the open brush.

Outside of a movie screen, I don't believe Elaine had ever seen a real gun in hand. She looked at the rifle and wasn't sure if it was for shooting rabbits or elephants, and didn't seem thrilled at the prospect of holding it. I tried to assure her, and smugly exhibited the muzzle and the polished walnut stock. I inserted a single .22 bullet into the firing mechanism and hoisted the rifle to my shoulder. I cocked the lever and took aim at a can forty to fifty feet away. I announced my target, pulled the trigger, and sent an empty Heinz tin flipping in the air.

"Here," I said, and placed the rifle on Elaine's shoulder.

"Look down the barrel at the guide and line up the next can with your eye. Hold steady, and squeeze the trigger." I held her elbow up and rested the gun against her shoulder.

A puff of dusty dirt rose abruptly within a foot of the can target. I placed another .22 bullet into the single-shot rifle. Elaine aimed and fired again without help. Another puff of dirt appeared, this time closer, just below the can. I could see her confidence building. A little more comfortable with the rifle, I had her insert the bullet and raise the gun to her shoulder and concentrate on the guide at the end of the barrel. She pulled. The can flipped in the air, and I could see Elaine was now a hooked marksman.

We shot up the cans between munching on sandwiches Elaine had packed. A few cars passed, but no one paid attention. We cleaned up our lunch bags and wrappings and left the riddled cans to disintegrate into the soil. Pleased with the success of our shoot, we got into the car and headed toward the San Fernando Valley.

It was hot and we kept the windows of the rear open, front and back. At the top of the drive, we entered a two-lane tunnel that took us under Mulholland Drive and headed down into the heat of

Shooting it up on Sepulveda Boulevard

the San Fernando Valley. We were engulfed with the rising citrus fragrance. The whole valley below was covered with orange, lemon, and grapefruit groves. Lines of eucalyptus trees divided the mirage of ranches spreading before us. We reached Ventura Boulevard, a basic two-lane road that ran the length of the valley from one end to the other. The heat and the heady fragrance of the citrus fruit made you gulp for air. Signs everywhere along the road scrawled an invitation to stop: "All You Can Drink, Fresh Orange Juice, 10 Cents."

We stopped; we drank. It was impossible to drink more than one glass. In the midst of the valley heat, you were given a glass of orange juice that was practically frozen. You touched the refreshing glass to your lips and the juice was so cold, one gulp would make the back of your head cramp in a freezing state. By the time it eased away, the next sip would freeze your brain again. We worked at finishing one glass of the “All You Can Drink.” We had no desire for a refill.

We drove west on Ventura, admiring the beautiful groves with an occasional cottage or ranch house and wooden barn nestled among the trees. We came to a road crossing marked Balboa. A hand-scrawled sign on the northwest corner advertised the property as a one-acre site with a small ranch shack in the center. It was listed at $2,000 and Elaine and I immediately got excited. Our thoughts were an unrehearsed duet. Why don’t we try to buy this and build a house after the war? We figured the angles we had in savings and the possibility of a loan from our parents. What a beautiful way to start our life together! We wrote down the address and contact name and drove home enthusiastically to announce and promote our plan.

My father, the builder, nixed the whole idea. “What, $2,000?” he boomed. “Why would you pay inflated war prices?” He once owned property and lost everything in the depression following WWI.

With Elaine at school and our evenings together, time passed too quickly. Les Silver came home on leave from Del Monte prior to reporting to officers’ training at Cornell University. One night Elaine and I, and Bud, who dated a girl named Regina, and Les and Laverne, his girlfriend from high school, made reservations for dinner and dancing at the Coconut Grove. We didn’t worry about fraternization while we waited in the entry for an overbooked table. It was Les, in his navy blue sailor suit, who tapped the shoulder of a man he thought was the maitre d’ and asked when he thought our table would be ready, When the dark-suited gentleman turned around, his sleeves revealed two golden stripes and his rank as a full lieutenant in the United States Navy. With profuse apologies, an embarrassed Les, the sailor, backed away, seeking the real maitre d’.

The music of Ted Fioritto was sparkling and flowed with melody and rhythm. Elaine followed my two-step, and I kept her close with my arm around her waist. The Grove, the ambiance, the costly extravagance was an evening we shared as a feeling of family. We danced, switching partners for a number to fulfill our social graces. As our last night together, we discussed futures, ambitions, and safe returns, while pondering the unknown ahead of us. We were excited that Les would become an officer, and joked that he could become a maitre d' after the war. Bud and I expressed our anxiety about entering our advanced flying stage, and not knowing what lay ahead. At evening's end, we parted, pledging to meet again when the war was over.

There was no way to hold back the days of liberty. Joyful, fruitful, happy, sad, all the emotional aspects had no bearing on the nonstop passing of time. On our last day of liberty, I took Elaine to the beach. We strolled the boardwalk from Venice to Santa Monica, walking on the Ocean Park Pier in between. We took a farewell photo and watched the sun settle in a shimmering sea. It was dark when we got home, and we engaged in a self-controlled necking session and shared our vows for our future. My promise was that once I earned my wings, I would come home and we would be married.

Liberty, Elaine and me, September 12, 1943

I stopped at Elaine's house in the morning, feigning an upbeat goodbye. She had early classes, and I saw little sense in her losing class time just to drive to the

Les Silver and me, after working out in front of Elaine's house

Me in my cadet "blues" with Les in his dress sailor suit uniform

train depot. I had managed to get two seats on the train to Corpus Christi, Texas, and my folks would drop Bud and me off at the station. Bud's dad was a potato broker and worked from midnight to noon, and it was difficult for him to get away. His mom didn't drive, so my folks had the last farewell.

Los Angeles was a city of about one million people. It seemed as though whenever we went to the station, everyone in the city was there at the same time. That was the wartime activity. Crowds, service-related, jostling, pushing, going, and coming. I shook my dad's hand, kissed my mom, and insisted on being dropped off in front of the train entry. Bud and I, in true Navy style, bailed out of the car and navigated our way to our train platform. We tipped a porter to store our bags, and made a tail-first landing in our assigned seats. Texas, here we come!

7

Flying at Corpus Christi

The Beam, Naval Air Training Center, Friday, January 14, 1944

There is much to be said about Texas hospitality. As soon as I arrived at my new cadet quarters, I stowed my clothes in an assigned chest of drawers, polished my shoes, and snugged my black tie in a neat Windsor knot. I checked myself as I prepared for a scheduled evaluation interview. I tried to look confident and poised. I opened the top drawer, and damned, if the biggest cockroach you ever saw didn't hand me my handkerchief. Now that was my introduction to Texas hospitality.

The primary training facility for naval aviators was in Pensacola, Florida, but with demands to produce a greater number of pilots, Corpus Christi was opened on March 12, 1941. Within two months, on May 5, 1941, the first group of 300 cadets started flight training along with 800 instructors and personnel. In June of 1943, history tells us that the third graduating class of Corpus Christi included George H. W. Bush, a future president of the United States, as the youngest cadet to earn his Wings of Gold. With the bombing of Pearl Harbor, the training rate doubled, and through the years, a total of more than 35,000 cadets were commissioned as naval aviators, with the title of Officer and Gentleman. With six auxiliary flight stations in addition to the main base, Corpus Christi became the largest pilot training facility in the world.

It took about eighteen months to train a naval aviator. Even after earning your wings, there would be advanced training for specific aircraft and duties before actually facing combat conditions. I thought of how fast the Army Air Corps had to get pilots and planes in the sky to fight the Nazi Luftwaffe. I received a letter from Mom Foreman with a picture of Jerry's grave in England. I thought of Jerry joining the Army Air Corps at the beginning of the war, and being shot down over England nine months after he enlisted. The urgency to get aircraft in the sky took precedence over the amount of training that was really required. Unfortunately, for many, their flight training came while learning on the job. I was grateful for the thorough amount of time given me by the Navy.

Flying in formation

Here I was, ready to start my next trip through the syllabus of flight. We were given several days of indoctrination, which included another physical: checkup, eye exams, and more shots. Our standard response was, "If we had as many needles sticking out of us as we had put into us, we would all look like porcupines."

My last flight at Livermore had been on September 2, and my first flight at Corpus was scheduled for the 27th, with Ensign Dalbec as my instructor. We had familiarization classes about our new plane, the Vultee SNV. A prelude to the Navy fighters, the Vultee was a single-engine, low-wing metal aircraft with two open tandem cockpits, covered with an enclosed sliding plastic hood and non-retractable wheels. It had a top speed of 180 miles per hour and was used for solo experience, instrument, navigation, radio, and formation flying. It was the primary transition to the advanced fighters and trainers of future aircraft. Ensign Dalbec gave me three one-and-one-half-hour dual flights on three successive days. On the fourth day, I received a fifty-minute flight check and was cleared to solo. I then spent the next hour and a half flying on my own. I familiarized myself with the plane and took a full review of the naval air station, a tour of satellite bases, the city of Corpus Christi, and a quick look at the Gulf of Mexico. I stayed away from the takeoff and landing patterns as instructed, until I came in visually on my own.

Our morning studies were heavy with navigation and instrument training. I was introduced to the Link Trainer, operated by lady sailors called Waves. I was enclosed in a stationary cockpit with a closed hood and the Vultee dashboard controls in front of

The Link Trainer

The Vultee SNV "Vibrator"

me. Sealed inside this mock-up cockpit, I took off as if I were flying the real aircraft. I was provided with an air map, and, by radio, was given an elevation to hold. I was told of the wind direction and velocity, to adjust to the tactical conditions, and instructed to fly to a given latitude and longitude and return to base. A large table and chart board were outside the Link Trainer, and an automatic marker traced my flight pattern on a matching map, according to my action of the controls taken from the closed cockpit. When notified by earphone to return to base and land, I followed my map and the flight procedures I had practiced in the air. According to my calculations, I followed my instruments, came in at the proper speed, nose slightly raised, touched down, pulled back the throttle, and cut the mechanical engine. The Wave and a seaman opened the hood on the Link Trainer and I triumphantly climbed out to see how I fared. "Congratulations, Cadet, you just 'ditched' in the Gulf of Mexico."

Hours of navigation and instrument study in ground school and repeated sessions in the Link Trainer finally taught us to a point of competence and confidence. To fly to a given point and return, with nothing visible other than the instruments in the Link Trainer, was the required goal prior to advancing to its practice in the air.

The Vultee aircraft was a sleek and sensitive plane that reacted quickly to any movement of its controls. Because of its powerful engine and its constant roar, the cadets referred to it as the Vultee Vibrator. We flew solo every day, racking up hours of familiarization and control and going through the routines learned in our primary flight training. My next dual flight, on September 11, was with an Ensign Tanacy for my first night flight over Corpus and the Gulf of Mexico. I adjusted to visual points along the shoreline, and after landing one and a half hours later, Ensign Tanacy climbed out of the plane, tapped me on the shoulder, and said, "Okay, you're on your own."

He outlined a prescribed flight route of almost two hours' duration. I was surprised and seat-weary, but the adrenaline set in and I took off into a late-night Texas sky. I was comfortable in the Vultee and together we completed the flight. I landed smoothly and was the last to follow the taxi lights on the runway. The mechanics were waiting, anxious to call it a night, and took the plane for refueling and readying for the morning flights. I dragged myself back to quarters feeling drained from the humidity, and tired, with an inner glow of accomplishment.

Combined with my ground school studies, I continued to rack up flight hours. I actually had a break one night and went to a movie at the base theater. There was a line of sailors waiting at the box office to purchase tickets. I got to the end of where the enlisted men stood and was called out by a base officer and reprimanded for waiting in line. As a cadet, and future officer, I was to go directly to the box office in front of all enlisted personnel and only wait if there were other officers or cadets in front of me. This was part of RHIP, rank has its privileges, part of learning how to be an officer, as well as a pilot. I felt slightly embarrassed walking past them, because most of the men, including some chief petty officers, were older than I was. I felt disrespectful. RHIP.

The Corpus campus was a vibrant conglomeration of activity. Aside from studies on navigation, astronomy, instruments, and radio, there were required calisthenics, hiking, cross-country, swimming, shooting, boxing, wrestling, tumbling, football, baseball, basketball, soccer, precision marching, and everything else I may have left out. Reading, writing letters, an open gymnasium, library, chapels, and base theater were all available to cadets if time permitted after fulfilling their flight and classroom obligations. I ventured to the base newspaper, the *Beam*, which was edited and run by the cadets. I would have liked to participate and contribute but just couldn't spare the time. I did draw a quick cartoon about my nemesis, the Link Trainer, which they ran in the January 14, 1944, issue.

My only other theater outing was when the Cadet Corps was invited to attend a special presentation by the well-known movie star Tyrone Power. He had been a private pilot before the war and had apparently gone through the Navy flight program and earned his wings as a second lieutenant in the Marines. The theater was jammed, and wildly enthusiastic applause greeted him as he came on stage. I think part of the cheering was directed at the stunningly beautiful woman who walked out on the stage with him. He introduced her to the audience as the librarian on the base, which I was sure would receive a rush of potential readers at the next opportunity.

Lt. Power sold a lot of war bonds for the Services across the nation and gave an upbeat, patriotic speech with many humorous anecdotes. The one I remember was when he said, "Last night I was walking on the beach at Corpus and it was loaded with cadets and girlfriends snuggled in the sand." He looked around at the crowd, "I accidentally stepped on some cadet's back, and a female voice piped up, 'Thanks.'"

Formation flying was the next phase of our training sequence. Each plane had to maintain an equal space to the next, flying a few feet above or below the wing of the other, maintaining a uniform distance while turning or twisting or in a uniform line, much like the Rockettes in Radio City Music Hall. It was the one aspect of flying I enjoyed most. We rotated in three-plane V-shaped alignment with a fourth in the center. We advanced to nine- and twelve-plane formations, practicing over the Gulf and then flying proudly over the city and back to our base. It took positive control of distance and power usage to stay in proper line. We took turns leading, flying inside with a minimum of power, careful of stalling, while the end planes on the outside flew full throttle to maintain the arc of the formation with equal space between the adjacent planes. The most fun for me was the conclusion, dipping my wing in turn, peeling off from the line, zooming down, and heading home, landing with the other planes in the group.

We had also checked out flying a low-wing single-engine, open-cockpit aircraft, built in San Diego completely out of plywood. It was called a Timms, smooth as glass, without a rivet to mar its surface, and extremely sensitive to the touch. It was used primarily for formation training and was really fun to fly, but I never heard of it afterward.

After accumulating a number of solo hours, the month of November '43 went back to a daily dose of dual time. Instructors concentrated on the proficiency of our navigation, instrument, and radio knowledge. Celestial navigation became an important part of our curriculum and required considerable study and practice. By mid-December, I had passed all my requirements, and with the members of my class, waited for our assignments to more

The Timms in formation

advanced flight training. Bud selected flying boats and would go on to the twin-engine PBY, built by Consolidated and considered the workhorse of the seaplane fleet. Milt Gibson went to multiengine bombers and would be destined to fly the PB4Y Privateer. Al Nadler's hopes for carrier duty came closer to fruition when he was assigned to Navy fighters. Each specialty was housed at adjacent bases to the Corpus center. I was assigned to the OS2U Kingfisher, a single-engine scout aircraft, set on a body-length pontoon, that landed and took off from the open sea. Most cruisers and warships were being equipped with catapults to carry a scout seaplane to cover and search for submarines, ships, planes, or for any enemy threat that might lie ahead. Whatever orders I might receive, this would be my last phase toward becoming a naval aviator.

Vultee Vibrators in varied formations

My first day of advanced training was a shock. I was re-introduced to the Stearman Yellow Peril, only this one was on floats. We were either lowered by crane onto the water or rolled down a concrete ramp. Our objective was to learn how to sail our craft on the water, take off in a choppy sea or smooth slick surface, handle rolling swells, large and small, and estimate the velocity of the wind and direction by the reaction of the ocean surface. I was cleared to solo on my fifth flight, landing and taking off in a variety of water conditions. At the conclusion of the flight, how you idled your engine and sailed to your receiver, whether it was the sailors at the landing ramp or the crane operator off the pier, was the true test of your competence. I couldn't help reflecting on my dismal attempts at acrobatics, as I was now training on a float aircraft that was never designed for slow rolls or loops. And to think I could have been "washed out!"

On the 29th of December, I was assigned to an Ensign Johnson, who introduced me to the Consolidate OS2U Kingfisher. This smooth, single-engine low-wing plane sat on a full-length float with

The Stearman Yellow Peril

two small wing floats on the end of each wing. The pilot sat in the front cockpit with a sliding hood and a gunner with twin .30-caliber machine guns in the tandem seat behind him for protection. This was the plane currently in combat operation and engaged in all the sea action wherever the American fleet battled. Ensign Johnson was pleased with my progress and the handling of the craft on the water. When I took the controls and guided the plane through the exercises I had learned, I felt I had arrived as a Navy pilot. After my second flight in the Kingfisher, a check ride with a Lt. Swindall cleared me to solo. I did so with rampant enthusiasm on New Year's Eve, 1943.

The next two months consisted of two to three flights almost daily. The emphasis on navigation, instruments, and radio control was a constant pressure toward perfection. The cost of training an individual pilot was too big of an expenditure to have him lost in the middle of an ocean without giving him every opportunity for survival. The relentless repetition of utilizing the knowledge learned, and the confidence and security it offered, would preserve the individual as well as the Navy's investment.

January 24, 1944, was my crowning moment. I sat in the rear seat of the Kingfisher, perched atop a catapult track. A cadet who checked out before me was at the controls. He gave me instructions on how to sit, and once cleared, shot off the catapult into the air, from zero to sixty knots within six seconds of track. We circled the dock, landed in the water alongside, and were hoisted by crane back onto the catapult track. The cadet climbed out and exchanged seats with me. It was my turn to shoot off the catapult. Upon being hoisted back on the catapult, I was allowed a solo shot before taking on the next cadet in line. I pressed my head back against the headrest to keep from whipping it backward, and watched the officer in charge, checking to see if I was ready. Again, I watched his hand signal as he waited my nod to go.

In that moment, sitting on top of that catapult, alone, holding the controls of an aircraft, ready to blast off an open deck and into the air, I recalled the newsreels I had seen at my Saturday matinee movie seared my brain in a microsecond flashback. "Oh, my God, look where I am!" I was still the poor Jewish kid from east L.A., sitting alone in a naval catapult plane, with officers and men preparing to shoot me off into the sky. This is what I had achieved. My eyes were steeled on the hand signal, and I signaled my ready, joy-stick in hand, as the officer dropped his forefinger to go. The blast from the charge whipped me along the track as I recalled my first solo flight at Lone Pine. Once airborne, I screamed out what no one else could hear, "Yippee . . . !"

I circled the ramp, landed smoothly in the bay, and carefully sailed to the crane. I was then hoisted up, ready to check out the next cadet for his first experience on the catapult. It was my turn to give him his instructions. After the next shoot, I climbed out and he took my seat. I wondered what went through his mind at that moment. I know it was an excitement each of us had to share within ourselves.

All the flight classes at Corpus were not equally timed for completion. Bud finished training in the PBY early enough for him to graduate on January 12. Al followed in Navy fighters on January 26, and I'm just not sure about Milt. I was scheduled for February 16. Earning my Wings of Gold and marrying Elaine was my high as I entered my last days at Corpus Christi.

Because there were limited ships that could accommodate the number of scout pilots available for sea duty, the scuttlebutt, or rumor, was that our Kingfisher squadron, upon graduation, was going to be assigned to flight instructor school. I couldn't have been more excited. That would mean I could be married and have another year in the States before going overseas. Our final flights in the OS2U Kingfisher were night checkouts. As we prepared our conversion from cadet to officer, our last scheduled flight was a three-hour-solo night exercise, February 14, 1944. With a large graduating group of cadets, we would fly over the Gulf of Mexico at prescribed elevations, zones, and times. Upon that final landing, our group would have completed our required hours, qualifying as full-fledged naval aviators. I would also have achieved my personal goal of catching up with Elaine's brothers as an Officer and a Gentleman. After waiting over an hour to use a pay phone, I was able to express my love and satisfaction in telling her I successfully completed my final course.

8

My Last Cadet Flight

OS2U Kingfisher

Rays of moonlight slanted through the slots in the overcast sky. At 2,000 feet the OS2U Kingfisher slipped above the dark clouds and burst upward into a bright evening sky. Competing with the moonlight, a few scattered lights from the shores of Corpus Christi squinted through the haze, and an occasional blinking light from random ships in the Gulf signaled their presence below.

My last cadet flight! I wiggled my wings out of joy and accomplishment. I could hardly believe that I was about to be designated a United States naval aviator. Again my thoughts went back to my beginnings. I had left Boyle Heights, in East Los Angeles, at the age of thirteen, and moved to West Adams when my Mom married my step-dad. It was a working-class community, made up of racially mixed groups, including a strong Jewish center. I recalled sitting in the matinee at the Bard's Theater at Crenshaw and Adams, watching Robert Taylor and John Wayne in windblown scarves, shooting down enemy planes on a movie screen, in a war inconceivable to this reality.

Why, at this time, on this particular flight, did my inner reflections cause my Jewish heritage to come to the fore? I was a nonreligious youth who went through a limited after-school religious exposure, but I never had a problem being Jewish. I had belonged to a Jewish Boy Scout troop, became an Eagle Scout, and competed equally with Scouts of all ethnic groups. My feelings toward my country were as strong as anyone's. Growing up in a depression and hearing that all Jews were rich and controlled the banks was a mystery to me. My mom was a single mother and struggled to keep us together by renting a room in an older couple's home. She had been raised in a Jewish orphanage in New York, and she fought to keep us together rather than having me repeat her childhood by placing me in Vista Del Mar, a Jewish orphanage in L.A., which today helps children of all ethnicities develop into well-functioning adults. The meager rent money paid to the older couple helped with their mortgage, and they cared for me during the day while my mom worked as a secretary for the Los Angeles County. This was my background, and somehow I felt that I was a representative of the Jewish community in which I was raised.

With my hands on the control of this sleek naval aircraft, I felt a surge of pride in my heritage and accomplishment, and felt equal to my flying peers. From my beginnings, I always felt that no one could be more American than I. When this war was over, I knew I could look anyone in the eye and dare them to question my effort and allegiance. I was pleased and proud, knowing that at the end of this flight, I would receive my Wings of Gold. It suddenly hit me. I realized I was back at the Bard's Theater, but instead of watching the big movie screen, I was now the real John Wayne.

My reverie passed and I concentrated on the moment. I came back to my world as I checked my instruments and flight conditions. Again my mind wandered. Our flight group of six had been notified that upon graduation we would be sent to pilot training school to qualify as flight instructors. We would then be sent to various bases throughout the country for at least a year's assignment. Rationally, the curiosity of combat was far less appealing than my thoughts of marrying Elaine. It meant we could be together while the time element of war continued to its unknown end.

And here I was flying solo in the dark of night with forty other aircraft in the sky. I made my turns, following the vectors assigned, alert and aware of the area shared by other aircraft in this night pattern. My security and confidence in my ability and in my plane was almost too relaxing. Such was my case that I was suddenly jolted by a loud *POP!* As dark as the night was below the clouds, my windshield shook and my hood was splattered with blackness. Oil shrouded my plane. Peering through the glimmers of light blown by the wind and the propeller, I effectively lost my front visibility, thrust into sudden darkness.

"Corpus Tower, Corpus Tower, Kingfisher 202," I called into my helmet mike. "Mayday! Mayday!"

The tower responded: "Corpus Tower, 202. State your problem."

"Oil covering windshield. Zero visibility. Cutting power. Over."

"202, Corpus Tower. Maintain glide setting. Circle wide to 80-degree heading. 202, what is altitude? Over."

"2,800 feet, Corpus. Dropping steadily. Over."

"202, Corpus Tower. Hold altitude if you can. Head 280 degrees until out of Kingfish flight pattern. Can you read? Over."

"Kingfish 202, read you loud and clear, Corpus Tower. Starting turn. Over."

I pushed the throttle forward and slightly raised the nose of the airplane. My eyes spied the control panel, checking oil pressure, airspeed, needle and ball, trying to hold the elevation. Banking into the 280-degree needle, conscious of stalling, I flew out of the circling pattern of forty other planes at various elevations. They were all flying at assigned heights on their last cadet flight.

I made contact again: "Corpus Tower, 202 on 280-degree course. Oil pressure dropping, throttling back. Over."

"202, Corpus Tower. Once through overcast you will parallel coast. Keep eyes open for strays. At 800 feet, seadrome will be ahead. Over."

With minimum power and the plane set in glide position, I kept checking my oil pressure with my eyes on the needle and ball, and banked into the 280-degree alignment. I tried slipping from side to side, kicking my rudders to visually see sideways any other lights of aircraft wandering nearby. As the plane dropped to the 2,000-foot elevation and into the dark overcast, I kept reporting my position while the tower cautioned other aircraft to safer elevations.

Radio control kept directing me as I repeated my airspeed and altitude. I flew through the black cloud cover, and from the sides of my cockpit, I spotted the lights of the seadrome dictating the area of the bay that paralleled the Corpus coast. With minimum power, and mindful of stalling, I continued slipping from side to side for visibility to line up the bobbing ocean lights that marked the waterway for landing. With everything in order, parallel to the shore, I lined my aircraft between the center line of lights marking the seadrome of Corpus Bay. With flaps down and small bursts of power, the evenly chopping water reflected alternating prisms of illumination as I kept the wings level and the nose slightly raised, and concentrated on my altimeter to tell me how close I was to the water. No slipping from side to side now. I mothered the joystick in my hand to anticipate a straight blind landing by instrument and feel. The altimeter kept dropping and melted to zero. I felt the pontoon caress the choppy water perfectly. I cut the engine and skimmed along the surface and settled in as smooth a landing as I had ever made. With the throttle full back, I wished my instructor could have seen that one. I loved that airplane and I felt it loved me back.

As the engine idled, I pulled back the plastic canopy. The plane bobbed forward in the water, and the warm Texas wind blew in my face as I stood up in the cockpit. With alternating shots of moonlight, I could see the oil that covered my windshield that could have been my demise. The lightly lit skyline of Corpus Christi never looked as good. My oil gauge showed a notch above empty as I taxied alongside the floating marine lights.

The towering concrete bulkhead at the end of the seaplane dock was silhouetted by lights well away from the sea lane. Two large searchlights played along the water's surface, suddenly lighting me up in the glare. An amplified loudspeaker directed me to follow the light. With the wind and the tide competing for my direction, I concentrated on sailing the OS2U toward a large crane backlit on the dock. I was concerned that if my wingtip or pontoon should touch the bulkhead, or damage the craft, my Navy flying career could be in jeopardy. The loudspeaker came on again: "Kingfish 202, cut your engine. Launch coming alongside."

A small Navy boat with lights on the side and a portable floodlight pulled alongside. The pilot of the boat skillfully aligned between my wing and tail and secured me to its hull. A sailor, under the direction of a junior officer, carefully stepped on the inner section of the wing, trying to lean away from the oil-splattered side. He reached into the empty gunner's cockpit behind me and released a cable attachment. Another sailor deftly handled the launch so we paralleled the dock where the crane had dropped a steel cable and hook to lift the aircraft out of the water. As it dangled overhead, I caught the cable and steadied it as a seaman hooked the chain to the attachment. I was instructed to sit down in the cockpit as the sailor nimbly got back into his boat. He had released our bond and carefully drifted free as the cable secured the plane to the crane. I bobbed motionless in the water, and the officer signaled the crane operator to raise me clear from the dock.

The lights caused me to cover my eyes as I felt the cable draw taut and the plane pulled up, sucking free of the water. We swayed slightly in the air as we were hoisted to the top of the bunker and gently lowered above a steel sleeve on the catapult rails. A waiting seaman had straightened the floating craft as it dangled from the crane. The crane operator then settled us gently into the catapult nest that lined the edge of the dock. Once secured, the sailors released the connection and helped me out of the cockpit to best avoid the oil splattered on the sides.

I climbed down to the deck and was met by the officer of the day. He was a full lieutenant in working khakis, carrying a clipboard to record my report. As I explained what happened, several platform crewmen went to examine the plane.

"Oil cap blown free, Sir," yelled one of the men that helped me from the aircraft.

Two other sailors, standing on the catapult rail, started wiping the oil off the skin of the plane. A large sack of rags was produced along with some cleaning solvents and strong arms to administer the labor.

As the lieutenant kept writing, I asked, "Any chance of getting another plane to finish my flight, Sir?"

"No way. By the time you tried to get back, all the other planes will be coming in. All we need is you going up while they're coming down."

I could see the plane getting cleaner as the lieutenant handed me his clipboard and asked me to sign the report. I glanced at my statement as written and returned it to the officer.

"Report back to quarters," he said. "Cadet dismissed."

We exchanged salutes, and I walked the length of the pier with my helmet and goggles in hand. I got to my cadet housing and removed my flight suit and waited for my flight group to check in. In response to all their questions, I exaggerated my experience.

The following morning after mess, we gathered in a small auditorium. A lieutenant commander congratulated us on our completion of our cadet training. We would graduate in two days with other squadrons in our battalion. He cited the values and obligations of a naval officer, the honor we had achieved, and the honor we were expected to uphold. Our graduating battalion would be sent for advanced training as fighter pilots, dive bombers, P-boat, and instructors. Ten percent of the graduates would accept their commissions as second lieutenants in the Marine Corps, and the rest as ensigns in the Navy.

Anyone who desired the Marines, or had a relative in the Marines past or present, was accepted first. If twelve percent of a class wanted the Marines, the first ten percent with relative connections had priority. If only eight percent of a class requested the Marines, the additional two percent was drafted from the pool.

Several more flight officers addressed the group. We were then released to pick up our official officer's uniforms that had been ordered several weeks prior.

Our navy blue uniforms had a single gold ensign stripe on the cuff of each sleeve. A single gold star was centered above the stripe, designating our rank as an Officer and a Gentleman. Embroidered gold wings were sewn over the left breast pocket of the jacket, designating us as U.S. naval aviators. The officer's cap had a gold Navy crest and a single gold braid stretched along the brim. We had also ordered khaki and green blazer uniforms for work and casual wear. There were other matching uniforms, gray and formal white, to be ordered as needed, depending on assignment. I tried on my officer's uniform and my mirror said I would never look better than this in my life.

We received a folder with general instructions, responsibility of rank, travel procedures, and a packet of photographs taken individually with helmet and thrown-back goggles, a leather flight jacket, and white scarf. The Navy had made ten copies, postcard size. It was like high school, except the Navy sent one copy to the Bureau of Personnel (BUPERS) in Washington, D.C. It would be used in the event one was involved in a heroic act, killed in action, or for whatever publicity would benefit the Navy. The other nine copies were given to each graduate to trade with fellow cadets or to send to family and friends back home. The following day, before graduation, each new officer would check out and receive his advanced assignment.

We were free. We packed, we wrote letters, exchanged pictures, went to the base movie, and anxiously relaxed. After waiting in the phone line, I connected with Elaine and told her I would notify her where I would be assigned, and arrange for her to meet me and get

OS2U Kingfisher

married. The excitement of graduation, my unknown destination, marriage, enveloped me with anticipation.

The following day our battalion was divided into various flight sections. When our Kingfish group was called, our team of six lined up to get our instructions. The three in front of me received packets for flight instruction school. My excitement peaked because that meant my overseas duty would be delayed, and as anxious as I felt for combat duty, the thought of marrying Elaine took priority in my heart. I stood as the officer in charge pulled up my documents. He glanced at me curiously as he held my packet and noted a large stamped HOLD on my folder.

"Cooper?"

"Yes, Sir," I responded.

"You have a hold on your orders. Seems like you are short a half hour of night flying."

I was shaken. "What does that mean, Sir?"

"Well, Cadet, it means what it says. You'll have to make up an hour of night flying before graduating."

"But, Sir," I stammered, "my class is graduating tomorrow."

"I guess they'll just have to graduate without you. You'll have to make up the hour of night flying and graduate with the following class."

My wings, my commission, my orders, my marriage, all placed on hold. After eighteen months of training, I was not going to graduate with my class. I was beyond disappointed. I was crushed.

The following three nights in Corpus Christi consisted of rain, wind, and hurricane conditions. All flights were on hold as I watched my flight group graduate and leave for their designated assignments. While my classmates were commissioned ensigns in the United States Naval Air Corps, I was still a cadet.

What I thought was my last training flight . . . wasn't!

9

Graduation and Orders

Wings of gold

When the storm lifted, I joined the following class of "Kingfishers" on their final night flight. Three hours later I went back to my empty quarters where arrangements had already been made for the next advanced class to occupy. I had gone through a second briefing and was told to report to quarters across the grassy parade grounds. I was to be dressed in my Navy officer blues, ready for graduation.

On February 19, 1944, well before 0800, I checked myself in a full-length floor mirror that again gave me the finest reflection I ever enjoyed. I wore my officer's uniform with the single gold stripe and the traditional gold star on my sleeve. My shiny gold wings were sewn above the left breast pocket, and my officer's cap with the Navy crest sat smartly on top of my head. I saluted the mirror and it saluted me back. I was an officer, an ensign in the United States Naval Reserve. I thought of Pearl Harbor, the war, eighteen months of the most physical, mental, and skilled training, completed. I was fascinated that the reflected image was really me. Even though my religious beliefs were basically agnostic, my Jewish heritage again came to the fore. I was proud to be Jewish and of having earned my Navy wings. I was now in a position to defend and represent my country and the advantages it had given me. I repeated to myself, I am a Navy pilot. It was my proudest accomplishment. I wondered, how do I top this? Where do I go from here?

I walked across the damp lawn to the quarters on the other side. Two cadets coming in from an overnight pass were walking toward me. As they came closer, they both stopped short and snapped a brisk salute. It was my first, and caught me by surprise. "Oh," I said, "knock it off. I'm not officially an officer yet."

They both looked at me, baffled, checking my ensign stripe and officer's cap, and mumbled, "Knock what off, Sir?" and then checked their own uniforms for some form of irregularity. The sudden power of rank struck me. I tried to explain to them that I was going to my graduation and that I was not really an officer yet. There was no comprehension on their part. Their concern was to get away from what they thought was a possible reprimand. Then I realized, they were me these past eighteen months.

I graduated with a class of forty-five newly designated Navy ensigns and twenty-nine Marine lieutenants. Standing with these bright and talented new pilots, I looked around, relishing my Jewish pride in being a part of this elite group. Yet, I couldn't help realizing that no other ethnic groups, Negroes or Mexican graduates, were taking their oaths as Naval pilots to defend our country. It was all white bread and me. After our swearing in, I responded to my first official salute by doling out a dollar bill to a base seaman. It was the custom at the time.

My biggest surprise came when I opened my orders. Instead of assignment to flight instruction school, I was directed to report to Banana River, Florida, in seven days to train in the Navy's largest twin-engine seaplane bomber, the PBM Martin Mariner. These orders were generally for those who had trained in the Consolidated PBY Catalina. I questioned the officer in charge.

"Sir, why are they sending me to PBMs? I have never flown a twin-engine aircraft, and I have never been in a PBY."

The officer looked at me. "That's no problem," he said. "You are a naval aviator. You can do it."

I telegraphed Elaine. I was disappointed about not getting flight instruction school because it might delay our getting married. I would keep her informed by phone or telegram daily. I joined three other graduates who were going to travel together to Jacksonville, Florida, and then I would go on to the town of Cocoa and check into nearby Banana River Air Base. The four of us, Ensign Dick Birk, Ensign Wayne Baker, and Marine Lieutenant Doug Ogilby, and I got along great. We ate together, shared cabs, rented adjacent rooms in New Orleans, and enjoyed the freedom from cadet bondage.

We toured the French Quarter and angled preferential seating at the Three Sisters, a popular tourist restaurant and bar. Service managed to filter its way through the crowded tables when a buxom woman, some twenty years older than we were, pulled up a chair to our foursome. She might have been a waitress, an owner, or at least a principal of the establishment. As she sat down, her bosom flared across the checkered table cloth as she leaned forward on her elbows, taking us all in.

"How you boys doing?" she asked.

After our confinement as cadets, it was difficult trying not to stare at her tremendous breasts, seemingly on the verge of bursting out of her blouse. It must have been obvious, and between the small talk, she casually reached over and took my hand and laid it flat on her cleavage. She then moved it side to side.

"Go ahead and feel," she smiled, and then made an open invitation to my friends. She held my hand firmly, and as a gentleman, I was not in a position to resist. My three companions put down their beers and accepted her offer. She obliged and we all ended up laughing heartily together. It's funny how a single insignificant, momentary act can leave you with a memory you carry for life. She must have spread many memories over a good period of time.

The four of us palled together. We roamed Bourbon Street, ate clams and oysters, tried different cafes, and listened to combos of jazz musicians. We took a tour to the cemeteries, and in between contacted our relatives and friends at home. Late nights and late sleep-ins, and breakfast or lunch in an array of restaurants and coffee shops, filled our days of freedom from the strict observance of cadet life at Corpus Christi. When the time passed, we checked out of our rooms and shared a cab to the train station. We pulled into Jacksonville, our final destination together.

Five days had passed since our transition from cadet to officer. This was the point where our orders would direct us to our varied

Ensign Wayne Baker, Lt. Doug Ogilby, Ensign Irv Cooper, and Ensign Dick Birk at the Hotel Roosevelt, Jacksonville, Florida, February 1944

futures. Individually, we headed to our final advanced training, dive bomber, torpedo bombing, and fighters. I was going to take the train from Jacksonville to Cocoa, and check in at the Banana River Air Base for my transition to the Martin Mariner seaplane, anti-submarine school. Our last goodbye took place in the Hotel Roosevelt. We had our photograph taken together, shook hands, and wished each other luck.

I have never seen or heard of them since.

CCNAS-1-19-44-6,000 3825

N. A. Designation
No. C-15413

NAVAL AIR TRAINING CENTER
U. S. NAVAL AIR STATION
CORPUS CHRISTI, TEXAS

NAVAL AVIATOR DESIGNATION
(Heavier-than-Air)

19 February, 1944

From: The Commandant.
To: Irvin S. COOPER, A-7(l), USER.
SUBJECT: Naval Aviator Designation.

1. Having successfully completed the approved course of training for Student Naval Aviators, and having met the requirements of Act I of Congress approved 24 June, 1926, I this day appoint you a NAVAL AVIATOR (Heavier-than-Air) and detail you to duty involving actual flying in and control of aircraft in accordance with Act of Congress approved 10 June, 1922, as amended 2 July, 1926.

CNO (1)

BuPers (1)

C. P. MASOI

P. H. Pierce
3y direction

10

The Mariner and My Wedding

PBM Martin Mariner

I arrived in Cocoa, Florida, a day early. I checked into the Navy base at Banana River. It was just north of the city of Cocoa where the Banana River ran parallel to the Florida coast. It was built specifically on the inland waterway paralleling the Atlantic Ocean so that the aircraft would not be exposed to high swells or turbulent seas. A series of concrete ramps, storing, and maintenance areas abutted the east side of the flowing stream. There were quarters for officers and men, and eating and entertainment centers. There was also a caste system in which all the new ensigns were assigned quarters together, ate in a separate dining room together, and basically did not fraternize with the flight instructors and other officers on the base. We were officers in a cadet environment. The one exception was that student officers who were married could invite their spouses to eat on the base on Saturday evenings, and dine with the base officers in the senior officer's dining room. All officers received a subsistence allowance and paid for their meals on the base. Unmarried officers who lived on the base paid for their room and board at a very modest charge. The base personnel had their own facilities.

The PBM Mariner was the largest twin-engine seaplane in the Navy. It was taking the place of the PBY Catalina, with greater speed, a heavier bomb load, and with a nose, tail, and top .50-caliber gun turrets. It provided two side hatches in the center of the craft that allowed two .30-caliber machine guns to fire from each side. The Mariner carried a crew of twelve, including three pilots, a plane commander and two copilots, and nine enlisted crew members of various specialty ratings. The head crew member responsible for the crew had the title of crew captain.

The average wartime flight ranged from twelve to fourteen hours. The pilots generally alternated, flying eight hours and navigating four. The Mariner had a double interior deck with the pilots and a navigation table on top, four bunks, a hot plate cooking tray, some with a small refrigerator, and a portable toilet. Three new pilot trainees were assigned to a plane. Joe Hudson, Howard Brown, and I made up our threesome, and we were assigned to alternating instructors for varying phases of instruction.

My first turn in the pilot's seat was a revelation. Like the officer said, "You're a naval aviator. You can do it." And I did.

I seemed to adjust to the twin throttles with ease. I enjoyed the alternating power of turning the aircraft easily from one side to the other. Learning to adjust the throttles to react slowly, anticipate the reaction, approach a buoy, and sail into a given position was achieved with practice and satisfaction. It was a thrill sitting in the cockpit ten feet above the water, taking off and landing. I was pleased to be as equally proficient as Joe and Howard, who had trained in PBYs.

Once settled, I found a motel in Cocoa. It had single rooms with a bathroom, and I made arrangements to rent Unit #7. One of my classmates, Milt Gibson, had married Jolene, his beautiful high school sweetheart and queen of their high school prom. Milt was six feet tall, a great athlete, and together the two of them looked like a movie star poster. They had taken the unit across the grass court from the one I reserved. All the rooms were rented by young married couples and turned over as each training session ended and a new group came in.

My next course was to arrange our wedding and get Elaine to join me. There were no facilities in Cocoa, so I went to Orlando and looked through the telephone book. I found a Rabbi Morris Skopp, who I learned had friends working and studying at U.C.L.A. I went to his home and made arrangements for him to marry us in his living room. Although my formal religious beliefs were limited, I did ask that the service be in English and that he provide a chuppah for the ceremony. A chuppah is a canopy constructed of four corner poles with a silk or linen fabric on top of an area about four feet by four feet. The bride and groom stand under the canopy while the rabbi recites the vows that the couple acknowledges. He explained to me that a chuppah required ten men in attendance to verify the union. The use of the chuppah was a tradition I had always observed, and I insisted on having it regardless of how few would be in attendance. Rabbi Skopp was a reformed Jew, and even though my request defied tradition, he agreed to my wishes. I quickly sent Elaine a telegram:

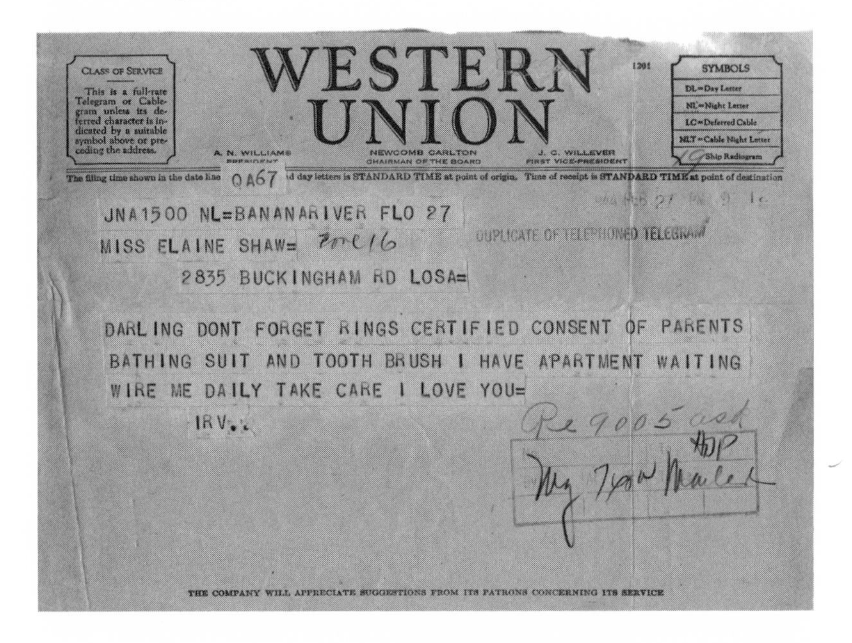

WESTERN UNION

JNA1500 NL=BANANARIVER FLO 27
MISS ELAINE SHAW=
2835 BUCKINGHAM RD LOSA=

DARLING DONT FORGET RINGS CERTIFIED CONSENT OF PARENTS BATHING SUIT AND TOOTH BRUSH I HAVE APARTMENT WAITING WIRE ME DAILY TAKE CARE I LOVE YOU=
IRV.

DUPLICATE OF TELEPHONED TELEGRAM

THE COMPANY WILL APPRECIATE SUGGESTIONS FROM ITS PATRONS CONCERNING ITS SERVICE

Elaine was nineteen and in 1944 Florida you were required to have your parents' approval to marry if you were under the age of twenty-one. After a series of phone calls and telegrams, Elaine was able to get a railroad ticket to Orlando, by way of Chicago. She would stay with relatives in Chicago for a day or two and then continue on to Orlando. The trip by train would take five days, with the last two from Chicago. She would arrive on Sunday, March 5. I planned our wedding for Monday, the 6th, and rented a hotel room in Orlando for the night before. I called Bud in Atlanta, and he planned to get a plane at his base and fly in for the day. I called George Woodford in Boca Raton where he was stationed as a flight coordinator. He had married his Dorsey High sweetheart, Betty Sommers, and they lived in a little cottage on the beach. Before they were married, her folks were unhappy that George was not Jewish, so I used to pick her up and then leave her with George when Elaine and I went out on dates. They had a wonderful marriage and they planned to drive up to Orlando for our wedding and then drive us back to Cocoa on their way home to Boca Raton. All arrangements were made.

Orlando was a small town but the train station was mayhem. Army, Navy, Marines, and Coast Guard personnel stopped and dispersed to every kind of training facility Florida had to offer. The mixture of uniforms mingled with wives, mothers, crying babies, male spouses, and every form of humanity, going back and forth and forming a mingled maze of congestion. Through this setting, with polite shoving, I found her. She was struggling with two suitcases as she stepped off the train. She was disheveled in a rumpled suit, loose-hanging scarf, silk stockings, and dress shoes. Unless you were in uniform, dressing in suits and ties and dresses and hats was the proper mode of attire in those days. Sitting on her suitcases for three days and nights in the aisle of the train crammed with passengers, scrounging for a sandwich or any kind of food at the infrequent engine stops, must have drained her stamina. The bathrooms and crying babies and the difficulty in movement reduced modesty to survival. My Elaine was pale, drawn, tired, and wan. I took one look and wondered, is this my beloved bride? My God, what have I gotten myself into?

She saw me for the first time in my officer's uniform. Her smile cracked the ashen vision I saw at first glance. The station was filled with many young ensigns with matching uniforms and gold wings, and I felt I was no longer unique. Elaine threw her arms around me, and if I had felt a fleeting second of doubt, it disappeared immediately. I grabbed her bags and tried to hold her arm at the same time while pushing our way to the outer skirts of the station's pavilion. We got a taxi in line and headed for the hotel.

Once in our room, Elaine showered and freshened up, her color lit up her face, and we babbled about our adventures to this point. She was hungry and tired. We ate leisurely in the hotel and returned to our room. It was suddenly awkward, and it was the first time we were in a double bed together. Remember, in those days, if you loved someone, the only way you could sleep together was to get married. And so we had waited.

Elaine had a wonderful figure and wore a sensuous night gown for this occasion. Modestly, I had showered and wore white jockey shorts as I turned off the lights and climbed under the sheet and light blanket. We held each other tightly. Elaine was willing. And I balked. In later years, I was chided for saying we had waited so long that I was willing to wait one more day until we were officially married. With the excitement and turmoil of the train ride and the marriage preparation, we held each other and fell asleep. I remember waking in the morning with a terrible ache in my groin.

After breakfast we talked about home, our families, and how my mother and her dad wanted to come to the wedding. We laughed when we realized her dad had bought her a round-trip ticket back to Los Angeles. I wired both families of Elaine's safe arrival and the impending afternoon wedding. After the ceremony, I sent another wire, signed "Mr. and Mrs."

George and Betty picked us up at the hotel. With due apologies, Bud had called to tell us bad weather prevented the Navy from releasing a plane for him to fly out of Atlanta. In the meantime, I had run into Paul Engles in the hotel, with whom I had gone through training starting in L.A. I asked him to come to my wed-

The wedding: George and Betty Woodford, Irv and Elaine Cooper, the neighbor, Rabbi Morris Skopp, and Paul Engles

ding, gave him directions, and he promised to meet us at the rabbi's house. George acted as my best man and Betty supported Elaine. Since the chuppah produced by the rabbi had four corner poles, he asked a neighbor if he would oblige by holding two ends in each hand, while George and Paul each held the others. The ritual was simple. When the rabbi discussed the symbolism of the chuppah, even in its unorthodox use, he described the covering as our first home. He elaborated on the meaning of home, the sanctity of marriage, the family, the passage of time, and our future life together. I was very pleased that I had insisted on the chuppah being a part of our ceremony. We said our "I do's," took a sip of wine, and as tradition prevailed, I stomped on the glass, which was wrapped in a small towel to prevent the shards from scattering on the floor.

I thanked Paul and the neighbor, expressed my appreciation, and paid the rabbi. We got in the car, had a late wedding lunch at a passing diner, and drove back to Cocoa to our real first home in the motel.

When we arrived, we got out of the car, gathered our luggage, and thanked Betty and George for being such an important part of our nuptial. Elaine slipped into her shoes, which she had removed during our drive back to Cocoa, and let out a scream of terror. We froze. "What?" She literally tore the shoe from her foot. A bee had somehow lodged in the inside corner of her open shoe and expressed its disturbance by stinging her big toe as she tried to put the shoe on. I helped Elaine hop to our room while George brought in our gear. I tried saying goodbye again while working to pull out the stinger. I looked for something to ease the pain, but Elaine's toe swelled and turned red.

It was not quite the honeymoon night we envisioned!

11

Life at Banana River

River Oak Hotel Court

The courtship of endless fantasies, phone calls, telegrams, and distant contacts prior to the proclamation of "I do's" was now a thing of the past. We were actually married. Odd that there were no courses in school on how to prepare to lead one's life, loving and living together as man and wife. But here we were. These were the days when loving couples had to get married in order to fulfill their desires and to savor each other for the rest of their lives. How does it compare with today's acceptance of trial and error? Casual sex, living together sometimes for months or years, culminating in marriage or separation with precious time lost in the interim, or perhaps a permanent arrangement with children of unmarried parents? I'm sure there has to be a thesis somewhere on this alone.

After bonding under the symbol of the chuppah in a strange home without family, and with the guidance of a rabbi found in the local telephone book, our first home was a motel room in Cocoa, Florida, on the bank of the Banana River. Elaine and I got to know each other in all the ways we hadn't imagined. Love, exhilaration, skepticism, and reality marked our experience as newlyweds. There were no plans ahead. The reality of war, the purpose of our location, and the training I was receiving at the Banana River Air Base was the reason of our being. My confidence and my skill and the ego satisfaction of my progress was most gratifying. Realizing that I was equal to my peers erased any self-doubt I may have had in my assignment. My days were fulfilled, and they ended with my return each evening to our motel home, and perhaps the exchanged question, "How was your day?"

Elaine's transformation from college student at U.C.L.A. to the wife of a training naval aviator 4,000 miles from home was an experimental adjustment, just as when I left my home over a year and a half ago. As I had become absorbed with my fellow trainees,

Elaine became a part of the newly-wed wives. Between them they learned where to market, where the local milkman made his daily rounds, and what local shopping was available. While their husbands trained, they developed a social existence, reading books, writing letters, walking the trail along the Banana River, making the bed, and waiting for the day's end and their husband's return. Elaine and Jolene spent considerable time together and could reminisce about places back home in Southern California. In this new environment, Elaine was introduced to a social activity unfamiliar to her past. It was called the "beer bust." One of the ladies of the Motel Social Club announced that she thought she was pregnant. To celebrate the occasion, she bought several cases of beer and arranged space in her motel room by pushing the bed halfway up the wall, and she had Glenn Miller, Tommy Dorsey, Harry

The day after the beer bust: Jolene and Milt Gibson on the lounges, left, with Elaine trying to recover, head down, napping in front, with our friends whose names I have forgotten

James, and other danceable records played in celebration of her announcement. I had a late flight that evening and when I arrived home the party was in full swing. I entered the room and the couples were laughing and dancing, and reasonably drunk. I couldn't see Elaine and asked, "Where is she?" That seemed a pretty hilarious question. They laughed and pointed floorward. And there she was, lying on the floor, with the dancers shuffling around trying not to step on her. "Elaine," I said, startled, "Get up. What's wrong?" She demurred, "I'm sick." I managed, with Milt Gibson's help, to get her back to our Bungalow 7. She got to the toilet with her head down into the bowl. "Beer," she said, "I never want to look at it again."

Even though her parents had sold beer in the family delicatessen, it was always available and nothing she had really tried. When offered a bottle of beer that afternoon, the Florida humidity and the cold glass seemed most appetizing. Elaine drank the first one down like a glass of water. It was refreshing and she kept drinking. It wasn't until she got to the bungalow dance that it caught up with her, and down she went. For whatever reason, her capitulation made the party a success.

In the same vein, I was offered beer in my emerging teens and just didn't care for the taste. My father was a carpenter contractor who went to work every day. He first loaded his truck with a full case of beer and then his tools. Each night he would return the case completely empty. "I'm just the middle man," he would say. Even though I never drank, my high school buddies loved to come to my house. My dad was a gracious host.

I successfully passed my familiarization tests of the Mariner, along with Brown and Hudson. Our next phase was instrumentation and bombing. We took turns in the pilot's seat, flying designated vectors, adjusting to wind currents over the Atlantic, and returning to our point of departure. We practiced daily bombing runs and procedures. As our training progressed, we were assigned full-day patrols along the coast of Florida, glued to binoculars looking for German submarines, and learning to man the .30-caliber machine guns in the Mariner's side hatches.

Our navigation assignments required learning the use of the sextant, to determine the latitude and longitude of the celestial bodies. We were allowed to take the instrument home to practice. Elaine became quite proficient in starting with the North Star. After several short night flights, we took our first all-night patrol, a ten-hour flight alternating between piloting and navigating. We were excited about our next assignment, a flight to Guantanamo, Cuba.

We had decided to celebrate by making a reservation for dinner with the base staff and senior officers. I was certainly aware of the phrase "rank has its privileges." As a new ensign, somewhat confined to the society at a specialized site, I was still impressed with the career service of so many men, young and old, enlisted personnel, and officers of varying rank. A commander or captain's cap, striking gold braid across the brim, commanded greater respect with each designated stripe.

We were seated at a long table between a lieutenant (j.g.) and a full lieutenant and their wives. At the head of the table sat a commander with the golden oak pins on his collar and three full stripes on his sleeve. Depending on how well he was known by the other officers, he seemed to be greeted and respected with a greater degree of affirmation. This was our first exposure to the measuring tape of rank.

With our limited social graces, the table setting was perfect: the center plate, with a salad plate atop, the napkin at its side, two forks and two spoons of varying size, two glasses, water and wine, placed one ahead and one askew. I always recalled the movies where formal tables were set that were completely remote to the manner in which we lived. The plates, the wine glasses, silverware, the napkins creatively folded, and here we were a part of this social circle. Elaine and I squeezed hands under the table cloth as a voice requested we bow our heads. After a short prayer thanking God for what we were about to partake, and the passing of the salad, I become most aware of rank and its privileges. A black naval mess steward entered the dining area carrying a large platter of steaks. He went directly to the commander's wife, holding a napkin under the platter before her. She selected her choice, which was deftly placed upon her plate. At this point, the steward walked to the other end of the table, displaying his ware in front of the wife of the lieutenant commander, the second-ranking officer at the table. Next came the lieutenant's wife, followed by the service to the wives of the (j.g.)'s, and then on to the ensigns wives at the table. Elaine was the last to select her choice before the steward headed back to the head of the table to present his offering to the ranking officer.

The steward whipped back and forth, serving each officer in order of rank, until the final steak on the platter was presented to me, as the lowest ranking officer at the table. That, with due respect, was the sign for all guests to wield their steak knives and go at it.

Many years later, in our civilian life, we made a trip to Israel and toured an army base near the Red Sea. Our tour group was invited to lunch under a large tent with a long dining table down the center. An Israeli general with a full beard was the host and he sat in the center, discussing and answering questions presented to him by the guide and group. During the discussion, the food arrived. The first person at the end of the table was offered his choice, then followed by a lady from Chicago, then reaching the general's staff sergeant, and then to the general himself. Everyone was served in the order they were seated. Elaine and I had to laugh to ourselves. No rank or privilege here.

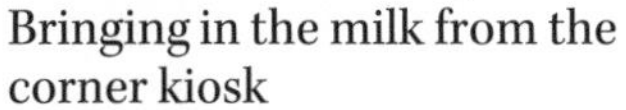

Bringing in the milk from the corner kiosk

Sunday attire at our motel home

I culminated my training experience by flying to Guantanamo Bay, Cuba. The flight, other than the destination, was uneventful. Brownie and I had walked to the chain-link fence that separated Guantanamo from Cuba proper. At 5:00 p.m., we watched the Cuban housekeepers pass through the gate to their homes on the other side. They returned the following morning to continue their cleaning chores on the naval base. I did manage to buy an embroidered tablecloth at the Ship's Store, which was my first gift as husband to wife in our marriage.

The following day, we flew from Guantanamo to Great Exuma, a Caribbean island, a 2.1-hour flight according to my log book. I was credited with .7 of an hour of pilot time. But for my first venture out of the United States, with the exception of Tijuana, Mexico, it was quite exciting. After reading the *National Geographic* as a schoolboy, I found out that the natives of the Caribbean really did balance baskets, produce, and varied products on their heads. The next day, a three-hour flight landed us at home in Banana River.

On May 19, 1944, I received my Combat Air Crew certification, and along with Crew 17C, Class No. 17 received our orders for leave. I was to report to Harvey's Point, North Carolina, to Combat Navy Squadron VPB (Navy Patrol Bomber) 27 by June 15. I was to be part of a new squadron preparing for assignment to the Pacific theater of action.

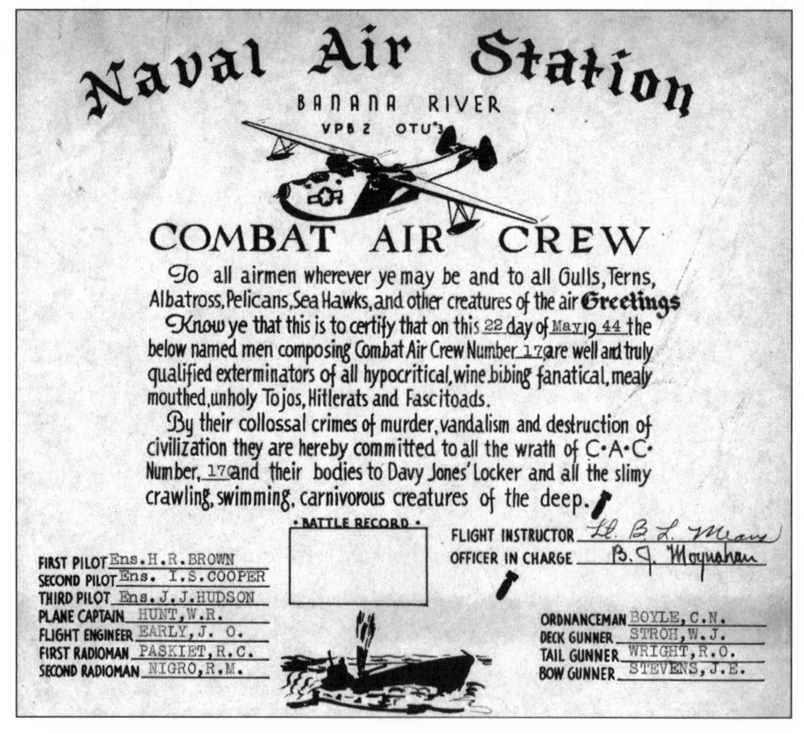

Naval Air Station
BANANA RIVER
VPB 2 OTU 3

COMBAT AIR CREW

To all airmen wherever ye may be and to all Gulls, Terns, Albatross, Pelicans, Sea Hawks, and other creatures of the air **Greetings**

Know ye that this is to certify that on this 22 day of May 19 44 the below named men composing Combat Air Crew Number 17 are well and truly qualified exterminators of all hypocritical, wine bibing fanatical, mealy mouthed, unholy Tojos, Hitlerats and Fascitoads.

By their collossal crimes of murder, vandalism and destruction of civilization they are hereby committed to all the wrath of C•A•C• Number, 17 and their bodies to Davy Jones' Locker and all the slimy crawling, swimming, carnivorous creatures of the deep.

• BATTLE RECORD •

FLIGHT INSTRUCTOR Lt. B. L. Means
OFFICER IN CHARGE B. J. Moynahan

FIRST PILOT Ens. H. R. BROWN
SECOND PILOT Ens. I. S. COOPER
THIRD PILOT Ens. J. J. HUDSON
PLANE CAPTAIN HUNT, W.R.
FLIGHT ENGINEER EARLY, J. O.
FIRST RADIOMAN PASKIET, R.C.
SECOND RADIOMAN NIGRO, R.M.

ORDNANCEMAN BOYLE, C.N.
DECK GUNNER STROH, W.J.
TAIL GUNNER WRIGHT, R.O.
BOW GUNNER STEVENS, J.E.

My certificate of completion from Banana River

12
The Wedding Reception

Our wedding photo

With three weeks left before reporting to duty at Hertford, North Carolina, Elaine and I arranged to go home to our families as Mr. and Mrs., or more formally, Ensign and Mrs. C.

It would be our delayed honeymoon, a sleeper berth on a Santa Fe Pullman train to Los Angeles. First stop: New York City. We checked into the McAlpine Hotel for $15.00 per night. We were as typical as tourists could be. We walked to Times Square, saw the Rockettes at Radio City Music Hall, took a carriage ride in Central Park, fed the pigeons, ate Italian, and sauntered back to the McAlpine. In silk stockings and high-heeled shoes, Elaine leaned on me and sighed out loud.

"My feet are killing me."

A voice from nowhere blurted an unsolicited response. "What's amadder, lady, dey make the sidewahks too hard fer ya?" as a typical New Yorker of the '40s passed by.

We laughed, and I thought of my effort at New York humor earlier in the day. We had gotten on a bus, and as I put change in the coin box, the driver asked, "Wheh to?"

My smart-ass retort was "Toity toid." The driver, unfazed, snapped back:

"Tanks."

Next stop: Washington, D.C. We made arrangements to meet Elaine's brother Harry, who was an engineer involved in high-security naval electronics. Having achieved my officer's status, I met him on equal terms and

Brother Harry, Elaine, and me in Washington, D.C.

we spent a pleasant afternoon together, visiting the White House, the Washington and Lincoln monuments, and additional tourist stops. We updated each other and reminisced about everything that got us to this point, and speculated on what the future held. Harry and I bonded well, and he expressed envy that I was going overseas.

Chicago was our next stop. Not a hotel room available for walk-ins, but we found a room in a fleabag hotel near the stockyards on the seedy side of town. The odor was horrific, and we even slept on top of the bed for fear of bedbugs and questionable linen. We met with an uncle of Elaine's, and he highlighted our stay by sending us to a great meal at the Black Hawk Restaurant on Randolph and Washington Streets. When we left Chicago, our berth on the train never looked as great and inviting. The Santa Fe took us to Los Angeles with stops at Kansas City, Missouri; Wichita, Kansas; Albu-

Elaine and me at the Black Hawk Restaurant, Chicago, May 1944

querque and Gallup, New Mexico; and the railway hub of San Bernardino, California.

The train station in Los Angeles was as busy as ever. We didn't anticipate the crowd that greeted us as we stepped off the vestibule. We soon realized they weren't greeting us but following the flamboyant singing cowboy, Roy Rogers, and his wife, Dale Evans, in full colorful western regalia. They wore matching ten-gallon hats, scarves, high-heeled boots, and white riding pants, and were getting ready to board the adjacent train to whatever their destination was. For us, it was just home at last.

We unpacked in Elaine's house. I felt awkward sleeping in Elaine's bed and bedroom, which had certainly been off-limits in our courting time. We had really come home to see our parents as a married couple. In spite of our desires not to have a reception, my mother persisted and made arrangements to have a large reception in the Park Manor Hall, near MacArthur Park, just west of downtown Los Angeles. It was set for June 3, and approximately 200 guests were invited to a sit-down dinner and reception. I know this was my mother's opportunity to get payback from all her friends for all the affairs and gifts she and my dad had doled out in previous years. Elaine's parents had a very limited social life outside of family and had no such designs.

In those days we didn't register for gifts nor were gifts even available. Because of the war, all production was geared toward manufacturing needed goods, and luxury products were not to be found. Whatever gifts we received, aside from a $25 war bond or a check here and there, were mostly good for donating to the Salvation Army. Typically, we gave away hand-carved bookends with Yosemite National Park imprinted in them.

Our leave at home was restless. We went to a photographer and took formal wedding photos at the insistence of our parents. We relived pleasant moments, walking the piers at Venice, Ocean Park, and Santa Monica. Most of our friends were in the Service, if not in school. We paid our respects to Mom Foreman, who had a large gold star honoring her son Jerry hanging in her front window. She was a Gold Star Mother and proudly remembered her loss.

We made arrangements to travel by train to North Carolina. I was anxious to see another part of the country and to join my new squadron, VPB 27, as a pilot on the PBM Martin Mariner. My base was called Harvey's Point, a twenty-minute drive from Hertford, a little town on the coast of the dismal swamp in North Carolina, some fifty miles south of Norfolk, Virginia. Elaine could stay with me through my indoctrination and training as long as we were in the United States. I was told it took about three months to form a squadron before I would be heading overseas. Elaine and I decided we would relish every moment we still had together.

We couldn't help but think of the future. As with all Service personnel, I would go wherever I was sent, to perform what I was trained to do, to complete my missions, and to hopefully return

Our view as the train pulled away. *left:* Elaine's mom, Sarah, and my mom, Evelyn *right:* Sarah with Manny and Evelyn, farewell

to the woman I loved. After that, would there be a world of peace? What would I do when the war was over? What jobs would be available? Would we have a home? Would we start a family? None of these questions could be answered until the present call to duty was completed. But the questions and uncertainty remained in our minds.

As provocative as our thoughts were, I think the same unanswered questions were in the minds and hearts of the people we loved. As we boarded the train for North Carolina and a future of unknown dimensions, we looked out of our window seat and saw my mother and Elaine's parents looking wistfully as the train started to pull away. All the questions we had asked ourselves could be seen in their faces as they saw their son and daughter depart together on their next wartime adventure. Elaine and I waved goodbye, and watched through the window as the train pulled away. We held each other, thinking that living on the other side of our country, on a dismal swamp, sounded ominous, except we would be together.

13

Hertford, N.C., and VPB 27

Welcome to Hertford, North Carolina

You'd think after a five-day train trip from the east to the west, and a five-day trip from the west back to the east, you'd get used to the "clickity-clack" of the rolling wheels on the iron tracks. After sporadic stops for water and coal and an occasional layover in a minefield of tracks, we finally emerged from our train to join a conglomeration of human naval stock in Norfolk, Virginia. Officers and sailors of every rank and order milled through the depot, coming and going, in every direction.

Naive, but resourceful, we found our way off the train and to the designated bus station with the wheels that would pass us through the town of Hertford. Our luggage was packed on top of the worn bus and unloaded at a nondescript stop in the middle of endless agriculture. We stood with a "where are we?" look when an elderly Negro couple with an open two-wheel cart greeted us. They loaded the wagon and moved along several unpaved roads until we came to a sign marked Church Street. It was the main paved entry going through the center of the three-block length of downtown Hertford, North Carolina. Upon our request, they directed us to the one drugstore in town that featured sandwiches and soft drinks.

We literally gobbled our food, and asked the lady behind the counter where we could find accomodation. She directed us to the home of Reverend White. He was the clearing agent for the rentals of the new tenant personnel. The installation of the new Navy seaplane base at Harvey's Point had suddenly opened the township of Hertford to a financial rental boom.

Married pilots and crews rented space in town while all others lived and worked on the base. We accepted a room on the second floor of a wooden frame house on North Front Street, a short block east of Church, that paralleled the Perquimans River and ran into Albemarle Sound. The rear yard backed up to the water, which lapped up to the property line in a steady, undulating rhythm.

At the end of its run, it appeared a murky red from the constant churning of its soil base. The official Dismal Swamp was inland of Hertford, but its name somehow carried over to the look of vegetation that broke through the surface of the water. There were two rental rooms on the second floor that would share a single bathroom between them. Hertford was normally a town of about 2,500 when all the kids were home. For now, with the war and schooling, the younger generation was gone and there was space for some 300-plus guests to fill their empty rooms.

We checked into our room, hung our clothes, and made ourselves as comfortable as possible. I left Elaine to set up housekeeping while I walked a block to the main street. A small Navy jump bus that made an hourly round-trip from the base to the town took me to Harvey's Point. With orders in hand, I cleared the check gate and reported to an office adjacent to a large PBM hangar. Here I met Ensign Evan Hushbeck, from Northern California, the duty officer of the day and the liaison for the squadron captain. He took me into the squadron office and introduced me to Lt. Commander Elwood Norton Chase II. As head of VPB 27, he was called Captain, while the first pilot of each aircraft was called PPC, or patrol plane commander. He was a career naval officer, six feet tall, straight back posture, blue eyes that seemed to penetrate and evaluate you from his experiences as one in command. He wore a khaki uniform with crisp ironing creases and gold wings pinned above the pocket of his shirt. He was warm and friendly, yet distant, but with a very professional stature. He looked like he had been sent from Central Casting to play this leading role. In returning his salute, I felt a radiation of leadership that heartened my feelings of confidence to serve. I felt warmly dismissed as Evan continued my induction into the squadron assignments and responsibilities. He was the captain's plane commander when the captain wasn't flying, and I was assigned to his crew as a second pilot. I would fly with Evan along with another pilot yet to be selected. Evan would fly copilot when Captain Chase took the controls, and then Evan would alternate with the other pilots so Captain Chase could have time to personally check out the new members of his squadron. I was welcomed and given a manual on the PBM-5, the advanced Mariner model, and informed of pending classes and a general flight schedule.

I walked through a large hangar where a new PBM rested on its temporary wheels. The plane looked enormous and I looked up at where the pilots sat, ten feet above its base, and felt a smug feeling of pride that it was the aircraft I flew. I marveled at the large twin Pratt & Whitney 2,000-horsepower engines as they nestled on either side of the PBM's gull wings. As pleasant as the moment was, I was shocked at seeing signs over the bathroom doors marked Officers, Enlisted Men, and Negroes, along with designated water fountains. I had black friends in school and was revolted by the public edict. I had read about the South, but it was always in a superficial way, and now I found myself living under rules totally contrary to my background. I checked the Officers' Club, the bar, and available food service. As in all Navy installations, officers could not use cash to buy anything but had to purchase coupons or chits and pay for them by turning them in for the amount they wished to spend. They came in denominations of 5-, 10-, or 25-cent tickets, and each base produced its own with no carryover to other facilities.

Back in town some of the renters were allowed kitchen privileges, but mostly for breakfast coffee or lunch, not to interfere with the homeowner. Cooking for yourself was not practical. In our kitchen, a heavy iron pot atop the front right burner seemed to have a constant butane flame cooking size 12 pig's feet. It left a rather unappetizing desire not to use the stove. The cafeteria at Harvey's Point served powdered eggs, powdered mashed potatoes, Spam, and foods reserved for advanced military operations. It was certainly not the fare served aboard naval vessels or established bases. The alternative was to eat at the Hertford Drug Store counter or a Greek restaurant that served meals at irregular times. We could store some things in the icebox next to the continuous boiling of pig's feet, but Elaine preferred a menu of corn flakes and a daily bottle of milk in our room.

July 1944 was hot and hectic. I would leave early in the morning and take the thirty-minute bus ride from Hertford to Harvey's Point. At the base, after coffee with toast or doughnut, I would attend ground school or hone my flying skills, dropping bombs, practicing navigation, firing machine guns at large nylon sleeves towed by smaller aircraft.

The training was constant and draining. Eighteen flight crews were formed, and a number of my Banana River classmates had reported for duty to our squadron, VPB 27. We were all assigned, two each to a PPC (patrol plane commander), as second pilots. We also received nine crew members of varied skills to make up our flying crew of twelve. The highest ranked enlisted crew member was generally a seaman first class, who acted as the plane captain responsible for the working crew. I was checked out and transferred from the captain's crew to Lt.(jg) Joe Eglies with another second pilot, Amos Krum. Amos was single and lived on the base. Joe was married and by sheer coincidence happened to rent the other bedroom in our house.

While I followed my routine, Elaine would get up in the morning and wait for the milk truck to stop and make its deliveries in town. She would buy the milk to go with the corn flakes she purchased at the drugstore's market section. Most of the wives socialized during the day, playing cards, reading books, writing letters home. Elaine was not a bridge or card player, but somehow got a job gluing seashells on earrings in a local home business. The pay was minimal as it could be, but her time was her own. Whenever I got back from the base early, we would walk along the shore of the swamp or on the ancient Chalk Landing Pier where members of the squadron would jump in for a swim. On occasion, Elaine would socialize with the other pilots' wives but be available as soon as I returned from the base. Her two closest friends were Bea Grady and Tee Brown. Joe's wife kept pretty much to herself until Joe came back each day. They had been married while Joe was a copilot in South America at the beginning of the war. Now on his second tour of duty, he was promoted to Lt.(jg) and PPC and had his own crew. Upon the safe completion of our first tour of duty, Amos and I, as copilots, would follow in his steps, go up in rank, and assume the responsibility of first pilot, or PPC. In most cases, we would form our own crew and repeat the cycle for our next tour of duty. Joe's wife was aware of the limited time they had together before he would be flying out to the Pacific theater. She lived with the fear of being left alone in Elizabeth City, New Jersey, waiting, again, for his safe return.

In addition to our flight schedule and ground school, squadron pilots were scheduled for duty as "officers of the day," to maintain a general order of all squadron activities. We were even assigned "shore patrol" duty, which required us to walk the streets of Hertford to keep order and to protect the public from any drunk or nonconforming naval personnel. On my night of duty, along with two squadron seamen, Tim Euker and John Dyky, a large tent revival off Church Street was of concern to us, but we checked the site several times and issued only minor warnings and had no problems. We enjoyed the spiritual singing, and I was inspired to make up a little poem:

Euker, Dyky, and me
When we were the Hertford S.P.
We had naught to do
But just quell the few
That attempted to go out on a spree.

Euker, me, and Dyky

The high point in Hertford was the weekend. The town hall, with seats for about 200 people, showed a different double feature each week. They stretched a twenty-minute intermission into thirty minutes so their patrons could go home to their bathrooms and return in time for the second show. If the women could hold off, most of the males relieved themselves among the trees that encircled the movie hall.

It was a Friday near the end of the month when our crew completed our flight and we were told to report to the medical dispensary for a series of shots required for overseas assignment. We walked between Navy corpsmen who proceeded to needle us in each arm. The porcupine joke went over pretty flat, but the announcement at the end of the line was most heartening. We were given a forty-eight-hour pass and did not have to report back to the base until the following Monday morning. We slapped each other on the back and let out some joyous yelps. The married group lined up for the bus ride to town, and the singles headed for the "O" Club on the base for a night of beer and drink. I thought it would be a great day to sightsee in Norfolk and find a nice meal.

At seven the following morning, Elaine and I walked to the bus stand hoping to catch the first bus out of Hertford for a full day in Norfolk. When we arrived at the curb where the bus stopped, a group of Negroes and a few sailors were waiting impatiently ahead of us. Elaine and I joined hands and walked to the rear of the line to wait our turn. It was awkward; the people of color all shifted out of the way, motioning us forward. We stood there as a bus rattled to a stop; the driver opened the doors and stepped forward to eye his morning cargo. He growled at the blacks to step back and motioned us and the other white passengers forward. I don't think they realized our embarrassment as we stepped ahead. I kept thinking of my title as an Officer and a Gentleman, and here I was behaving as neither. I tried to imagine making a scene in this setting of such local protocol. It was unjust, and I thought, even if I were to allow an older black lady to proceed ahead of me, the bus driver was in command and would take over in a most unpleasant manner. I wondered if those waiting behind us would even understand our motives of making an issue to treat each other equally. I know it would only make their situation worse.

We boarded the bus as directed, our muscles unfamiliarly tight, and settled in the front seats with the other white passengers. The Negroes followed, dropping their coins in the box, and then worked their way to the rear of the bus. It was a rocky ride with fifty miles of stop and go, with Southern humidity and shimmering tobacco fields in the morning sun. We got out at the bus terminal in Norfolk, and upon the direction of a sympathetic bystander, headed toward the center of town.

The morning streets were crowded: shopkeepers, defense workers, civilians, and Navy personnel of every rank, all walking in every direction. We bought a cold lime drink at an open stand and started tourist walking toward the center of activity. Souvenir, novelty, and military shops lined the streets. We walked in and out of many stores, but the wartime fare was not very attractive. The humidity was enveloping when we saw a movie theater advertising AIR CONDITIONING. I was very warm and aware that I was perspiring, which was slightly unusual for me. We went to the box office, purchased tickets, and entered the theater for some form of respite. The air conditioner was a massive swamp cooler on the roof, but it did give us a measure of relief. The movie was *The Ox Bow Incident*, starring Henry Fonda. In addition to our general physical discomfort, the movie certainly didn't lift our spirits. I wondered how the film's unjust murder affected the Southern viewers.

After the show, we decided to find a nice place to eat and head back to Hertford. As we walked down the street, we passed a storefront Navy first aid station that handled all sorts of emergencies for the personnel in town. I looked in and saw a Navy corpsman sitting at a desk.

"Pardon me," I ventured, "would you have a thermometer I could borrow?"

The corpsman jumped to his feet, eyed me closely, and invited me to sit down. He opened a drawer and withdrew a wrapped thermometer. He removed the cover and inserted the instrument under my tongue, and started taking my pressure at the same time. "Pulse okay, but your temperature is 103, Sir."

I got up and thanked him and told him I would be heading back to my base.

"I'm sorry, Sir, that will not be possible."

I took Elaine's arm and started to leave. A young doctor, a full lieutenant, appeared and set his arm on my shoulder.

"You can't leave. We have to take you to the hospital for observation."

"I'm okay," I resisted, "I'm just going back to my base."

"We'll take care of that, this is just a precautionary procedure." Another corpsman appeared, and the doctor directed they bring a car around. Within minutes, a gray Navy-marked sedan appeared at the curb, and Elaine and I were seated in the backseat. Two corpsmen drove us to the hospital and checked me in. As an officer, I was given a room with two beds, and told to undress and wait for a staff doctor. A long hour passed until a doctor entered, carrying a chart. He went through a verbal evaluation of my condition, followed by a quick routine of standard tests. I was told they had already notified my squadron of my confinement and that I would be held for observation for a couple of days. I knew this was a reaction to a battery of shots I had taken the day before I left Hertford. They wanted to be sure.

Elaine kept me company and decided to check with the naval aid office in the hospital as to where she could get a hotel room. It was too late for the bus, and she wanted to spend the night in Norfolk and return to the hospital in the morning. This was not the free, relaxing, tourist day we had planned. I had never spent a night in a hospital before and here I was, feeling healthy, with a slight sweat, and listed as an object for observation. I was worried about the loss of any flight time and where Elaine would stay. She kissed me goodnight and headed downstairs to inquire about whatever accommodations were available. Her departing words were, "I'll see you in the morning."

HERTFORD, NORTH CAROLINA

Ensign Howard Fischer and me (right rear), fraternizing with younger crew members

The front of our North Front Street residence

Early evening on the Chalk Landing Pier

Elaine dunking on the Chalk Landing Pier

14

The Duvals

Staring down from Southern bedroom walls

It was too late to catch the last bus to Hertford. Upon direction from the nurse's station, Elaine went to the hospital entry where a naval aid and information desk had been set up. A motherly-looking woman in a tailored gray jumpsuit smiled benevolently as Elaine approached. A Navy Aid badge was pinned to her strap as she asked, "May I help you?"

Elaine returned the smile. "My husband is an ensign and has to stay overnight in the hospital," Elaine said. "I know the hotels are full and I was wondering if you know where I could rent a room for tonight."

Mrs. Duval, as her name appeared on the brass badge, appraised her presence as Elaine explained her situation. "Oh, you poor dear," said Mrs. Duval. She glanced through a worn ledger with nothing to report. Looking up at Elaine she continued: "You know, dear, my son is an ensign too. He's on some ship in the Pacific and I think you should just come home with me tonight. We have a spare bedroom and I could bring you back to the hospital in the morning."

"Thank you," Elaine said. "I'll be glad to pay for the night." Mrs. Duval brushed her offer aside. "Don't be silly. I'll be off duty in about twenty minutes and you'll just ride home with me."

As Elaine tried to thank her again, Mrs. Duval shook her head from side to side.

"No, no, no. And please, just call me Nellie."

The ride in the 1940 maroon Buick took about half an hour to reach a two-story brick house of modest pretension. Mrs. Duval stopped her car in an oval driveway of crushed gravel in front of a brick walk to a brick porch to the brick house. Casual green shrubbery contrasted the brick with almost matching green shutters in need of an uplift of paint. The two steps up to the brick porch centered on a recessed entry to a heavy front door. It had the grain of oak with a leaded glass inset above the detailed rails and locking panel. It too was lacking a finish. A coat of varnish would require needed ration stamps in place of items of greater priority.

From inside the entry, the walls and furnishings reflected Southern decor. Hand-crocheted doilies protected chair and sofa arms, head rests, and cabinet and furniture tops. Mrs. Duval showed Elaine the guest room on the first floor. She then climbed the stairs to the master bedroom on the second.

A tired crystal chandelier hung from the center of the guest bedroom ceiling with two matching sconces on opposite walls. A comfortable chair with an ottoman was placed in the corner. On one side of the four-poster double bed stood an oak side table. A tarnished gold Jesus hung on a dark wood cross centered on the wall behind the bed. A bureau with a knit doily on top featured an oak picture frame inset with a family portrait. It must be of Nellie, her husband, and a teenage boy, looking out at the guest room from its stand. There were two pictures of flowers in somewhat matching frames. A certificate of service from a local Methodist church hung proudly on the adjacent wall.

Elaine set her purse down, wondering where she might wash up. She sat in the chair and checked the limited reading material on the side table next to it. A classic, *The French Revolution* by Thomas Carlyle, and a New Testament Bible were the only books evident.

With her eyes closed, Elaine relaxed, recalling the day. The ride from Hertford to Norfolk, the light lunch, the movie to cool off in, and the stop at the Navy first aid station in search of a thermometer. My temperature read over 103° and the medics would not let me leave. Elaine thought of me, who had never been sick, lying in a strange hospital bed, nursing a higher-than-normal temperature and not being allowed to leave. Her thoughts stopped abruptly as Nellie Duval entered the open door to the room. She had traded her naval aid jumpsuit for a more comfortable housedress.

The side door of the house opened and a man entered, looking very lawyer-like. He carried a large brown leather briefcase and nodded to his wife in mutual acknowledgment of their presence. He set his case down and walked wearily into the entry parlor. He stretched in the chair as Nellie brought Elaine in and introduced her to her husband, Mr. Duval. He was of average height, with a fairly stern face and white sideburns to match the color of the small beard on his chin. He asked Elaine where she came from and remarked about the uncomfortable humidity of the day. It seemed cordially friendly until Mr. Duval turned and stared intently at her.

"Cooper, hmm, are you Jewish?" he asked.

With Elaine's limited worldly experience, the question seemed reasonable, she thinking there might be a relationship he wished to explore.

A little surprised, she smiled and said, "Yes, I am."

"I thought so," was the somewhat exasperated reply. "The biggest jeweler in Norfolk is Coopers. And they're Jews."

The overwhelming silence that followed left Elaine confused. She stood there. They stood there. There was an awkward silence. Elaine excused herself and walked timidly back into the guest bedroom.

Nellie looked at her husband, shocked and bewildered. A Jew in their home? Elaine caught her words as she closed the door. "And to think I just changed the linen."

Panic rolled through her being. Elaine had never been subjected to such a feeling of ostracism. What do I do? How do I get out of here? Her mind groped all the possibilities. The daylight became night. If she walked out on a strange dark street in a strange dark city, where would she go? She felt danger in and out, and her heart beat with an uncomfortable rhythm.

She closed the door to her room to reason out her apprehension, struck by the actions of strangers she had never been exposed to before. Helplessly, she decided to wait it out until morning.

In her room, Elaine could hear muffled voices. She was not asked to dinner. She half-slept through the night sitting in the chair. In the morning, she could smell bacon and coffee, but was not invited into the kitchen. The Duvals had breakfast and Nellie explained, "I know Jews don't eat bacon."

They got into Nellie's Buick and rode silently back to the hospital. Elaine muttered a "Thanks" to Mrs. Duval and came up to my room. She quickly used the bathroom, and then I heard her experience.

My squadron had been notified of my confinement, and I was told I would be kept for observation for the next two days. I was diagnosed as a victim of "cat fever," the result of the multiple shots I had taken prior to my forty-eight-hour leave. I would be kept in the hospital for two more days. By now I was really upset. I felt perfectly normal but could not leave, I was eager to get back to Hertford and my squadron, and I wanted to confront Mrs. Duval and ask her if her son and I were fighting this war on the same side.

We decided that Elaine would go back to our room in Hertford and I would follow in two days. The thing that pleased me most was that before Elaine headed for the Norfolk bus terminal, she stopped at the hospital drug store and bought a one-pound box of Whitman's Sampler chocolates. She sent the box to Mrs. Duval with the following note: "Thank you for your hospitality. Elaine Cooper."

Somehow, my day of confinement elevated my physical perception to normal. Thinking I might be released the next day, I asked Elaine to find a room for the night so we could go home together the following morning. With ample time, and with the help of the hospital, she found a room available in a nearby residence. She bought a small travel case and some undergarments at a local dry goods store and checked into a modest bungalow owned by a widow with the name of Thompson. When Elaine appeared at the door, Mrs. Thompson gushed over her, pleased that I was serving my country, and welcomed her into her home. She was a small woman, in her late sixties, with a sweet smile and remarkably smooth white skin, and wanted to do anything to make Elaine feel comfortable for the night.

After an offering of ice tea, Mrs. Thompson showed Elaine her guest room, which turned out to be almost a replica of the nightmare she sat up in the previous night. Jesus hung over the oak headboard, a table and lamp by its side, and an ornate framed certificate of contribution to the Presbyterian church graced the wall. Mrs. Thompson, with fullest sincerity, wanted to make sure Elaine felt at home. As seemingly wont in Southern conversation, between the talk of trivia, Mrs. Thompson asked in a most passive way, "And what church do you go to, dear?"

Having seen the framed denomination on the wall, with outward calm and inward trepidation, Elaine casually answered, "Baptist."

Mrs. Thompson beamed, and the cordiality continued through her stay.

It was the following morning that the doctor assigned to my case insisted I stay for a full five-day isolation prior to my exposure to the members of my squadron. I had Elaine leave early enough to catch the bus back to Hertford while I sweated out the balance of my sentence.

15
The Bus Ride to Hertford

The Newbold-White House, built around 1680, believed to be the oldest brick house in North Carolina

Norfolk's intercity bus terminal was bustling with naval and civilian commuters. Ticket windows marked "Whites" and "Negroes" had lines of both. Nearly everyone carried luggage, service gear, or cases with a generally high profile of wear. Shopping bags and cardboard boxes wrapped in twine were more evident in the Negro lines. Restrooms displayed signs indicating the color required for entry and use. A waiting area for those who had purchased tickets was divided between whites and blacks. Coin-operated Coke machines with wooden cases stacked alongside offered unappetizing bottles of soft drinks, in both segregated areas. Flies, unconscious of the color line, drifted from stack to stack and settled on the sugar-sweet tips of the bottles. Several floated inside half empties, resulting from a binge, too saturated to fly free, too confused to find the only exit.

Elaine bought her ticket and waited in the outer area, gasping from the heat and humidity. The number eleven bus to Elizabeth City and Greenville was called. Between the two cities lay Hertford, a stopover for the bus, and a ten-minute walk to the rented room of the boarding house where we stayed. What had seemed so bleak a place to live now appeared a haven of security.

As a crowd formed, Elaine lined up at the double white line scuffed by heel marks and tire tread. Number eleven was having its destination sign reversed from Norfolk to Greenville. The driver, winding with one hand, engaged in discussion with a non-visible conductor outside the open window of the driver's seat.

As the bodies pushed against each other, edging toward the unopened door, the bus motor continued to run, its exhaust fumes puffing like a giant cigarette, blue smelly odors permeating the open covered port. The driver finished changing the destination sign and slipped back into the driver's seat without a loss of dialogue. He pulled the door lever, whacking it open as the first bodies pressed onto the two-step entry. The driver looked tall and lean, sandy haired and leathered skin, in his early fifties. His eyes squinted, gray pupils and a cheek wart with blondish hairs growing out of it. He shuffled bus tickets, made change, checked destinations, and drawled greetings and instructions in a voice of grating boredom. He had dark glasses on the top of his head, and Elaine noticed the sweat stains under his arms in the short-sleeve bus-blue shirt he wore. He accepted her ticket, and raised his eyebrows and said, "Hertford? Hmm."

Elaine found a window seat about eight rows back in the bus, too far to benefit from the small electric fan over the driver's windshield, but grateful for the crack of air over the upper half of the window. She set her small overnight case on the floor after removing a tissue and wiping her face. A man in his mid-forties, collar open and a tie at half mast, carrying a seersucker jacket and a newspaper under his arm, moved into the seat next to her. He eyed her with interest but tried to look the opposite. Elaine stared out the window. The man sighed, opened his newspaper, and continued to read from the middle of an article previously started. The driver continued taking tickets, adjusting fares, and ordering passengers to their seats in a monotone habit. The man next to Elaine became oblivious to the jostling and loading of the bus, engrossed in the war news of the day. The temperature in the bus was rising as the motor idled and the people cargo with suitcases and boxes continued to press through the aisle.

Now the Negroes stepped through the bus door. The driver collected their tickets. "Git to the back of the bus," he drawled.

Elaine felt a twinge of shame. She saw the sign over the windshield at the right of the fan, NEGROES BACK OF THE BUS. She mused with an uncomfortable sensation. The whites get on the bus first, taking all the seats closest to the front. Then the Negroes board, working their way through the aisle until they reach the rear.

The separation made Elaine cringe, almost challenging her to go to the back of the bus as a symbol of apology for Southern behavior. She thought of two Negro girlfriends she sang with in girls glee at Dorsey High, and tried to imagine them in this situation. She reflected on her Jewish experience in the Duval house, and her emotions ran from fear to bewilderment to disgust with the reality of this South.

As the bus filled, the humidity seemed to build with each added body. Motor fumes kept wafting through the frame of the bus, alternating with the odors of the bodies and clothing, sweaty and perfumed. Elaine recognized two sailors from the base, boarding with small-issue overnight bags. One scrambled for an open seat, jostling the other who stood in the aisle. The bus was filled. A uniformed starter, who was previously out of view talking to the driver, appeared at the entry, one foot on the step. He exchanged words about schedule, time, and driver replacement, and waved his hand forward as he stepped away from the bus.

The boarding doors pinched closed, and a gear shuttered and churned through the transmission as the bus jerked forward. The aisle people moved together backward then forward in unison with the motion of the bus, holding on to overhead rails and seat handles as the bus turned onto the street. Hot air came through the upper windows of the bus, giving momentary relief in its movement. The sailors whacked each other playfully as the driver shifted gears and rolled into high. Elaine tried to lower her upper window, struggling with a rusty latch in order to admit more air. The disinterested man in the seat next to her immediately came to her aid.

Elaine thought of spending the night alone in the ramshackle house. The others may be in, but they kept pretty much to themselves. When the fellows were on duty or flying, the women would occasionally get together and discuss home, the war, the duty, and the unknown orders that would inevitably separate them from their husbands. All except Jane Eglies were newly married. She had been through this once before, fourteen months ago when Joe first came for his training, going off to the Caribbean on antisub patrol as a copilot. Now he was my plane commander, ready to take his crew to the Pacific as part of a new tactical squadron. His wife was quiet, not interested in forming temporary friendships. After fourteen months of separation from Joe, she savored their minutes together, knowing that when this squadron was formed, another separation lay ahead. Where, and how long, were the constant gnawing questions. Elaine's feelings were no less painful.

The bus jostled along, seats full, aisle crammed. Each time it turned a corner, its body creaked out loud with the pain of overload, no rest or care. There was nothing to love in this bus. Its frame seemed as weary as most of its passengers. It was driven with indifference by a caustic and emotionless driver. Each time he picked up or dropped off a passenger, his exasperation with his cargo of commuters and travelers was more evident than the last.

"Git to the back of the bus," he commanded as a tall, wiry Negro with gray hair and overalls and sandals boarded.

"S'cuse me, s'cuse me," he said, working his way slowly to the rear of the bus, protecting a bundle of greens he carried in one arm. He found his designated section holding on to the overhead rail, and balanced the change of momentum as the bus struggled through the streets of Norfolk.

Occasionally, the driver would relax and exchange friendly banter with a familiar passenger. They would swap greetings, transmit salutations to wives or mutual friends, and discuss town events, indifferent to all others aboard. At least he kept the bus moving, allowing the humid air to pass through, limiting the now stifling odors and fumes from building up further.

Once clear of the city, the bus headed out Highway 17, paralleling the Dismal Swamp on its town-to-town run. It stopped at isolated outposts on the road, swapping passengers, on and off, while carrying a maximum load. Elaine was grateful for her seat by the window. She thought of the times she had to stand, and fought an impulse to exchange her seat to a standing pregnant woman who boarded at the last stop. She was happy when a seated sailor gave up his seat and joined his crony hanging on the overhead rail for balance. There still existed, she thought, some manners and courtesies in mankind.

Green fields rolled by the window. Working the acres of tobacco, field hands could be seen in the distance, fading then evident in the waves of heat that tricked the eye. After a long stretch, the bus pulled up to a dilapidated stop, the bus sign askew, a bench with broken back rails occupied by a lone customer. She was an elderly Negro woman, heavy, dark, in her late years, holding a shopping bag close to her thighs.

With his usual indifference, the driver stopped the bus fifty feet past the bench and opened the doors. The old lady waddled to the entry, and with considerable effort, hoisted herself onto the landing of the bus. She had money in hand and gave it to the driver. He accepted with disdain, slammed the doors shut, and lurched the bus forward. The aisle people swung forward and back, and could feel the transmission shift to drive as the bus picked up highway speed. The new passenger pushed her bag in front of her, saying "S'cuse me." She could make no forward movement because the aisle was now jammed. The driver, aware of the lack of progress, snapped his usual "Git to the back of the bus!" Again the old lady begged, "S'cuse me," one leg still on the bottom step, the doors rattling ominously behind her.

The speed of the bus allowed more air to tumble through the open windows. Elaine's hair was blown in several directions, but it was worth the relief it gave her. There was no relief in watching the old lady, half on the upper step, half on the lower. She wished she could help her come forward.

The driver was upset. "Git to the back," he bellowed, so loud that conversations in the bus died. Curious passengers crammed their necks to see who defied his command. "S'cuse me," she said again, and then looking toward the driver, pleaded, "I'm tryin'."

She got to the top step precariously. It was difficult for the white passengers to move. As the aisle people squeezed back, they blocked the full aisle, restricting passage to the rear. Many eyed the situation with interest. There was no room for the lady to pass.

Again the driver commanded, "Now git to the rear of the bus." His frustration weighted his foot on the gas pedal, the bus speed increased, full throttle down the two-lane highway.

"Please?" the old lady asked. The aisle was closed. Until some passengers got off, she was physically restricted to the front of the bus.

"Now, damn it," shouted the driver, "move back!"

Only the wind hurtling through the upper windows could be heard. All passengers watched the impasse with curiosity.

The bus jolted. The driver had hit the brakes, released the pressure, and pumped again. Passengers fell forward; the old lady, dropping her bag, hanging on to a seat handle, stepped back a step, one foot on the landing, one foot above.

"Damn it. I said git back," yelled the driver, still pumping the bus to slow down. Before it lurched to a stop, the entry doors exploded open, startling the old lady, struggling to hold her balance and her bag.

"Git out," he shouted, "git out!"

Her appeal was lost as she was commanded out in the middle of the highway, miles from a stop or visible civilization. She backed off the bus carefully, as the passengers, save those in the rear, applauded.

The bus jerked forward. Elaine's face turned gray with shock, staring frantically as the bus left the old lady and picked up speed along its route.

It was the passenger next to Elaine who observed her reaction with nonchalant interest. Her eyes were wide with incredulity as she tried to comprehend the scene that had passed before her. She started to speak, but only "I, I can't believe . . . " came out.

"If you think that's bad," said the passenger with the seersucker jacket, "the driver happens to be the minister of the Baptist church in Edenton. Preaches every Sunday!"

16

The Stork Club

Milk, a drink of choice

If you're active and confined, and suddenly released, there is a sudden spontaneity to your step that you had normally taken for granted. Leaving the hospital before noon of the fifth day, even tolerating the bus ride to Hertford, was exhilarating. With all the medical diagnoses, I had merely sustained a high fever reaction from the series of shots I had taken the day before I left Hertford. I told them, as I knew, it was a short-lived reaction generally known as "cat fever."

The old wooden house on the edge of the swamp looked comforting after the stay in the hospital. Walking past the kitchen, even with the unappetizing pig's feet still protruding out of the open iron pot, was a comforting sense of familiarity. The creaking floor in the rented room had a feeling of home, but it was Elaine's greeting that washed away my hospital ordeal.

I caught the Navy's jump bus to the base and reported to Ensign Austin Puvogel, who was the squadron officer of the day. I went to the ramp and caught Joe and Amos and our crew as they just returned from another familiarization flight. I was greeted warmly as they brought me up on the coming schedule. In a couple of days the squadron was going to fly to Key West, Florida, to be given advanced courses in antisubmarine warfare by the Boca Chica training unit. The courses would consist of advanced gunnery, navigation, mine laying, simulated attacks on submarines, dropping bombs, and actual live torpedo runs on varied targets. The program would take a little over two weeks to complete. Captain Chase said that the wives could join us in Key West if they traveled at their own expense. I was excited to tell Elaine and have her make travel plans with Brownie and Grady's wives.

Before I could get back to my room in Hertford, an emergency announcement was made requiring all flight personnel, pilots and crews, to report immediately to their aircraft. A tropical storm was making its way toward Cape Hatteras. The storm threat was of such force that all aircraft were required to evacuate. The destination: Floyd Bennett Airport in New York.

I called Elaine to tell her and to notify the other wives that their husbands would be leaving to save their aircraft from an impending hurricane. No one would have time to leave if they lived off base. As I spoke, the wind was picking up and the waves in the Sound were starting to churn.

As each crew filled its roster, their planes were lowered down the ramp, checking their takeoff procedure, and headed into the wind for flight. With all aboard our plane, Easy 12, we were launched into the Sound, and two and a half hours later, in the settling dusk, the lights of New York's skyline came into view. It was the first sight of the City for many of us, and the dramatic view emblazoned an experience that only New York could produce.

We contacted Floyd Bennett's tower and were told that all buoys were taken. We were informed that additional buoys were set up in the East River and to land and tie up until further notice. We swung our plane around, paralleling towering buildings, gawking at the sight, and visually lined up the East River in the reflected light, throttled back, and dropped our wing flaps. With our Mariner seaplane, defying the distraction of the shimmering surf, we landed smoothly on the lightly wind-chopped water. This was a far easier maneuver than the one made by Captain Chelsey Sullenberger in the Hudson River many decades later. The key to his feat was keeping his plane's wings level, with gusting wind sweeping through the adjacent canyons of high-rise street buildings, nose slightly raised, and not allowing his wing tips to deflect to the water, causing a disastrous wing over. While he landed on the belly of his land-based plane to stay afloat, we landed on a water-tight hull with floats on each wing tip, to balance and maintain our stability.

We taxied in the river, turning on a handheld spotlight on to locate a buoy. We found several in a spacious cluster, and after tying up to one, three other planes from our squadron joined us. Our radio said to sit tight until dawn. The attraction of the skyline was maddening. The lights kept blinking a welcome that I felt I had to answer. I asked Joe about calling in for permission to go ashore. He was sure the response would be negative and decided he would take one of the four bunks and catch some sleep. Amos sat in the cockpit, content with a cigarette in his hand, just looking at the view.

I asked our plane captain, T. J. Smith, where the life rafts were stowed. Smitty produced one from the rear storage of the aircraft. I checked with some of the other pilots in the planes tied up near us, and with a positive nonpermission conspiracy, several of the copilots decided to abandon ship and row ashore if I produced a raft. The side hatches were open, and Smitty helped me lower the eight-man deflated raft outside the plane. It was too big to inflate inside, so by setting the carcass outside, I held the tow rope and released the air canister. The raft inflated and thereby produced the required transportation from plane to shore.

With Smitty's help, I crawled out of the side hatch and into the raft. I removed the oars and pointed the bow upstream to counter the current. I rowed to the nearest plane and picked up Howard Brown in Easy 14. We picked up three other pilots and rowed the raft to the shore. We pulled it up the embankment and tied it to an available power pole.

We walked about a block through a vacant lot of weeds and emerged on a street parallel to the river. We finally caught a wandering cab, and the five of us crammed into the car as the driver asked, "Where to?" The group wanted to go to a bar and since I had been here once, they looked to me for leadership. I could only remember the name of a famous night club, and I blurted out, "The Stork Club."

The suggestion was received with enthusiasm. The cab driver was quite familiar with the spot and wound his way through packed streets and wartime traffic and dropped us off in front of a crowded, bustling club with men, women, and service personnel jamming the doorway. As we peeled out of the cab, our military status opened a line to the club's entrance. We swaggered forward in our khaki work uniforms, tilted officer's caps, and gold Navy wings on our chest, and were directed ahead of all waiting patrons, straight to the people-packed bar. The bartender saw us coming in, cut other requests, and shifted his attention directly toward us.

"What'll ya have, men?" he asked.

I think Brownie started first and asked for a "Coke High," which I discovered was a mix of Coca-Cola and a shot of rum. As the bartender pointed his finger in affirmation, the other three asked for the same.

Suddenly, his finger pointed at me. I rarely went to a bar and didn't care about drinking, so contrary to my friends' request, I asked, "Would you have a glass of milk?"

That brought a wild laugh from my rowboat partners. The bartender acknowledged my request by snapping his fingers with a "You got it!"

It was pretty funny to them, and as we reached in our pockets to pay for our drinks, the bartender assured us they had already been covered by an older man sitting at the end of the bar who had watched us as we entered the club. We looked to see who it was and saw a gentleman with a substantial look and a buxom lady on the stool next to him. We thanked him by giving him a short salute, which he returned in kind. Although there were other military men and women in the club, as naval aviators, we were treated most royally.

Someone next to us at the bar leaned into us and asked confidentially, "Where you fellows comin' from?" To say we brought our planes to New York to escape a hurricane was not very glamorous. So Brownie answered by saying, "We just flew in from England." That lie immediately prompted the offer of another round of drinks.

It was late when we left. We were lucky to find the lot where we left the raft. They were "high" and kidded me. Not that they heard, but I explained how my dad offered me a glass of Scotch when I was thirteen years old. Even though he told me it would make a man of me, it tasted like I thought L. B. Hair Oil at that time would have tasted, and I just spit it out. I never liked the taste, and although alcoholic drinks were always available to me, I just never had an interest in drinking. We all got back to our planes, and after wrestling the raft back to each plane, I finally got to mine and Smitty pulled in the raft, deflated it, and stowed it away. I slept the rest of the night in the copilot's seat next to Amos. I never knew he snored.

When I awoke, Smitty and Smokey Stover were frying bacon and eggs on our portable stove. They had already sent up cups of hot coffee to Joe and Amos and me, and had already taken care of the rest of the crew. The storm down south was passing, but we flew up to Floyd Bennett and waited for an all-clear. We got on base but slept on the plane before heading home the following day. When we took off, we circled the island of New York, admiring the beautiful skyline, and headed down the coast to check on our life in North Carolina.

The hurricane had grazed Hertford before heading back out to sea. Its winds were so bad that Elaine had feared for her life. She didn't have time to join the other women and ended up lying under our bed, alone and frightened, waiting for the roof to blow off the house while the walls and fixtures swayed wildly. Sudden blasts of wind and rain pelted the house, followed by a series of irregular blows that seemed ready to disintegrate the structure as each blast followed the next.

Upon my return, Elaine was still in turmoil. I tried to calm her and then offered a consolation. Upon our landing at Harvey's Point, we were told that the squadron would be leaving for Key West the following day. We had made arrangements for the wives to take a train from Cocoa to Miami and then transfer to a bus line that would travel the 160 miles across the Florida Keys to Key West. I would arrive ahead of her and arrange housing for our stay. I would have two more weeks of training, and we could squeeze in two weeks of sunshine, swimming, and relaxation in the southernmost point of the United States.

17

Sea to Shining Sea

Sally Rand, the exotic dancer

We reached Key West! As in all communities near service bases, housing was at a premium. After a little-over-six-hour flight from Harvey's Point to Key West, the single pilots checked into the base officers' quarters and the married men went out looking for a place to reside. I found a single room between the Navy base and the heart of downtown Key West. It had a straw mattress and a full-cover mosquito netting draped over four corner bedposts hanging from the top to the floor. After a tedious bus ride across the Keys, Elaine arrived the following day and was somewhat surprised at the luxurious accommodations I had found. A straw bed?

Our squadron went through a vigorous training program. All crews practiced dry runs and attacked and dropped bombs and dummy torpedoes on simulated targets. We practiced mine laying, expanded our radar and gunnery skills, and culminated our training with each crew dropping live torpedoes at a moving target. As a unit, VPB 27 scored better than any other Mariner squadron that had taken the course so far.

We had only one night flight and considerable leisure time between exercises. Elaine managed a lot of poolside relaxation and was voted the "Gal with the Best Figure." Most of Elaine's poolside suntan time was spent with Berteale and Tee, Brownie and Grady's wives. When Elaine offered to go to the nearby snack bar for lemonade, she was joined by Betsy, wife of one of the other ensigns. As they walked the path toward the refreshment stand, Betsy said she visited a local Baptist church to see if she could volunteer her services while in Key West. She was delighted they accepted her offer. She then asked Elaine if she, and I, would like to join her at a Saturday night social at the church recreation hall. Elaine declined to answer, saying she would have to check with me if I had made any other plans. On the same beat, Betsy asked, "By the way, honey, what church do you go to?"

Elaine balked for a second and the thought of "here we go again" flashed through her mind. She casually answered, "I'm Jewish."

Betsy stopped abruptly in her tracks. She placed her hand on Elaine's shoulder and stared directly into her face. Betsy said she had never really known a Jew before. As Elaine pulled away, Betsy concluded, "You do have high cheek bones."

We did not go to the Baptist social that Saturday night.

On a break from my training one afternoon, I saw an immaculate OS2U Kingfisher bobbing in the water but secured at a private dock. It turned out to be the personal aircraft of the base commander. After inquiries as to its availability, I was given a one-hour check ride by a Lt.(jg) Mapa, and then free use of the craft while in Key West. I took a half dozen flights, sometimes carrying an enlisted sailor along for a ride in the backseat. I would usually fly visually sixty or seventy miles over the Gulf, carefully staying twenty-five to thirty miles away from Cuba. When I got back to the base, I would make a deep-dip wing over, rev up my engine to show off I was home, and skim smartly on the water and tie up at the dock that I had left. I would join Elaine at the pool, and then we'd be free for the evening. We ate mostly at the Officers' Club while the singles, both officers and men, went into town and checked out every bar.

One memorable evening in Key West was our visit to a club featuring Sally Rand dancing with her flowing ostrich feathers, crisscrossing her figure in a tantalizing manner. It was considered very sexy at the time. The most eventful memory was of one of our happy-go-lucky pilots, Ensign John Doyle, who met a young girl on a blind date. Within three or four days they made arrangements to marry, and the last I heard, some sixty-five years later, they were still a family and happily wed.

Our squadron made excellent scores in all our courses and readied to leave and apply our skills in battle. In contrast to all the flying I had done, Elaine had never been up in an airplane. For the trip back to Hertford, I bought two tickets on a National Airlines plane from Key West to Miami. We would fly together, and then I would bus back over the Keys to fly home the following day.

The National Airlines plane, a twin-engine Lockheed Lodestar, took off for the worst, bumpiest fifty-minute flight imaginable. As a passenger, not behind the controls of that plane, sitting in my Navy uniform with gold flying wings attached to my chest, I was turning green with nausea, and embarrassed to be seen by the public. Fortunately, with my brown bag securely folded in my back pocket, I barely managed to contain myself. Elaine felt "woozy" but managed well and wrote home about the fun of her first airplane flight. We toured Miami, lunched, and I put her on the train to Hertford and promised to meet her the next day. I bused the 160 miles back across the endless Keys and prepared for the morning flight home.

Harvey's Point and Hertford had not changed in our absence. While going back to our normal routine, our crew took a short assigned flight to Norfolk and landed in the sea and tied up to a buoy from the seaplane tender Barnagate. A motor launch took us to the ship, about the size of a destroyer, where we had dinner in the officers' wardroom and slept aboard ship in double-tiered bunks. The crew followed the same procedure in their quarters, and we returned to our base the following day. This was a familiarization of things to come.

As a squadron, we had completed every phase of training and now prepared to leave for the West Coast. We had completed 296 training flights and 983.4 hours of flying time, in addition to completing a ground school curriculum prior to training at Key West. On October 28, 1944, the first five planes left for the naval air station at Alameda, California, basically across the bay from San Francisco. Elaine and I made arrangements for her to go home by train. On November 2, Joe Eglies, as plane commander, Amos Krum, and I, along with our crew and squadron radio and radar officer, Ensign

Bob Ogram, with our worldly possessions stashed in travel bags throughout the plane, took off in Easy 12 for the ocean on the opposite side of our country. We made our last takeoff from Albemarle Sound at Harvey's Point in a wide climbing swing over the Atlantic Ocean, and headed westward with the rising sun behind us. Flying across mountains, valleys, rivers, and cities in a loaded seaplane was a unique experience. We flew a little over nine hours according to our schedule, with plenty of fuel to take us to Eagle Mountain Lake in Texas. I didn't see a mountain and the lake didn't look much like an eagle, but we headed in and made a smooth landing in the short, choppy water lapping the confined shoreline of a lake within a shallow mountain range.

Once ashore, refueled with gas, instead of lounging around an available recreation facility, I was anxious to see whatever sights were available. Fort Worth was twenty-six miles west, and a special bus was on hand. My curiosity prompted me to sightsee the town and just window shop along the streets of a strange new city. It was in this setting that two pairs of hands grabbed me from the rear on both sides of my body. They weren't threatening but so unexpected I was caught off guard. They belonged to two rather attractive young ladies, smiling and tugging gently on either elbow. Before I could respond, I felt a meaningful squeeze and a provocative lure, "Hi, Big Boy, would you like to have some fun?"

As much as I was startled, I got the message. "I'm sorry, ladies," and I flashed my wedding ring, "but I am a married man."

Undaunted, they looked at me, and frowned. "What's that got to do with it?"

"I—" and before I could continue, they both spoke with a knowing smile, "What she doesn't know won't hurt her."

I thanked them for the offer and peeled their arms off me and strode briskly ahead. It gave me some material to brag about with my friends, and it clarified my feelings that if I were to cheat on

Elaine, whatever gods there were would not allow me to return home safely. My God was my fidelity, comfort, and security.

The next day, after an eight-and-one-half-hour flight from Texas, we landed in the Bay of San Diego, in undulating swells of the glistening Pacific Ocean. The fog was so thick along the northern coast, and heading south, that we were not allowed to proceed to Alameda. It took several days before they would let us take off, with less than a five-mile visibility. The irony, of course, was that once in a war zone with zero visibility, they rarely curtailed a mission.

The skyline of San Francisco was certainly no comparison to New York, but flying in over the Golden Gate Bridge was an exciting introduction to the naval base at Alameda. The planes were pulled up on the ramp, and the quarters, maintenance, clubs, ship's store, and facilities were real Navy, organized and superior to anything we had seen. Off the base, hunting for rental space in a city of constant flux was another ordeal. I did manage to find a one-room bachelor apartment with minimum furniture, in Berkeley south of the University of California. Elaine took the train from Los Angeles and joined me within a day. Our new home was a commuter bus ride to and from the base, but included a morning ordeal of slow-moving traffic through the only two-lane tunnel connecting the mainland to the base. For the next two months, with some advanced training flights, our squadron was assigned to ferry aircraft from Alameda to Kaneohe Bay, Hawaii.

Our initial training was to fly to the halfway point of the 2,100 miles to Hawaii, encounter a picket ship stationed midway, and return home, using a sextant and radar for navigation. One of the most fascinating flights that I recall from those days was in ferrying a PBM to Hawaii, leaving it, and returning a day or two later with other crews as passengers in a land-based Navy transport. The plane we ferried was taken to the skies early in the morning from

Alameda Bay. Before we left the Golden Gate Bridge, at 1,000 feet we were enveloped in a low cloud cover about 2,000 feet thick. We climbed through rather quickly and burst into a clear, open blue sky with the sun brightening the world above. We set our course and made a series of adjustments by dropping and tracking wind balloons for drift and speed. We made radio contact with the picket ship halfway through the flight and adjusted our course, still unable to see the ship or the water below. The cloud cover was constant. We rotated pilot and navigation seats, and some fourteen hours into the flight, we still had no visible view of the water below. Our radar came up with land ahead. We lowered ourselves through the overcast and about 1,000 feet above water, we saw the ocean for the first time since takeoff. We could see the Hawaiian Islands under the cloud cover in the distance, and we congratulated ourselves on a navigation well done.

At this time, the sea between the mainland and Hawaii had been cleared of enemy subs. The Navy and Marines were pressing forward in the Pacific, retaking captured islands from the Japanese. Severe battles and casualties were recorded daily, and Elaine and I knew that after all the training venues we had been through together, we would soon be separated, and the real test was about to begin.

Courtship, romance, and marriage, entwined with the separation of family and friends, settling unsettled in strange and impersonal places, can strengthen a couple's resolve or cause the breakup for individual solace. In our case, we were grateful for the time we had together. We were realistic that we had not laid roots as a couple but as participants in a transient lifestyle brought on by a world at war. From a tiny corner of southwest Los Angeles, we had shared an experience of living in areas of the United States that could have happened in no other way. We would relish our adventures and look upon them as an enrichment of the life we planned together. It was agreed that once I left for the war in the Pacific, I would promise to come back while Elaine continued her studies at U.C.L.A. Upon my return, I promised to complete college and we would start our real life together. Whatever time I had left at Alameda, we would share and enjoy every free moment as if it were our last.

18

Kaneohe Bay, Hawaii

Joe Eglies and me, Honolulu, November 13, 1944

After training flights halfway to Hawaii and back, and later with a skeleton crew to deliver PBMs for advanced duty, our first official flight to Kaneohe Bay was November 12, 1944. Joe, Amos, and I rotated seats, each flying eight hours and navigating four. I was fascinated that we took off in the Bay at San Francisco, circled past the high-rise buildings, headed west over the Golden Gate Bridge, and set our flight plan toward some dots in the Pacific Ocean over 2,000 miles away. We flew for sixteen hours, seeing nothing but water below and stars up above. In the middle, we encountered clouds and flew blindly, adjusting for wind on our automatic pilot. By a blip on our radar, we picked up the picket ship slightly off our course, and made the necessary corrections to continue.

The rays of the radar work like a rock dropped into a pond. When the rock hits the water, a circular ring flows outward. When that ring hits an object, it returns to its source. The radar sends out an electrical impulse in the same way. If the impulse hits an object, it will bounce back and a light appears on a screen. If there is nothing to reflect the flow of the water or the response to the electric charge, both will dissipate within a given distance, indicating no obstructions ahead. The PBM's radar was good for about 120 miles. The flow of the water by the rock in the pond would depend on how large the rock and how large the splash. The radar indicated the distance between it and the unknown object that returned the impulse.

Based on our airspeed of about 120 knots (138 miles per hour), we followed our radar until it picked up several blips together, indicating we were within 100 miles of the Hawaiian Islands. Dropping down through the clouds from our 6,000-foot elevation, we flew along until we could see our goal. Kaneohe Bay was on the eastern side of Oahu, and we were able to fly directly into the base. Throttle back, wing flaps down, we eased along the tops of a heavy swell. Joe raised the nose slightly, and our Mariner touched neatly on a crest and rolled safely into the surf. Our time read 16.2 hours in the air as we taxied toward the ramps and were pulled up on the concrete landing.

We checked in, unloaded our gear, arranged our quarters, and after a quick bite of food, showered, took a short nap, and readied ourselves to explore our tropical surroundings. We were told we would return to the mainland in a couple of days, with all pilots and crews to be ferried back together.

I met Joe and Amos in the entry lobby of the officers' billet. There was a pool table in the middle, and four pilots from a different squadron were racking up balls to break. We were in Hawaii, and we decided to go shop for a real Hawaiian swimsuit and shirt. Two other pilots joined us, and the five of us found the Kaneohe Ship's Store, loaded with merchandise unseen in public retail displays. Aside from naval pins, insignia, and personal and military supplies, the brightest array of Hawaiian shirts and swim shorts hung on long display racks and neatly organized tables. As a group, we individually sorted through the colorful supply, asked each others' opinions, and made our selections. With our choices in hand, we headed for a cashier counter where a motherly-looking saleslady asked if she could be of further service.

It was an awkward moment for us. Hawaiian swimsuits were full and colorful and came without built-in supporters. It was necessary to purchase an individual supporter, or "jock strap," as it was known. There were none to be seen on the shelves. The five of us lined up at the counter, still looking, and too embarrassed to ask. Finally, Amos spoke up, "Uh, do you have, uh, supporters for the, uh, swimsuits?"

At five foot nine and one-half inches tall and a full flying weight of 155 pounds, I was the slightest of the group. The saleslady looked at us benevolently and smiled, as we each held our selected swimwear in hand. I was last in line as she pointed her finger at each one of us and said, "Medium, medium, medium, medium," and paused to look at me, and said, "small."

I assured her that I required a medium-size supporter, but had one hell of a time living down that remark.

With time to spare from our duties, Joe and I were anxious to visit Honolulu. We joined a group of other pilots to make the trip into town on a rather worn yellow bus with a wizened old Philippine driver at the wheel. Heading into town, the bus barreled up the narrow two-lane incline and suddenly disappeared in a heavy gray cloud. The passengers' concern was most evident as it appeared the driver's eyes barely cleared the dashboard, and all swore at least one wheel of the bus was turning freely over the side of the road. A shock of rain splattered the bus, and we suddenly emerged from the clouds and rattled into the terminal in the heart of Honolulu. One of the pilot passengers feigned faith by falling to the ground, pretending to kiss the earth, grateful for a safe bus landing.

Honolulu was a revelation for me. I saw a black sailor with a Chinese girl riding comfortably in an open street-car, and combinations of dark Portuguese and Caucasian companions. The streets were filled with yellow, black, brown, and white people completely integrated in a seemingly compatible society. It was a stark comparison to what one would see in any stateside city. I thought to myself, if the world were like this, who could command superiority over anyone? No one could call anyone less than them because everyone was a part of everyone else. I learned that it was only the native Hawaiians who frowned on interrelationships with those other than their own ethnic core.

We ran into several members of our squadron, who were raised mostly in the East and knew nothing about Hawaii other than what they had read in the *National Geographic.* I ran into Jim Grady and realized that his wife, Tee, and my Elaine were probably together in Alameda at the same time.

Joe and I visited Waikiki Beach. I knew that through the years the beach had been broad and other times storms had reduced the sand exposed to the surf. I was disappointed to stand on a street paralleling the beach within fifteen feet of the water's edge. Where had the beach gone? As a challenge to myself, I crossed the street and ran full force toward the beach. My foot left the curb and I jumped to the water's edge, without touching the sand of Waikiki Beach. I enjoyed a strange satisfaction while Joe thought I was a little crazed.

We risked our lives again riding back to the base in the ramshackle bus, but managed to arrive safely at Kaneohe. I promised myself to bring Elaine to Hawaii to share my Pali experience. We had delivered five PBM-5Ds, and a like amount had been ferried in by another squadron from Alameda. Over 100 of us, pilots and crew, were to return to the mainland in one of the largest four-engine cargo seaplanes in existence, the Martin JRM1 Mars. Only four of them had been built and were currently operational. It was made by the same company that produced our Mariners and was considered one of the best aircraft ever built.

We seated ourselves along the cavernous walls of the Mars and prepared for an all-night flight home. As usual with most flight crews, sleep was easy under any conditions. About midway in the flight, the cabin door opened and the copilot checked his human cargo. He looked around and announced through the sound of the motors, "Anyone want to sit up front?" Sitting close, wide awake, I was the first to jump up with a "Yes, Sir, here."

I entered the large cockpit area, past the engineer and navigator's table, and slipped into the right copilot's seat. I was greeted by Lt. Commander Baker, the PPC of this giant aircraft, adjusted my earphones, and stared out over the vast cockpit controls. A large windshield with only the night showing through was above the four engine throttles, surrounded with buttons and switches and a reflective radar screen in the center. In what was a prelude to future airline technology, Captain Baker showed me the plane's navigation system. He had me dial a radio control number that drew a line across the screen from Seattle. I then repeated the procedure by drawing a line from Los Angeles. On the screen, the two lines crossed and moved together forward toward the mainland. It was the precise point where the two lines crossed that indicated exactly where we were over the Pacific Ocean. We could easily adjust our position to head into whatever destination we chose. A far cry from navigating by sextant and calculating the wind! Several hours after I returned to my seat, the Mars made a smooth landing in Alameda Bay, 15.4 hours after takeoff, of which I logged, and could boast, 1.3 hours as copilot.

Through all our training sessions from Hertford to Key West to Alameda, we constantly flew with different crews. Aside from my initial flights with Captain Chase and Evan Hushbeck, I seemed to be pretty well set with Joe Eglies. As a Lt(jg), Joe was one rank above me, in addition to being the plane commander; all of the copilots were newly trained ensigns. When Amos Krum joined us as the second copilot, I learned his rank was the same as Joe's. There were several in our squadron who had been officers in other branches of the Navy and had applied for flight training in that capacity. Joe was quiet, soft-spoken, precise in decision and movements, and very proficient. Amos was also the quiet type, with a dry sense

Joe Eglies and Jim Grady, September 1945

of humor, very mechanical, and a very good navigator. His only negative was the constant cigarette that lived in his mouth. Every time we got into our plane, you could smell the gas fumes before takeoff. Joe would command, "The smoking lamps out," until we got airborne. I used to complain to Amos that I knew we would never get shot down in battle but that one day he would light a cigarette and we would all blow up.

Posing in Honolulu

Our duty at Alameda was somewhat relaxed, with time to visit San Francisco and enjoy the amenities of a bustling city and environs. Elaine and I took as much advantage as possible, not knowing which day would be our last together.

Despite our lighter work detail, everything was not always smooth at Alameda. On one flight to Kaneohe, Lt. W. J. McGuire overshot Hawaii by 300 miles and set a record of 21.3 hours in the air before landing at Kaneohe. Lt. McQuillan's plane was let down the ramp, and when he hit his throttles preparing for takeoff, the plane spun crazily in circles. A propeller had been installed backwards. Lt. Welch had an engine go bad 400 miles into the Pacific and had to jettison fuel and limp back to Alameda on one engine. Joe Eglies had to cancel our trans-Pacific flight because our trim tabs were reversed. In all, our squadron had ferried thirty-two planes to Kaneohe when our final orders arrived. VPB 27 had logged

1,042 flights with a total of 4,163.5 hours from its commissioning in Hertford to its position in Hawaii. On November 25, three staff officers and eighty-four enlisted men set sail on a small escort carrier, the USS ATTU, CVE-102, as it passed under the Golden Gate Bridge heading to Hawaii to set up squadron headquarters at Kaneohe Bay. Each flight crew was assigned a new PBM-5 aircraft, and a specific date for departure, ready for the war in the Pacific.

Elaine and I spent our last day together on December 2, 1944. After all our wonderful adventures, it was really time to part. A short distance from the ramps at Alameda, we were able to kiss goodbye, wondering when next we would meet. I carried my flight bag to the plane and watched as our crew stowed their gear through the open hatch. I climbed the ladder to enter, and with a final wave goodbye, the panel was closed and our plane was lowered down the ramp into the water. Elaine watched as the late afternoon sun settled into the horizon of the Pacific. Our new Easy 12 Mariner pushed away from the ramp. A heavy thrush of water kicked up as we hit our throttles and headed into the bay for takoff. Elaine was standing on the tarmac near the ramp and I tried to wave a final goodbye. I wasn't sure she saw me, but she did see us lift off the water and head upward toward the Golden Gate Bridge. Elaine's last view was the transition of the mighty Mariner as it turned into a speck and disappeared into the early evening air. I did know our thoughts meshed; when would we see each other again?

19

Kaneohe Bay, Part 2

Newspaper ad lauding the PBM Martin Mariner

It was a long, tedious flight to Kaneohe Bay, requiring a number of adjustments because of variations in wind and gusts. We logged 16.9 hours from Alameda to our destination in Hawaii, and another hour to be pulled up the ramp and unload our personal gear. This was our formal introduction to the Pacific War. Pilots and crew checked into their quarters, eager to find out what lay ahead. Captain Chase and Lt. McQuire had moved into a cottage adjacent to the Kaneohe airstrip. The cottage served as the squadron headquarters with communications and orders issued daily. In the evening it played host to the established singles and drinking buddies in a seemingly ongoing beer bust. That was one part of my Navy career that I seemed to have missed out on.

Prior to our first assigned flight, many of the crews decided to name their aircraft. Joe seemed quite democratic in discussing it with our crew and wanted to use a name we could all bond to. I was in panic. If I were the PPC, I would have announced the name as "Sweet Elaine," or something personal to me. I didn't want to fly in a plane named after some other woman. We batted around several ideas, and strangely enough, Joe came up with "C'est La Guerre."

I knew it was French, and the crew members, most of whom had left high school without graduating, were completely perplexed. Aaron Long, our gunner from Biloxi, Mississippi, asked, "What does that mean?"

I don't know why, but Joe, who rarely used profanity, didn't say, "This Is War." Instead he said, "In French, it means like, Tough Shit!"

That brought a loud laugh and certainly a name good enough for everyone to agree on. The name was proudly painted on the side of Easy 12, and that would carry us through to battle. I was greatly relieved to be able to fly under a nondescript title, and not some other woman's name. Most plane commanders named their plane after a wife or girlfriend.

We were informed that our duties in Kaneohe were to make regular search and antisubmarine reconnaissance flights, as well as continued practice in selective training missions. We were being prepared to cover the actions to be taken directly against the Japanese mainland. Our first flight was a training one to Hilo, Hawaii, where we made evasive maneuvers against fighter planes practicing against us. We made joint attacks against a submarine target with another PBM and had continuous gunnery practice and bounce landings under various sea conditions.

Our first mission was to find a Japanese sub reported to have been spotted northwest of the Islands. We were sent out into a menacing storm in the middle of the night. We tried circling the area where the report had been made, but the ocean was so rough it was impossible to cover. Low clouds rolled in and the wind kicked up severely as we tried to stay below the clouds but above the gigantic swells of a defiant sea. It was impossible for radar to pick up any target because the waves were so high they obliterated the screen. We found ourselves flying blindly when suddenly the wind flared with such hurricane force that it twisted the plane in uncontrollable gyrations. We fought the controls as pressure tried to suck us up into the storm. Joe had nosed the plane down and, with his command, we both pushed our yolks forward with as much strength as we had to keep a ripping wind from pulling us upward. The mission was fruitless, and the flight became one of self-preservation. We worked to stay below the swirling storm, concerned that our wings would literally be torn off the plane, wondering how our wing floats could stay attached to our wings. The rain smothered our windshield, and Amos and the crew had strapped themselves in to keep from hurtling against the bulkheads. We endured the rage of weather and reversed our flight plan back to Oahu. As we approached the Islands just before dawn, heading to Kaneohe, I suffered my only case of vertigo. I swore we were going to be blown into the mountains adjoining the seadrome, but Joe's steady hand and his eye on the needle and ball brought us into a safe, rough sea landing with me, helpless, at his side.

It was the following night; a raucous Christmas Eve party was taking place in the Captain's cottage. The weather was too bad to attempt Honolulu, so those of us too lazy to walk to the Captain's celebration mostly gathered around the pool table, joked, and shared bottles of Four Roses whiskey, which I passed. At the same time, the same scenario of the night before had Lt. Harry Beaty assigned to repeat our mission, looking for the same suspected Japanese sub north of the Hawaiian Islands.

Again, the weather was so violent, once in the storm, impossible to search, he called for permission to return to base to attempt a night landing instead of waiting until dawn. With approval to return, Beaty headed back and faced a swirling wind landing in the dead of night. Between rain and storm and mountain swells still rolling through the Kaneohe seadrome, the plane crashed, killing half his crew, including second pilot, a friend, Ensign "Ross" Pennock, and five enlisted members, for our squadron's first fatality. I can't say how long the party played on until we were notified. The storm subsided, and on Christmas Day, once again we were assigned a day patrol to find the elusive sub. After a nine-hour search we had nothing to report.

Back at our quarters, a lone pilot was practicing different bank shots at the pool table. As I approached, I recognized Milt Gibson from Lone Pine and Susanville and our last residence at Banana River with Jolene and Elaine. We exchanged happy smiles and brought each other up to date since we'd last seen each other. While I was sent to Hertford and VPB 27, Milt was sent to copilot the PB4Y Privateer, a four-engine attack bomber.

The Navy's need for long-range aircraft had led to the adaptation of the Army's Consolidated Liberator. Milt's squadron had completed its training courses and was set to fly to a forward base on one of the recaptured islands within the next few days. Milt was rather upset. In response to my concern, he blurted out, "I'm flying with an asshole that's going to get me killed. I don't know if he thinks he's flying a single-engine fighter or just takes crazy show-off chances." Milt shook his head and went on. "He tries to get as close to every target as he can. He overpowers every dive and pulls up faster than our syllabus recommends. Our crew gets bounced around, and we don't know what to expect every time he takes the wheel. He doesn't follow procedures and takes everything into his own hands. We get minimum time behind the wheel. We never know what the hell is going on. I don't know how you would report a PPC without getting yourself in trouble." We ended up wishing each other good luck and remembering each other to our respective wives.

Even though we sent crews out for antisub patrol, reconnaissance, and Dumbo flights (air-sea rescue missions) to pick up downed airmen, we never stopped training between flights. Two days after a practice gunnery flight, we were notified that on December 30 several skeleton crews would be ferrying PBMs to the Philippines. Our first stop would be a six-hour flight from Hawaii to Johnston Island, which I had never heard of before. It turns out that the island was really a coral reef sticking up about two or three feet above the ocean, essentially a man-made atoll divided into two sections by a seadrome in between and an airstrip on one of the sections. When our turn came, we took off, and after six hours of flying we should have reached Johnston Island. It was a day flight and with radar, binoculars, and an unlimited view, we could see nothing. I had noticed what I thought was a slight splash on the ocean surface, which we passed without any response from our radar. With nothing in sight but ocean, an hour later we turned back and headed toward the splash. It turned out to be Johnston Island. The seadrome was set between two outcroppings of coral, and we made a smooth landing between the islands. We taxied to a seaplane ramp and were fueled for the following day's flight to Kwajalein. With nothing to do before turning in, I joined some of the crew fishing for tropical fish off a low wooden dock above a coral shore. With an open hook, several aquamarine-colored fish were snared and flipped onto the wood planks. The resident company cat, with a bobcat tail and looking more like a grown puma, snatched them as they fell and had a continuous, fresh, wiggly fish dinner with great satisfaction that night.

Two incidents happened at Johnston. We watched a PBM that forgot to close the rear tail hatch before taking off. As the plane thrust forward nose high and rear down, water rushed into the open hull, overloading the rear of the craft, like an anchor pulling the plane back into the water. The more power the pilot gave, the higher the nose went and the more the tail went into the sea. He cut the engines as the plane started to fill with water. After a frantic call for help, safety launches got to the plane in time to keep it from sinking.

Then a NATS (Naval Air Transport Service) DC3 aircraft came in to land at Johnston in the dead of night. The pilot asked for the runway lights to be turned on. It was New Year's Eve, and the controller accidentally lit the seadrome lights between the islands instead of the runway lights. Just as his wheels were about to touch down, the pilot identified the water surface from the reflection of his landing wing lights. He gave his engines full power and pulled up in time to avoid a possibly fatal landing with his fixed-wheeled aircraft in the seadrome of Johnston Island. He landed safely on the now-lighted Johnston Air Strip.

We spent New Year's Eve on the isolated atoll with little celebration, except for a good turkey meal, and started the new year heading for Kwajalein. Amos was flying copilot and I was at the navigation table. I got on the mike to inform the crew that we were about to cross the international date line, placing us a day behind our time. I calculated our speed and distance according to the charts, and at the precise moment announced, "We are now crossing the international date line." It was funny watching some of our crew looking out the plane windows at the ocean floor, complaining they couldn't see it.

We found Kwajalein Island after a ten-and-one-half-hour flight and spent our second New Year's Eve in two days with another turkey dinner at a remote atoll in the middle of the Pacific Ocean. We slept in service tents with outhouse facilities exactly one year after the Marines had captured Kwajalein in a fierce three-day battle. Of the 3,500 Japanese holding the island, only 51 survived and were taken prisoners. Kwajalein was the largest coral atoll known. The following morning, back on our plane, we left Kwajalein for the island of Saipan.

Saipan was Japan's key defensive post, 1,300 miles from the Japanese mainland. On June 13, 1944, after a punishing bombardment from a flotilla of naval battleships, 8,000 U.S. Marines from the 2nd and 4th divisions stormed through the clear, pristine surf from 300 landing craft and controlled a beachhead six miles wide. They sustained heavy losses, but three days later, units of the Army's 27th Infantry Division landed and took control of the As Lito airfield, damaging hangars, buildings, and probably unflyable planes. The Japanese had 30,000 troops and 20,000 civilian families and workers stationed on the island outpost. The Americans invested 71,000 troops in the taking of Saipan. We lost 2,949 men and suffered 10,364 wounded, for one of the most costly battles of the Pacific.

VPB 27 ferry pilots at Saipan. Left to right: Lt. Miller, Ens. Doyle, Ens. Cooper, Ens. Batista, Lt.(jg) Eglies, Ens. DiBenidetto, Ens. Fink, Lt. Dunbar, and Lt.(jg) Krum

With no way to resupply Saipan and 24,000 soldiers killed, Emperor Hirohito ordered the remaining troops and civilians to proceed in a banzai attack against the Americans. Those who survived were ordered to commit suicide and be honored as heroes. Over 20,000 suicides were recorded, leaping from Suicide Cliff and Banzai Cliff, which I understand are tourist attractions on the island today.

We landed on the west side of Saipan. A concrete ramp had already been built in anticipation of a heavy seaplane involvement in the final Pacific battles. A tractor pulled us up, and we stretched our legs and curiosity. On the clear surf next to the ramp, I noticed several Japanese-looking tennis shoes, washing in and out with the surf, divided with a single notched slot for the big toe and a full cover for the other four toes. I noticed one shoe with a foot still in it. On the other side of the concrete landing, a large yellow Caterpillar tractor was digging a six-foot-deep hole. Joe, Amos, and I watched several Marines throwing a stack of disheveled Japanese bodies into the hole. Two Marines with sacks of white lime were scattering it generously over the corpses until the supply had been disbursed. The tractor went to work, scooping the dirt back over the mass grave and trundling across it with its weight to compact the fill. A Marine took a flat panel from a wooden supply box and nailed it to a makeshift wooden stake, which he posted on top of the earth. He had scrawled with crude black paint: 32 JAPS BURIED HERE.

This was my first exposure to the actual remnants of war. I could not believe that we, the United States, would bury the dead, objectively, without identification, with a complete lack of emotion. It was done out of necessity to discourage any possibility of disease. From our position, we could see Marines still in the mountain above us, shooting flame throwers in crevices and caves still not cleared from some holdout defiant soldiers.

Within 500 yards of this mass grave, I saw a coral path to a crisp, outlined area of white crosses, boxed squarely in a straight military-style formation. I am definitely not religious, but because of my Jewish heritage I gazed over to see if any Stars of David were represented among the Christian crosses. I was rewarded when I saw several interspersed and felt proud that we were part of America's effort. In later years, I learned that a Captain Ben L. Salomon, the surgeon of the 2nd Battalion, had defended his patients on Saipan from Japanese soldiers, and then manned a machine gun to enable his patients to be evacuated. After the battle, his body was recovered with ninety-eight dead Japanese soldiers in front of his position. Captain Salomon was awarded the Congressional Medal of Honor posthumously and was the third Jewish recipient from World War II.

Our next stop from Saipan was to an atoll no one had ever heard of. It was called Ulithi. It had been used as a Japanese seaplane

Along Leyte airstrip, Philippines. Front row, E-12 skeleton crew: Long, Garlitz, Smith, Stover, Snyder. Back row, pilots: Krum, Eglies, Cooper

base but was abandoned as ineffectual and too difficult to develop and maintain. The Americans arrived in September of 1944, and the Seabees built a 3,500-foot airstrip, a radio station, and storage facilities. The reef ran twenty miles in length with a ten-mile width, 80 to 100 feet in depth. Six thousand workers were brought to the atoll and turned it into the largest naval base in the world. Most importantly, supplies, floating docks, and fresh water could all be processed and stored without having to return to Hawaii. Several kamikaze attacks had been made on the base with some losses, but the Marine pilots kept the atoll secure.

After our overnight stay at Ulithi, we took off for the Philippines to deliver our planes. I logged 3.3 hours of our 6.6-hour flight time to Tacloban, in Leyte Bay. We tied up to a buoy along with a dozen other Mariners and were boated to the USS Tangier, a former cargo ship converted to a seaplane tender. Another one-night stand and we prepared to return to Hawaii. In the morning, the ferry pilots and crews were taken by small landing craft to the edge of the Tacloban airstrip that paralleled the surf line of the bay. The weather was hot and humid, the water was warm, clear, and shallow, and our shirts were wet with sweat. As the boats approached the shore from the tender to Philippine soil, approximately 100 yards away, one of the pilots from a different squadron stepped on the ledge of his boat, threw his right fist into the air, jumped into the water, and shouted, "I have returned!"

The reaction was immediate. The 100 or so occupants of the other boats all jumped into the water, landing waist-deep in with their clothes and shoes, hurling their right arms into the air, and in a mixed vocal unison, charged toward the beach, yelling, "I have returned! I have returned!" mocking our General Douglas MacArthur's famous photo op.

Wet clothes and soggy shoes survived the humidity, and our fiery crews boarded a NATS R5D and landed in Hawaii, on the Kaneohe airstrip, on January 6, 1945. It was great getting back, but where do we go from here?

20

Saipan, in the Marianas

PBM using Jato (jet-assisted takeoff)

My thoughts returned to my high school friend Jerry Foreman. His mother sent me a photograph of Jerry's grave in England. He was shot down flying his P-38 fighter nine months after joining the Army Air Corps. The comparison of his limited training to almost two years for me made me well aware of my remarkable advantage. Having just returned from ferrying aircraft to the Philippines, my first assignment back at Kaneohe was even more training: night flights, simulated bombing and torpedo runs, bounce drills, antisubmarine exercises, and, finally, checking out the newest innovation, Jato (jet-assisted takeoff), which consisted of two highly compressed air tubes attached to each side of our aircraft to provide immediate extra power under certain takeoff conditions.

One major difference between a land plane and a seaplane is the surface of operation. A runway can be wet or dry, calm or windy, but always a steady surface. Taking off and landing in water is rarely the same. The water can be choppy, which helps break the contact of the step in the seaplane's hull, and lifts it off the water once proper speed is attained. If the water has giant swells, without enough power to fly you might be at the top of the crest, and then the swell drops and you're hanging in the air without enough airspeed to keep you up. The result is that your plane goes down as the swell leaves and you hit the bottom of the trough hard enough to explode the 2,000 gallons of gas carried in your tanks. The following swell again launches you into the air, and without sufficient power you could come crashing down again into the sea. In reverse, when the water is smooth and free of wind, the suction holds the plane to the surface without allowing air to get under the step and freeing you to take off. The pilots, with full takeoff speed, would rock their yolks forward and back, trying to break the bond between the plane and the water.

Now we were introduced to Jato. If you were on the top of the swell, instead of crashing back down into the sea, with torpedoes or 500-pound bombs, hitting the Jato button would give you ten immediate knots of speed, and help keep you airborne. On a smooth surface, after attaining flying speed but unable to break the suction between the plane and the water, hitting the button would give you an immediate jolt, breaking the bond and allowing you to lift off the water. Timing was the key to Jato training, and we never stopped learning.

Our last indoctrination course was a short flight again to Hilo, Hawaii. We spent three days aboard a seaplane tender in Cook Inlet. We learned about life aboard ship, the operation procedures between our aircraft at buoy, and insight into what we might expect living in the actual war zone.

We did learn that our squadron would be sent to Saipan at the beginning of February. We would conduct antisubmarine patrols, reconnaissance, and air-sea rescue missions (called Dumbo), and attack small shipping as needed. Just before we left, on January 25,

IN MEMORY

Lt. Jerry Foreman
1921–1943

1945, Lt.(jg) Ted Connally, returning from a routine patrol, made an emergency landing in the open sea two miles from our station at Kaneohe. The plane crashed in heavy swells and burned, killing copilot Ensign H. M. Anderton, four squadron crew members, and three other enlisted men along for the ride from another squadron. Several others on the flight were seriously injured. And we had yet to face our enemy in an actual war zone.

On February 10, Captain Chase led the first section of planes from Kaneohe to Saipan. After his first stop at Johnston Island, he landed in Tanapag Harbor, Saipan, three days later and set up headquarters. After some passionate letter writing home, Joe, Amos, and I took off with our crew in Easy 12, C'est La Guerre, on February 14. We followed our previous flight plan and joined the rest of our squadron on schedule. We were pulled up the ramp, and from the cockpit we could see what looked like small bonfires all along the coast next to our concrete concourse. As we exited our plane, we were greeted at the bottom of the ladder by a number of Seabees selling Samurai swords, Japanese helmets, and cat's-eye beads taken from the Tanapag surf and made into attractive necklaces. The going rate was $25 or an exchange for a fifth of Four Roses. Each officer in our squadron was allowed to buy two fifths a month at a cost of $4 each. When the Marines came out of the hills where they pursued their Japanese enemies, they were willing to pay $100 for a bottle, on the theory that when they got their pay there was no place to spend it, save some high-stakes poker games.

With Joe Eglies and Amos Krum at former Japanese hangar, Saipan

Seabees greeted each arriving plane like natives thriving on tourists as they arrived for the first time on a foreign shore.

As new residents of Saipan, we discovered that the so-called genuine engraved Samurai swords had been made from the springs of confiscated Jeeps and that the camp fires were really forges for making copies from a single captured sword. Most Seabees were a little older and had enlisted because of their work skills as carpenters, mechanics, welders, and members of the construction trades. Once the Marines secured an attack position, it was the Seabees who followed and set up the facilities for an operating base. They were savvy in a business way, and I'm sure many returned home with enough "earnings" to start their own enterprise when the war was over. Business was brisk on Saipan as each new plane landed and was greeted by enterprising Seabees.

We were housed in tents with wooden floors and ate in a Quonset hut mess hall with several free days before starting our twelve- to fourteen-hour flight patrols. Saipan was still a combat zone, and you could still see Marines in the mountain landscape, blasting their flame throwers at persistent holdouts. Joe and I borrowed a Jeep and drove around the secured coastal areas, seeing a blasted concrete bunker and shattered buildings. We saw a half-dozen disheveled Japanese soldiers, hands tied, of the few captured alive, squatting on a dried grassy slope with several armed Marine guards doing their job.

We were assigned to Fleet Air Wing One and were primarily used for day search missions and night antisubmarine patrols. The island of Tinian, some twenty miles off the east coast of Saipan, had Army B-29s taking off on daily bombing flights to Japan, as well as from other islands along the Marianas rim. We spent an afternoon on Tinian watching the B-29s take off and land, wondering which one of these might go down in the ocean and if we were the ones to bring the crews back. We would fly Dumbo coverage in case a bomber or fighter escort hit the water.

We were on constant alert and aware of Japanese fighters making an attack on our relatively slow and vulnerable Mariners. On one flight between Saipan and Japan, we were attacked by a Japanese "Oscar." As he came at us, we dived low over the water so the fighter could not get below the unprotected part of our plane. Our top gunner, Long, fired at him, but after a quick burst, he took off. We felt he didn't follow through because he didn't have enough fuel to engage us. Our .50- and .30-caliber guns in our nose, sides, and top could repel close encounters from all sides. By breaking off, he denied us the opportunity to test our capability. This was a highlight after many long hours in the air that were mostly fruitless, boring, and tiresome.

A small wooden stage with rows of wooden benches had been built by the Seabees. One evening we were rewarded with a USO show featuring Arthur Donovan, who refereed the Joe Louis fights and all the boxing matches in New York and anywhere else that required his talent. He told inside stories and humorous anecdotes about Louis and other contending fighters in various championship matches he had refereed, which kept a large group of Army and Navy personnel, Marines, and Seabees well entertained. We were sitting in the rear of the amphitheater when a stray bullet came out of the hills above and hit the dirt in front of our bench. It skidded harmlessly, spent, in the dust.

Since Kaneohe and Saipan, the formation of our squadron, pilots and crews, had been constantly shuffled around. Here, at Saipan, every crew seemed to be well established. Joe Eglies, whose real first name was Franz, was my PPC, and Amos Krum and I had pretty well established ourselves as his copilots and navigators, although we all shared equal responsibilities. Our enlisted flight crew was led by our crew captain, Tommy "T. J." Smith, AMM2c, from San Diego, California. The eight crewmen in his charge ranged in age from eighteen to twenty years, mostly enlisted out of high school without graduating, anxious to serve their country. As officers, we had to maintain a professional distance in the relationship between ourselves and the men. Flying together within close proximity for endless hours, sharing coffee, bunks, and portable potties, broke down many of the expected formalities. If a crewman had a close personal relationship with an officer, it gave him a sense of prestige with his peers, that someone would be looking out for him or favoring him. We all shared a bond between our plane and our duty. Once outside our aircraft, salutes and expected courtesies were in mutual order. Penalties were leveled against signs of disrespect, and in general the relationship between pilots and crews was always above standard. Within the plane, formalities were far more relaxed.

Since all the aircraft could not fit on the concourse, most of them were tied to buoys in Tanapag Harbor, in between dozens of Navy ships of every size and purpose. News of a heavy storm brought concern to Saipan Control. It was decided that a pilot and three

At Saipan: Bill Hollgan, Otho Edwards, Irv Cooper, Howard Fischer, and William Mulcahy

crew members should man each aircraft in the event of a weather emergency. I was sent with a skeleton crew of Smokey Stover, Al Bradford, and Henry Bale to babysit C'est La Guerre, tied to a buoy several hundred yards from the ramp. The launch bounced through rising rough waters and took us to our craft along with other crews to theirs. Once in the plane, we made sure everything was tied down and sea anchors and life vests secure in place. Smokey joined me in the cockpit to relax and talk and wait out the storm. The storm didn't wait. The water started to rise and fall, and the plane pulled from the buoy with a wrenching jerk. I had Bradford double-check

E-12 "CEST LA GUERRE" CREW
Front row: Alvin Bradford, AMMF3c; Arthur Young, AMM3c; Thomas Smith, AMM2c (plane captain); Edgar Garlitz, ARM3c; Howard Bale, AMM3c. Back row: John "Smokey" Stover, AOM2c; Arthur Snyder, AOM3c; Lt.(jg) Amos Krum; Lt.(Qg) Joe Eglies; Ens. Irvin Cooper; Aaron Long, ARM3c; Arthur Snyder, AOM3c

the cable, making sure we were tight to the buoy. Rain suddenly hit us like a bomb as it pounded the plane's aluminum like uncoordinated drummers in a bad symphony orchestra.

I sat in Joe's seat on the left and watched as the wind kept pulling our chain taut to our buoy. I felt the jolt as the full pressure came to bear on the connection between plane and tie. The waves in the harbor started to rise and just as quickly subside. The plane floated upward and downward, from crest to trough. The variations between the gusts of wind were so erratic, I was concerned how long we could remain tied. I had my crew put on their Mae Wests (life jackets) and earphones for emergency instructions. I announced that it would be necessary to start the engines and keep them at idle but ready to use. I asked Bale and Bradford to check the sea anchors if needed. The sea anchor was a large metal ring hooked to a tapered canvas top and a smaller canvas funnel at the bottom. When cast into the water on either side of the floating aircraft, the smaller bottom held water from passing through and acted as a surface sea anchor by holding the turn on whatever side it was placed. Tripping it sideways would let the water pass and eliminate the drag. On the opposite side, a duplicate sea anchor could replicate the first, and the pilot could make sharp turns or adjust to a forward drift by commanding use of the port or starboard sea anchors. I was fearful of opening the side hatches because of the possibility that a high side wave might splash into the plane. Both Bale and Bradford would have to act precisely, as directed, on command, in order for me to control the alignment of the plane. The pull and tug was severe. I had Stover check the hydraulics, and I turned on the engines. They sputtered and started, and I moved the throttles forward when the wind hit us directly and eased the power off to synchronize the velocity against the pull and tug.

With my hands on the twin throttles and my eyes on the storm outside, I saw an enormous wave rolling in front of me. As it hit, we were suddenly on top of a mountain of water and I could see a naval vessel a hundred yards away disappear in the base of the onrushing water. Within the span of a thought, the positions were reversed. A bolt of wind hit us straight on, and I pushed my throttles forward to maintain my position. The plane shifted to one side, further from our buoy, and I realized our chain had broken and we were on our own in this merciless storm.

I notified the men, realizing we were cast free between a number of large ships that we would have to avoid. I emphasized again that everyone secure their life jackets and stand by for immediate orders. The ships in Tanapag Harbor had tremendous chains tied to heavy anchors that made 45-degree arcs from ship to water. Should our wing or wing float hit one in the dark, our plane could lose its balance, tip, and sink. I cautioned the crew to report any danger they saw immediately. It was Bale who assured me over the mike, "It's okay, Coop, we're with you."

I was furious. In the midst of this turmoil, I didn't need palsy assurances. It was the first time I felt the responsibility of an officer to an enlisted man. This was not the time for equal rapport. This was the time for a professional response, a direct, "Yes, Sir," or "Aye, aye, Sir."

Against normal radio silence, I had turned on the transmitter and tried to get instructions. "Saipan Tower, Saipan Tower. Peter, Bogey, Mike, broken free from buoy. Request instruction to bring ashore? Over."

No response. I repeated the call several times, guiding the plane between ships and other planes, still tugging at buoys and trying to weather the storm. The static was harsh when it suddenly broke with, "Peter, Bogey, Mike, Saipan Tower hears you. What is your position? Over."

"S. Tower, Peter, Bogey, Mike floating free, broken chain, engines idling, no buoy to tie to, request permission to ramp. Over."

"Peter, Bogey, Mike, ramp closed, can you maintain position? Over."

"S. Tower, water too rough between vessels to control position. Seadrome swells extremely heavy. Ramp only clear opening. Peter, Bogey, Mike. Over."

I kept pushing the throttles forward and back, kicking rudders right and left, trying to maintain a neutral position in an unrelenting sea.

"Peter, Bogey, Mike, stand by for emergency crew. Careful grounding craft at ramp. Can you read? Over."

The gale was defiant. Bursts of wind. A sudden calm. I kept adjusting the throttles to stay within our parameter. The rain peppered the windshield as I focused on staying clear of anything near. My reaction was tense, and there was no sense of time from breaking loose at the buoy to the frustrating radio communication and wondering how long I could control my plane.

"Peter, Bogey, Mike, landing crew at ramp. Proceed with caution. Do you read? Over."

"Loud and clear. Approaching ramp. With care. Over."

I eased the throttle, spotted the ramp buoy, reversed the props, and had Bradford in the entry hatch to secure a rope tie to the buoy, which was a bouncing target. To our luck, the gale took a breath and momentarily subsided as the plane and buoy rose on the same elevation. Bradford leaned out, caught the ring, and secured a rope to the buoy just as the wind was about to nudge us away. Two sailors, waist-high in the surf, fastened the temporary wheels to the hull and signaled the Caterpillar to pull us up to the concourse. They tied the plane as firmly as they could. The wind streaked across the tarmac, docking and straining the tie-downs holding our Mariner to the concrete. Would any other planes break free?

We checked everything inside and climbed down into the rain, waving thanks to the the landing crew for coming out in this weather. They weren't too happy, waiting for another emergency on its way to the ramp. I still felt exhilarated. I was proud to have brought our plane in safely and wanted to give myself a medal for my efforts. My crew brought me back to reality. They knew we were in trouble, but they also knew I was trained to control their plane. As rough as it got, they expected me to bring their plane in safely. As a team, they were happy to be ashore. I realized for them, I just did the job they expected me to do, and they did the job I expected of them.

I did talk to Bale. "You're in the rear of the plane and can't see what's ahead. When I ask you to do something during the course of operation, I expect nothing but a quick response." I felt a little embarrassed and didn't want to come off like a snob, but I continued. "When this war is over and you and I are in tweeds or whatever civilian clothes, you can call me Coop or whatever you want, but as long as we're in this Navy together, my name is Mr. Cooper. I will never give a frivolous order. But when I, or Mr. Eglies, or Mr. Krum, give an order on our plane, we expect it to be done with respect and as quickly as possible. Your response could be your life or the rest of the crew if not done quickly. You're not in a position to see what's ahead of us or what information we have learned. I respect what you have to do and expect you to respect what we do. If we do everything together, as a team, we will all get home in one piece. Everyone in this crew has a responsibility to themselves and all of us." I paused, and then added, "You and the crew did a good job tonight. That's why we are here."

We were standing alone under a covered supply shelter dividing the path between the tents of the officers and crew. Bale looked at me and gave me a snappy salute. I looked at him and said, "Knock it off." I realized that when the crew got together they probably referred to their pilots as Joe, Amos, and Coop, as did all the other crews identifying with their pilots.

The weather had a schedule of its own. After displaying its temperament, the next few days provided us with tropical breezes and clear skies. When not on patrol, the mild conditions offered us an opportunity for some good pickup softball and basketball games played on makeshift courts. It may sound like a touch of normalcy, but Saipan was still a combat zone. There were many isolated pockets of resistance, and the Marines continued to blast hidden caves and crevices with flame throwers and hand grenades. Submarines still plied offshore in cat-and-mouse encounters, perhaps more as observers than in direct attack, with little hope of escape. Our squadron flew constant fourteen-hour-day and -night flights, attacking small enemy ships and recovering downed airmen on rafts floating in the sea.

The squadron was made up of eighteen flight crews plus a staff of operations, administration, gunnery, and radio-radar officers and personnel. The USS Onslow, a seaplane tender the size of a Navy destroyer, moved into Tanapag Harbor. Captain Chase, with the first six flight crews, moved aboard. The USS Yakutat followed, and another group of six transferred from land to ship. The USS Shelikof, the third of the tenders, dropped anchor, and we moved aboard with the last six crews. All the tenders were similar to the ones in Norfolk and Hilo that we had used during our indoctrination. The quality of life certainly improved. We went from saltwater showers and mixed Spam dinners to chicken, beef, and pork and nightly desserts, clean sheets and laundry, and, most surprising for me, a personal-issue napkin ring that I would use at each meal. VPB 27 finally had a place to call home.

We lived aboard ship, launched to our aircraft tied to designated buoys, and continued a heavy flight schedule with few results. Our enemy may not have shown up beneath the sea or in the skies; its only ally was the temperamental sea that passed the Saipan shores. Every landing and takeoff was a new experience, and the squadron pilots developed dramatic skills to handle the challenge. On most of the morning and evening takeoffs and landings, off-duty crews would be watching from the decks of the three tenders we occupied. Some of the most skilled efforts would prompt a spontaneous cheer from fellow Mariners hanging on the railings of their ships.

We flew cover for planes attacking Iwo Jima, and from a distance we could see the shelling that bombarded the island. On Saipan, we saw many wounded Marines brought to the island for flights to hospital bases in Guam, Hawaii, and the mainland. They were brought in on stretchers, and you could see the blanket lying flat where a leg was supposed to be. I recall someone pinning Purple Hearts on top of the covers, but most of the patients were medicated and oblivious to what was happening. If they were conscious, they were grateful to be alive.

On this note, we received our orders to proceed to Kerama Retto, a group of islands about twenty-five miles southwest of Okinawa. The islands were in the process of being cleared, with little resistance, and sharp-pointed coral was being blasted from under the water of a two-mile-long seadrome planned for a seaplane operation. The underwater clearance offered plenty of depth for planes to land and for supportive ships, military and supply, to make haven within the contours of the islands. In several days, as soon as the ships anchored, we would join them and participate in the protection of a proposed major sea base to launch final attacks on Japan. Like the public, until now we had never heard of a place called Kerama Retto. What we did know that the public didn't was the contribution that would be made by the seaplane, particularly, the PBM Martin Mariner. It was part of the contributing assault that helped end the war in Japan and bring about the defeat of the Imperial Japanese empire.

21

Welcome to Kerama Retto

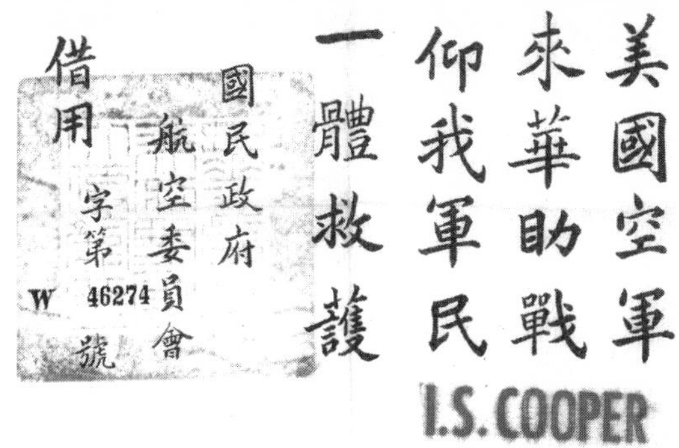

Pocket flag carried by American pilots fighting against Japan

With a world at war, most people were aware of London, Paris, Berlin, Moscow, Stalingrad, and the many satellite cities that felt the bombs of the Nazi and Allied aircraft that blanketed Europe. As the war in Germany was nearing its end, America shifted B-29s and other aircraft to the Pacific in the final push against Japan. As more Navy, Marine, and Army units moved west to the Pacific, the realization that fewer would return brought a new geographical education to so many families involved. Unless you read the *National Geographic*, you might have had a limited knowledge of Hawaii, Tahiti, Hong Kong, Shanghai, and Tokyo. But to receive the final news of a lost son, father, uncle, or brother on an unknown Pacific island was an even deeper pain. The reports of correspondent Ernie Pyle, the heroics of "Pappy" Boyington and his fighting P-51 squadron, the news of the Flying Tigers, and the Battle of Midway all brought new and exotic names to the public's attention. They now learned about Guam, Tarawa, Guadalcanal, Kwajalein, Peleliu, Saipan, and Iwo Jima.

They never heard of Ulithi, the largest sea base in the world at the time. Who knew of the thousands of ships that were to be assembled there, carrying planned occupying troops, supplies, ammunition, tanks, trucks, freshwater, and fuel, setting up for the invasion of Japan? No one ever heard of Kerama Retto and the contribution of the PBM, the Navy's most formidable seaplane, in ending the war.

Who knew what or where? We knew at this precise moment that some 100,000 Marines and Army soldiers were battling 150,000 Japanese, eye to eye, rifle to rifle, bayonet to bayonet, in heat, rain, and mud, establishing control within 1,300 miles from the heart of Japan. Our seaplanes were the few craft that had the range to clear waters until closer landing strips and facilities could be built on a conquered land base in Okinawa.

We were scheduled to be among the first occupants assigned to Kerama Retto. Six seaplane tenders, including our Onslow, Yakutat, and Shelikof, left Saipan on the 26th of March, 1945, for the three-day voyage to our new frontier. The Marines had cleared the mostly agricultural islands that made up the protected anchorage, which the Japanese never considered as an area that would appeal to the Americans. Apparently, they never realized it had enough space and depth to house capital ships, carriers, and the varying supply services to develop an actual naval base. They could not imagine that such a force could possibly get a foothold that close to Japan. Navy intelligence must have pondered its likelihood and decided that establishing a seaplane base would eliminate the long-distance flight attacks from the Marianas and the Philippines, and that such an effort was feasible until closer airfields could be established. It totally surprised the enemy.

On the morning of the 29th, as our tenders were ready to pull into Kerama Retto, we finished our last land-fed breakfast at Saipan and took off to join them as they dropped anchor in our new base of operations. Joe and Amos lifted C'est La Guerre from a warm, choppy sea into a rising sun that amazingly resembled the Japanese flag. I sat at the navigation table, and two other planes from our squadron, flying on each wing, followed us west in a loose formation. We all rotated seats in flight, and three and one-half hours later I switched from navigation to copilot and looked forward to landing in our new home. As we approached the closely scattered islands that made up Kerama Retto, a long string of Navy ships cruised directly across our bow, passing between us and our newly designated base. I was monitoring the radio and set up our IFF circuit, which gave out a signal identifying us as friendly aircraft. We all felt a glow of pride to be a part of such a massive Navy operation, doing more ogling than actual participating. Flying at 6,000 feet, Amos squeezed between Joe and me, looking out the windshield, trying to identify the various classes of vessels that made up the fleet in front of us. The line of Navy warships, anywhere from two to five to ten miles apart, streamed endlessly along the southern coast, passing our entry into Kerama Retto, for as far as we could see.

As we approached the line of ships, we heard an explosion and observed a black cannon cloud close to our elevation and a modest jolt to our plane. We could see the source of smoke from a cruiser's cannon, and Joe jumped on the mike, "What the hell's going on? We're Peter, Bogey, Mike, heading to our landing. You guys blind? Over."

A voice, evidently from the sighted cruiser, responded. "We don't care who you are, you cannot cross our line unless you have ten miles' clearance between ships. Do you read?"

To emphasize his point, another black cloud burst high to the side to make sure we got the message. Annoyed, we flew south along with our companion Mariners for half an hour, paralleling the ships in line before finding a space wide enough to cross. Once on the other side, Amos navigated our way back to the original point of entry, and we could see the group of islands as they appeared on our charts. Any man in the Navy will tell you that the Consolidated PBY was really the only long-range seaplane they knew about. The PBM, with its massive bulk, twin tails, unique gull wing, and machine gun turrets, was something most had never seen. Our PBMs were making their first real appearance, ahead of most aircraft because no land had been taken to set up runways. We could easily have been mistaken for a Japanese seaplane, except for our IFF signals, but getting hit by one of our own would certainly have been no consolation.

As we flew into Kerama Retto, we saw six tenders scattered between island points with planes already tied to buoys. Motor launches were cutting a swath between them and their ships, picking up crews that had landed ahead of us. The lengthy seadrome was obvious, and our group landed loosely on uneven swells, looking for our mother ship. By radio, we each lined up our buoys, and Smitty opened our forward hatch as we cut back our engines and coasted smoothly to our bobbing buoy. Smitty secured our plane to the ring, we turned off all equipment, and we completed our exit procedures. A small fuel trawler lined up alongside, and Bradford coordinated the refueling, readying the aircraft for takeoff as soon as we were directed. The following day, our plane was loaded with antisubmarine bombs for a scheduled flight that night.

Back aboard ship, we had our dinner in the comfort of our wardroom, at somewhat normal dinner hours. The crews ate in cafeteria style, generally open all hours because of the varying shifts employed by the ship's hands on watch or duty. There was always a sign at the head of the cafeteria line, TAKE ALL YOU WANT, EAT ALL YOU TAKE. The fare was far superior to the packaged rations issued to the land-based troops fighting for the capture of their goals: a hill, a village, an armored conclave. After our dinner, we took to the ship's rails to watch several of the earlier arrived planes take off for immediate all-night patrols. The very first flight was led by Lt.(jg) Hushbeck, the captain's PPC, searching for submarines or ships or anything threatening our position. Our scheduled flight for the following evening was to patrol the Chinese and Okinawa coasts. Each pilot was issued a package of Chinese money, and everyone was given a nylon kerchief imprinted with a Chinese flag. It described us as American aviators helping the Chinese in the war against Japan, and asked for their help in returning us to our units in the event we went down in Chinese territory. We were also told that any ship or launch or junk that had a motor was probably controlled by the Japanese and should be sunk, beached, or destroyed. Any boat without a motor or with a sail was probably Chinese and should not be harmed.

We turned in to sleep and awoke in the morning to find several large ships moored between the islands. Hushbeck had returned from an uneventful search, and other Mariners had resumed their patrols. It was midday when sirens screeched and red flags were hoisted above the ships. We ran out on deck and were cautioned to return. Many of our crew members were assigned to machine gun stations and small gunnery batteries aboard ship. A picket ship hovering between Okinawa and Japan had been attacked by kamikaze aircraft and relayed the warning to the gathering ships in Kerama. Along with several other pilots, we donned metal helmets and slipped out on deck to watch the action. We waited and watched and waited until we heard the roar of a ship's loud cannons booming behind an island buffer. A lone Japanese aircraft streaked low overhead at an altitude of about 2,000 feet, and rolled over and headed down for a target we couldn't see. I couldn't imagine how many ships had anchored in our lagoon until I saw the sky filled with cannon and gunfire from a variety of potential targets. Halfway down the arc of its trajectory, just as it rolled over, the kamikaze plane blew to pieces, and its debris scattered harmlessly in the water below. The gunners on our ship cheered and waited until an all-clear was declared and the red flags were pulled down.

Our first night patrol lasted well over fourteen hours, from dusk till dawn. Our prime concern was for Japanese submarines, identifiable only by radar, if they were to surface at night. We were equipped with a Fido bomb, which when dropped on a suspected target could travel five miles underwater by magnetic attraction. Within that distance, the bomb would attach itself to the sub's metal hull and create an explosion, not strong enough to sink the sub but sufficient to identify its location. We would then drop one of our two 500-pound bombs and follow with the second, with enough power to sink or expose it to the surface. We never had that opportunity. We spotted some lights along the China shore but never received hostile fire. Before we landed back at Kerama, we had to jettison our bombs in the open sea rather than chance the bombs exploding in a rough open-sea landing.

Upon our return, we learned that a lone Japanese swimmer had climbed into one of the buoyed Mariners and attempted to blow it up. His grenade or bombing device was so wet that it refused to explode, so he tried physically to damage the aircraft but couldn't sink it. From that time on, all Mariners tied to buoys at night required a pilot and three crew members to stay aboard. That meant that Joe, Amos, and I, as well as all other crews, would spend every third night aboard their plane. Smokey Stover, Al Bradford, and Henry Bale would make up my plane watch.

Kerama Retto became home to a variety of ships and even more seaplanes, aircraft carriers, cruisers, tankers, Liberty ships with supplies, fuel trawlers, destroyers, and mine layers, all anchored in the Kerama lagoon. Some islands became sites for shipboard garbage, with a continuous fire consuming the waste. Other sites were set up for recreation, beer-drinking parties, and swimming beaches. And most days were host to kamikaze attacks with some tragic success. Ironically, as more ships gathered in Kerama, our retaliation contributed to our losses.

I was grateful that our tender, equal to the size of a destroyer, was among the smaller ships anchored between the island groups. The kamikazes that got past the picket ships en route to the end of their journey would aim at the larger ships to sacrifice their lives rather than the smaller craft. As the first kamikazes came in, all the ships raised their machine guns skyward, following the suicide plane to its target. If the plane wasn't hit high in the air, the machine guns followed it down with a vengeance, firing until it disappeared into its target and causing a loud explosion. Unfortunately, the lower it got, the machine guns from one ship would end up aimed at deck level of an adjacent ship, hitting the other ship's gunners. On one such occasion, a seaman on our Shelikof was hit by a gunner from another ship. He was carried bleeding into our officers' wardroom and laid out on a full-length table. The ship's doctor, a gynecologist from Texas, seemed slightly out of his element, until his corpsman whipped out a tourniquet and restricted the bleeding.

On one occasion I saw a kamikaze go through the deck of a carrier, exploding in a sick bay and killing a number of men scheduled to return home the following day. In another incident, I saw a fighter plane take off from a carrier behind one of Kerama's little islands. As it climbed into the air, a gunner on the other side of the island, not realizing it was an American plane, shot at the aircraft, which exploded and fell back into the Kerama waters. At the same moment, a plane had taken off after the first one, and the pilot, seeing what had happened before him, powered forward for as much height as he dared, rolled over, and bailed out, pulling his parachute and landing in the water near the pilot before him. I remember in my mind writing an imaginary condolence letter to the first pilot's parents describing their son's loss in action, in a place in the Pacific they never heard of, Kerama Retto.

Some twenty years after the war, Elaine and I took a trip to Japan. The tour guide, who seemed about my age, and I kept eyeing each other. I think we both wondered what we each did in the war. Once I got to know him, the discussion came up, and he told me he had been a kamikaze pilot. With further explanation, I learned they had more pilots than planes, and after waiting around a lengthy time, he was placed on a small ship and sent to sea. The most revealing portion of our discussion was that I learned that kamikaze pilots were not volunteers. They had been selected by their service and given their assignment. Regardless of what they personally felt, they could not shame their family by refusing such an honor.

Had I been assigned kamikaze duty in the Japanese Air Force, I would have tried to make friends with the commander, or at least to the equal of a Navy yeoman who issued orders, to put me at the bottom of the list until they ran out of planes. By the same thought, I think of the the burden the American commanders had in sending squadrons of fighters, torpedo bombers, and dive bombers to attack a fleet of enemy battleships, carriers, and auxillary ships, aware how many might not return. They counted on the aircraft, the training, and the skill of the American pilots to do their job and return safely. Backing them up were seaplanes, submarines, and rescue ships outside the perimeter of battle, to pick up and save any downed pilots and crew. It seems the Japanese fought to die, while the Americans fought to live.

On April 12, 1945, prior to an all-night fourteen-hour patrol off the coast of Korea, we received news that our commander -in-chief, President Franklin D. Roosevelt, had died in Warm Springs, Georgia. He was the only president we knew growing up. His vice president, Harry S. Truman, took the oath of office, and we knew very little about him or his background. As we wondered about the war and the future of our country, it took second place to the uneventful mission we had the following night.

22

Combat at Kerama

PBM resting at its buoy when not in flight

The anchorage at Kerama was so spread out and the invasion by the Fleet Air Wing was so successful, it took me some thirty days to realize what we really accomplished. The very first day we landed, five Mariners covered the invasion fleet that night. Our crew flew on the second night of our arrival, and our squadron alone accounted for 2,182 hours of patrol, averaging 70 hours a day for those first thirty days.

The whole idea of the seaplane initiative was to repulse the threat of the Japanese submarine to the increasing number of ships entering Kerama Retto. We had been denied the use of our skills from our years of training because, at this stage, the Japanese had few submarines left to challenge. Records claim only two contacts with submarines had been made during the Kerama invasion. We thought we had one, and I'm not sure if it was ours that was counted. Perhaps they were both the same?

After several all-night flights, we were assigned a day patrol on the 10th of April. Our radar picked up a blip some thirty to forty miles from our position, and we eagerly chased it down. Once within visual range, we thought we saw the splash of a conning tower or the drag of a submarine antenna submerged in the sun-reflected water. Joe ordered us to prepare sonar tubes for casting into the sea from the open side hatches of our plane. The name *sonar* is an acronym for Sound Navigation And Ranging, and its original use goes back to the early 1800s. Today's sophisticated sonar technology reacts under water as radar reacts in the air.

Joe laid out a drawing in the cockpit covering a five-square-mile box. Our sonar tubes were marked in five different colors. On the first corner of the square, Joe had me call out a blue, and Smitty pulled out the antenna attached to the length of the three- or four-foot tube and released a small attached chute that allowed the tube to drop vertically into the water. When the bottom of the tube hit, a plastic seal broke and a cable attached from the antenna to a radio receiver dropped 100 feet underwater from the surface of the sea, ready to pick up any form of motor sound and transmit it to our earphones in the cockpit. Joe flew in a straight line for five miles, and I signaled the release of the second tube, marked purple. Joe banked hard right and flew straight ahead for the next five miles before dropping our third tube. We hit all four corners and then crisscrossed the area, dropping our fifth different-colored tube dead center in a laid-out box in the ocean.

In Kaneohe Bay, we had taken sonar classes and spent a number of hours listening to underwater sounds. We were taught to differentiate the gurgle of fish, whales, dolphins, and other sea creatures from the sound of a responsive ping emitted from any metal or motor under water. Joe, Amos, and I concentrated on the sounds coming from the different-colored tubes. If we were to pick up the slightest ping from a corner yellow and then receive a stronger echo from an opposite corner red, we would know which way the sub was moving. If there were no sound at the green corner, we would know the sub was not in that area. We could determine in which direction a submarine was moving by listening to the response of our underwater ears.

Once we confirmed the possibility that an enemy was submerged within our sonar-covered area, we released our Fido bomb explosive that could track a submarine within a five mile radius. Once it followed and touched the metal clad hull of the submarine, it would detonate and cause a large explosion, but not strong enough to sink the sub. The charge coming up from the water would expose the location of the sub, and then we would drop two 500-pound depth charges at the site. This would normally cause extreme damage and could sink the sub. Unfortunately, our Fido found nothing.

Assuming the sub had spotted our aircraft, it could have submerged out of sight, cut its engines, and lay silently at the bottom. We were now engaged in a cat-and-mouse game. We had only a limited amount of fuel to wait out the time. We kept circling the area, listening for sounds, and put out a call for other aircraft or surface ships to take over. It was a long, tiresome day with no solid results. After a number of hours, the sonar tubes filled with water and sank to the bottom of the ocean, not allowing a sub or surface vessel to salvage the equipment. Two days later, one of our squadron planes, piloted by Lt. Welch, picked up a sub contact thirty minutes after takeoff and spent a day repeating our experience. He dropped two bombs on the site, with no visible evidence, and received a "submarine probably damaged" assessment.

While we established our routine aboard ship and our scheduled flight assignments, the Army and Marines were engaged in the deadliest bloody battle of the Pacific. Aside from the daily kamikaze attacks at Kerama, and the more probing flights around China, Korea, and Japan, our adversary came in the form of defiant weather and temperamental seas. Every takeoff and landing was a new experience. Heavy fogs would envelope Kerama Retto, and with the use of Jato to take off in the rough swells, the seadrome would be covered with such a layer of smoke, it was impossible to see. It seemed most night flights were all done by instrument. Many planes could not take off on time, and returning aircraft from an all-night flight had to circle Kerama until visibility let them land in the treacherous sea.

When not flying an all-night patrol, our every third watch aboard the plane was physically tiring. Bradford and Bale took their guard duty seriously, with guns in hand, mostly resting and guarding atop the Mariner's wing in the warm, humid evenings. On Bradford's free time, he had rigged up a music system to a small turntable that somehow had shown up in our plane. I would play the record "Moonlight in Vermont," as sung by Margaret Whiting, over and over, and even learned all the words. I seemed to spend considerable time talking with Stover, a ranking ordinance mate. He was very bright and personable. We talked about home, school, the war, ambition, and our peacetime pursuits. Protocol was relaxed until business was at hand. We all had respect for each other's jobs.

Each pilot in the squadron had been assigned a ground duty job, and somehow I, with only two years of college training, was appointed education officer. I sent for study courses from the University of California, Berkeley, and offered those who wanted college credit for their correspondence classes an opportunity to fulfill their needs. I had written several letters to high school principals describing some of the Navy courses crewmen had passed in order to advance their ratings in specific classifications. I had success in getting science credits for some and an actual high school diploma for another. I also wrote a letter on Stover's behalf, recommending him for officers' training. (At the war's end he became an officer and in civilian life became a business attorney in Walnut, California.)

After our day with the submarine, we flew four all-night flights in a row, every third day. On one, we shot up and beached a motor launch trying to hide in a coastal inlet. On another, we patrolled directly into the mouth of the Yangtze River and were attacked by several Japanese fighters. We dived low over the water and escaped in the night. Coming back at dawn from an all-night patrol, we would leave the China coast and encounter a combination of fifty Chinese sampans or junks, fishing with nets in a loosely organized group. If we carried bombs we had to jettison, we would drop low over their sails, wiggle our wings in a friendly gesture, and then drop our bombs a mile or two away. The concussion was so heavy that the explosion blew the fish from the depths of the ocean to the top of the sea. The fishermen then rushed with their nets to haul in their catch as the fish floated to the surface.

Somewhere in the second week at Kerama, the six crews on the Shelikof were requested to appear on the fantail of the ship. A small table had been set up, and Captain Chase stood with Executive Officer McQuire and Administrative Officer Richard Kendrick. As the crews lined up on each side, Captain Chase made a short speech extolling the good work performed by the crews in front of him. With that, he called the pilots and crew of each aircraft, exchanged a snappy salute, and presented each member, individually, with the Air Medal for five combat contacts with the enemy in flight. Naturally, I was pleased. This honor was very difficult to receive in the Navy, and I figured that now that the Army's B-29s and other aircraft had been diverted from Europe, the Navy would emulate the Air Force practice of recognizing every fifth successful mission completed by their crews. In my mind, I couldn't compare our flights to the horrendous formations that the Army flew over Europe and the losses they encountered on every run. Those crews never thought about if they were to be shot down, but when. Yet when the Army pilots thought of duty like flying twelve to fourteen hours alone or with another aircraft, flying all night or all day, low over enemy territory, exposed to ship, shore, and air fire, it may have seemed incomprehensible. I guess we each live within our own training and comfort zones.

I made a drawing back in 1944 about our squadron's probable awards. It seemed to get a laugh then, and now suddenly ended up in the wardroom of all three ships. The ongoing joke was that instead of receiving a Purple Heart, we would all receive a "Purple Shaft."

Between flights, life aboard the Shelikof was not unpleasant. Excellent meals, ample letter-writing time, reading, card games, acey-deucey, and general conversation. My time socializing was mostly with Howard Brown, with whom I had gone through considerable training; Austin Puvogel, a conservative New Yorker who was against my liberal Los Angeles views; New England's Eddie Raymond, who was always excusing himself to write "Loretter a lettuh"; and Bill Holligan, tall and lanky and just a sweet guy. There was no fraternizing with crew members aboard ship. Joe, Amos, and I did spend time talking together.

On one of my nights aboard ship, the weather was storming and the sea was rough. I was grateful not to be on the plane watch or in flight. The Shelikof reacted, unlike the larger ships, by constantly rolling and tugging at its chain. Sealed from the rain and wind outside, the interior of the ship was hot and stuffy. I could feel a nausea and seasickness coming on to me. If I had been a sailor, I would have taken all my voyages by rail. My defense, at this early evening hour, was to climb into my top double bunk in the officers' quarters and try to sleep it out. I had succeeded except that somewhere around a quarter to twelve, I was shaken awake by Yeoman Hummer. "Mr. Cooper, wake up, the captain wants to see you," he kept shaking.

"What? Me? What about?" I came out of a daze. Hummer repeated his call. "The captain wants to see you."

I was totally baffled. Why me? What have I done? What does he want me to do? I climbed down from my bunk, wearing shorts and T-shirt, and grabbed my khaki pants and shirt. I pulled on my loafers as Hummer held out a full yellow raincoat and wide-brimmed rain hat. "The captain's gig is waiting for you."

I staggered through the passageway, climbed the ladder and through the hatch, crossed the wardroom, and headed outside toward the midship deck. The wind pelted the rain in my face as I climbed down the ladder to the captain's gig, waiting to take me to the Yakutat. The swell raised the launch to my level, and I jumped in and got under the canvas cover as the pilot gunned the motor and pulled away from my ship. The Yakutat was about a half mile from the Shelikof, and the swells rode high and low with the wind and rain blowing unevenly in all directions except seemingly ending in my face. The launch skillfully sidled up to the ship, and two crewmen grabbed the ladder for me to climb aboard. Up and down, the water level lashed against the hull until I reached the top. Once on deck, in the wind-scattered rain, I whipped out a perfunctory salute to the officer of the day, who advised me to follow a crewman to the captain's cabin.

I removed my rain gear, but my pants and shirt showed signs of the storm's penetration. I knocked on the captain's door, trying to hold my balance as the Yakutat rolled from side to side. My thoughts raced. Why was I called out to see him in this weather? Again, what had I done?

I was told to open the door, and I did. Captain Chase was sitting in a chair next to a desk with a single bed alongside. He sat in his shorts and T-shirt and still looked like he was playing a role from Central Casting. Aside from some papers on his desk, a framed photo of an attractive woman, whom I assumed was the captain's wife, stood regally in one corner.

"Captain," I uttered. "Ensign Cooper, Sir?"

His eyes surveyed me. "Cooper," he said.

"Yes, Sir," I said.

"You don't drink, do you?"

Surprised, I looked at him. "Well, not really, Sir."

"Good. I'd like your monthly chits if you don't mind."

The captain was referring to the two chits I was issued to buy two fifths of whiskey each month. Totally startled, I somewhat stammered, "Yes, Sir."

"Good. Dismissed."

The ride back in the captain's gig was an adventure in itself. The skillful crew that operated the boat maneuvered through the wind and the rain and the rolling sea, and got me back aboard the Shelikof in once piece, but slightly doused.

I told everyone that the captain wanted me for a secret mission.

23

April 27, 1945

Attacking a Japanese convoy

Dressing for a regularly scheduled flight was a routine I took seriously. My full-length flight suit had a series of pockets, zippered and buttoned, located from chest to waist, from arms and legs. I used to wear comfortable penny loafers in flight but, after attending a survival training course, switched to a high-top boot for practical purposes in case we went down. I carried a package of mixed-size fishhooks, small rolls of nylon fish line, a compass, and a pack of chewing gum. I kept a picture of Elaine in my breast pocket. I wore a seven-inch leather-sheathed knife and a .38 Smith & Wesson six-shooter pistol strapped to my waist, cowboy style. A downed survivor told me what he missed most in the weeks it took him to get back to his unit was a toothbrush. Naturally, I carried one with a shortened handle tucked somewhere in my leg pocket stash.

April 27 started as a normal day, scheduled to take off at dusk, fly all night along the Asian coast hunting for the usual prey, from submarines to trawlers, small ships to shore encampments, to downed pilots, to capital ships or aircraft. Every flight was an adventure in itself. Every takeoff and landing, unlike Albemarle Sound or Alameda Bay, was a challenge to the skill of the pilots in battling the changing conditions of an unrelenting sea. One day calm, the next day frenzied. Every patrol bomber pilot will describe the constant boredom of flying twelve to fourteen hours, scanning the ocean with ten-power Navy binoculars, or concentrating for blips on the radar screen between the two pilot seats, and returning to base with nothing to show for their efforts. To find a single dot of a downed airman, or a raft with a full flying crew, to aid in their rescue, would be their reward for the time and training it took to get there.

Not all of the crew prayed before each flight, but I couldn't help but observe some members crossing themselves and saying a quick prayer to Jesus before taking off. Whatever help it brought,

I was grateful for the support. I always remembered the boxer who crossed himself just as the bell rang starting a fight, and someone asked, "What does that mean?" The answer: it didn't mean a damn thing if he didn't know how to fight. Because of an unusual amount of activity aboard ship, with more boats than usual tying up at the gangway ladder, I had a moment of premonition. I found myself reflecting on the only Hebrew phrase I could remember, which was from a Passover Holiday prayer, "Mah nish tanah ha-laylah hazeh," which means, "Why is this night different from other nights?"

My agnostic mind recalled it only from the joke we told as kids. It was King Arthur reviewing his Knights at the Round Table. He inspected each one as they stood at attention, erect, in shining armor, trim, holding a glistening sharp sword. When he came up to the last one in line, he was aghast to see slumping before him, a figure disheveled, dirty, and displaying a sword tarnished with rust. It was said that from King Arthur's lips came this ancient Hebrew phrase, "Mah nish tanah ha-laylah hazeh." Why is this knight different from all other knights?

I soon found out why.

After dinner, we were called for a special briefing in the wardroom prior to our scheduled flight. Joe, Amos, and I left our quarters oddly curious as to what was going on. We entered the room with Otho Edwards and his two copilots, James Bistodeau and Bill Holligan, who were also scheduled to fly that night. Our executive officer from the Yakutat, Lt. William McQuire, had just come aboard ship with his copilots, John Doyle and Wally Tschida. They entered the room from the outside deck as we entered from the interior passage. We were surprised to see them in our wardroom filled with strange pilots, not from our squadron. There were crews from VPB 208, a squadron that had been on their tenders with us at Saipan and now here at Kerama. As we entered, they shifted around the tables in a half circle, giving us room to complete the loop, facing three briefing officers we had never seen. An easel with a large pad clipped to the top was placed at the end of the table. After acknowledging everyone's presence, the lieutenant in charge addressed the group in a straightforward, businesslike manner.

"Gentlemen," he started, "we expect PBMs to make history tonight."

We all looked at each other with great curiosity, and then back at the speaker, who continued: "Our target is a small Japanese task force some 900 miles up the Yellow Sea. We have no aircraft that has the range to attack and return, and I'm sure the Japanese are aware. Your Mariners are being equipped with two 2,000-pound torpedoes, one under each of your gull wings. You will take off from Kerama and fly at 200 feet above the water until 100 miles from your objective. You will then drop to 100 feet, and as you get closer, drop down to 50 feet to stay under their radar. As the force comes into view, you will line up a target, make a single strike with full power, and return to base. This whole exercise is based on surprise; something the Japs will never expect."

The briefing officer made some marks on the easel pad, which were somewhat ignored. All the pilots stood motionless, concentrating on the description of the mission, trying to absorb the instructions. This was an assignment far different from the routine, boring patrols about which we constantly complained. One of the plane commanders of VPB 208 flicked his hand for recognition and asked about the element of risk. One of the other officers of the briefing team leaned forward and spoke slowly. "This whole operation is based on surprise. We expect all of you to get through, and—" several seconds passed before he went on, "at the very worst, it's possible—" again a pause, "possible upon the worst conditions, that three of you might not make it!"

I stood stupefied. I knew the three crews from our squadron exchanged looks with the three crews of theirs, each wondering if it would be us or them. My Hollywood background always seemed to transport me to a movie moment. I immediately thought of John Wayne, comprehending, in celluloid, the odds of not returning from a death-defying battle. Except this was not a movie. I kept thinking, were they willing to gamble six half-million-dollar aircraft and seventy-two lives to surprise a Japanese convoy and convey a message that the United States could hit them anywhere at any time? My immediate thoughts flashed to Elaine and the future we had vowed to share. Everyone's heart pounded, yet everyone stood casually erect and exhibited a professional air of competence and confidence.

After further briefing, one of the officers in charge took out a coin and flipped it to see which squadron would attack first. The other squadron would follow two minutes later, full throttle at 200 knots. VPB 208 would go first. We would follow behind.

Our group of three would be led by Lt. McQuire in Easy 2 in a loose formation, with Otho Edwards in Easy 17 on one wing and our Easy 12 on the other. The briefing ended with "Fly safe, good luck."

I could feel the blood churning through my body as we joined the group of pilots exiting the room. Edwards's crew and our crew had been standing on the deck, wondering what all the newcomers were doing on our ship. As soon as they spotted us, they converged around Joe and Amos and me. "What's happening, where are we going?"

Joe explained our mission.

"We will fly almost a thousand miles with two torpedoes and hit a Japanese task force of supply ships, tankers, and destroyers. We will fly in two formations, with Squadron 208 going in first, and we will follow two minutes later. There will be total radio silence, and everyone will be at their gun stations and flight assignments."

The crew yelped with joy at the thought of seeing real action. Our top gunner, Long, pumped his fist in the air with excitement, shouting, "We're going to get those bastards!"

Our crew, which was two to four years younger than their pilots, felt an adrenaline high on hearing the news, excited, behaving like going into battle was a high school football rally.

I wanted to yell at them to calm down and tell them there was a good chance of not making it back. Instead, stoic and positive, we addressed their specific duties. This is what we had been trained for. My own thoughts ranged from the preparation of flight to the thought of never seeing Elaine again. I recall my consolation in thinking that if I did not get back, she would have my $10,000 G.I. life insurance policy and be able to live out her life independently. For me, it was comforting.

It was nearing dusk as each crew prepared to follow their flight instructions. Once the launch removed the other officers to their ships or planes, the full Shelikof crews were taken to our planes and prepared for takeoff. We all wore our Mae West life jackets. Joe and Amos adjusted their Smith & Wessons in their shoulder holsters and kidded me about carrying my pistol cowboy-style on my hip.

Once in the plane, we checked the torpedoes under our wings. The machine guns had been loaded by an ordinance crew. Strings of .50-caliber machine gun bullets for the top, nose, and tail turrets and abundant rounds of .30-calibers for the two machine guns at the waste hatches were stacked on both sides. Each member of the crew went to their assigned station as we checked our weight disbursement for the least flight resistance. The enthusiasm was now focused on doing our job.

We climbed to the cockpit on the upper deck. Joe took the controls on the left and I sat copilot on his right. Amos took the navigation table and laid out his charts and flight plan. Because of his seniority, it was agreed that we would swap seats when we attacked the target. Joe and I went carefully through the checklist as the last rays of the sun glittered between two small island peaks of Kerama. Again the alternating flashes of the sun resembled the design of the Japanese flag before disappearing into the horizon. We tested the rudder, flaps, tail, and all other movable parts in accordance with our flight manual. I called each station for clearance and received a snappy, "Aye, aye, Sir," and we were ready to go. Joe had flipped the ignition switches on, and the twin 2,000-horsepower Pratt & Whitney engines responded. I called Smitty to cast off from the buoy, and we drifted away, still checking controls. The water was choppy as we taxied toward the seadrome. We could see the three planes from 208 lining up for takeoff, wingtip to wingtip. They hit their throttles and thrust forward, half covering their craft in high ocean spray. They continued with their heavy load until they had the speed to become airborne and disappeared into the approaching darkness. We joined with Edwards on either side of McQuire's wings and hit our throttles in a similar manner, and after a long run broke our bond and took to the air.

We leveled off at about 500 feet above the water, and once cleared of Kerama and any possible ships in the area, away from the other planes, we had everyone test their guns by firing a few rounds. When all were satisfied, Joe announced that the smoking lamp would remain out, and that there would be no radio communication until he gave the clearance. We followed each other in a loose formation on radar, holding on automatic pilot for about two hours before deciding it was time to drop to 200 feet. A few stars had drifted out and with a partial moon with limited brightness, you could catch reflections of ever-increasing swells with waves hitting waves and possibly aiding our protection from enemy radar. Joe checked my control at flying straight and level at the 200-foot elevation, without autopilot. "If you get tired, yell, and we'll relieve you. But stay steady."

With my hands on the yolk and my eye on the altimeter, holding the elevation and following the instruments was tedious and physically draining. In the darkness of the night with the sea pounding below, it was like flying over a splashing inkwell, maintaining a speed of 140 knots without the luxury or the freedom to vary the course. My arms were taut, my legs stiff, and the constant concentration was lost in the responsibility of duty. I was so engrossed in the aspects of the flight that I barely thought of what might meet us at the end. Time dragged on until, just under 100 miles from our target, we picked up the blips of the Japanese convoy. I reluctantly traded seats with Amos, and Joe dropped our elevation to 100 feet above the water. I felt like a third shoe, frustrated at the prospect of being defenseless and unable to share in the physical action that lay ahead. As Amos adjusted to the feel of flying the plane, Joe dropped down to 50 feet above the sea, trying to lose us in the reflective waves, hiding from the enemy's radar. To maintain our spacing with the three planes ahead, Joe increased our speed to 155 knots.

Straddled between Joe and Amos, I focused on the radar screen with Joe while Amos concentrated on keeping the plane low and level. With about ten miles to go, the radar blips on the 208 aircraft blended into the blips of the task force. They roared over the string of ships, and the sky lit up like a 4th of July fireworks display at the Los Angeles Coliseum. Joe hit the throttles, and the Mariner reached its maximum speed of 200 knots, good for only a five-minute burst. Without hesitation, we thrust forward as the sky exploded in a violence of fire and smoke. The three planes ahead cleared low over the darkened silhouettes of the ships, now lit up by their own firepower. As we leveled our wings to launch our torpedoes, thousands of fireflies, which turned out to be tracers from enemy machine guns, whipped randomly in our direction, pitting our plane with bullet holes. From our top gun turret, Aaron Long broke radio silence. "Our Father who art in heaven . . . "

With Amos and Joe concentrating on a target, I yelled, "Get the fuck off the mike!" before he could finish his prayer. Long in the top turret, and Bradford in the nose, fired their .50-caliber guns ahead as we dropped to ship's level. Two large freighters appeared in front of us. I yelled at Joe and pointed to the right, the larger of the two. Joe skidded over, leveled his wings, and motioned Amos to release our torpedoes. Flares, tracers, and cannons turned the night into a pulsating daylight. As the weight of the torpedoes dropped from our plane, we felt a slight jolt passing over our target and an immediate explosion that knocked me to the floor of the cockpit. I was the only one in the plane not strapped in, and I was startled to find myself on the deck. Joe and Amos were wrestling with the yolk, trying to level the plane as our right wing dipped severely with a loss of control. Joe had flooded the engines with fire-suppressing foam as we cleared our target and headed upward into the night.

Within a couple of minutes we were far enough away from the ships to lower our speed to 140 knots and circle back to our base. I managed to get on my feet, grateful we were still flying. A large cannon blast had made a hole in our right wing, and we could see a metal flap whipping in the wind where the hole blew through. The stabilizer controls did not react, and it was necessary to overcontrol to compensate for the effect of the drag caused by the open gap in our starboard wing.

Radio silence was broken, and while the other aircraft reported in, I checked the damage to our plane. Our nose gunner was safe, and just behind him, under the pilot's deck, my heart pumped frantically when I saw Smokey Stover at his station, covered with blood.

Metal flap from cannon hole in wing

Bullet holes in C'est La Guerre

Cannon hole in PBM wing

"Oh, my God, Smokey, are you hurt bad?"

"I'm okay, Mr. Cooper."

The hydraulic line above his station had been shattered by bullets, and the red fluid emptied above his head and saturated him down to his knees. No actual wounds and, in spite of the many bullet holes in the plane, no one was hit. All alive and well. The report from the other aircraft revealed several crewmen hit, but not life-threatening. All six of the planes were riddled with bullet holes as we headed back home to Kerama.

Joe gave me his seat and asked me to level off at 4,000 feet. He stretched and then assessed the condition and damage to the plane and personnel. The controls were heavy. I relieved Amos from the strain and wrestled with the yolk and left rudder until Joe returned and took back his seat. We alternated flying by hand with the aileron out and only partial use of the hydraulic system. It was like driving a car without automatic drive, except on a much larger scale, and required physical strength to hold the wings level and keep the plane in line.

We arrived back at the seadrome in the morning light. I logged over eight hours of flying on our twelve-hour flight. I relived the attack and the explosion and the concern over whether our wing would hold until we landed. I felt amazed that we all made it and grateful to get back. While Jesus pulled a number of the crew through the ordeal, I thanked my savior Elaine for bringing me home.

All the planes had called in and reported their damage. As each one landed and cut their engines, twin boats were waiting to come under either side of the plane. By holding both wings up, the hull of the plane was kept from settling in the water, preventing the bullet and shrapnel holes from flooding and sinking the PBM. As we landed in the water, we were held by two such crafts and towed to

Hoisting PBM aboard the Pine Island

the stern of the Pine Island, one of several large seaplane tenders that could hoist two planes on its deck and start making the repairs for them to fly again. Smitty was on top of the wing and connected the Mariner's bulkhead ring to the tender's cable, and a crane pulled us out of the water and set us on its deck.

The cannon hole in the center of our right wing was large enough for a person to crawl through. Had it hit ten feet closer to the body of the plane, the cockpit would have been blown out and only five of the six aircraft would have returned. I was proud of our Martin Mariners. A communication from General Douglas MacArthur's office expressed the same admiration:

P.S.N.Y. 3-29-44 1M

MAILGRAM
U. S. NAVAL COMMUNICATION SERVICE

DELIVER THIS MAILGRAM TO COMMUNICATION SYSTEM IMMEDIATELY UPON RECEIPT FOR DISTRIBUTION AND HANDLING AS A REGULAR DISPATCH

FROM: U.S.S. CTG 51.2Ø

DATE 28 APRIL 1945

Mailed by: (Place), (Time)

ACTION TO: VPB-2Ø8/VPB-27

INFORMATION TO:

Classification	X
Plain	
*Restricted	
Restricted *Officers only	
*Secret	
*Confidential	

Special Instruction

RELEASE

* If not encrypted by originator do not retransmit by radio without thorough paraphrasing and encrypting.

THE TASK GROUP COMMANDER TAKES THE GREATEST PLEASURE IN OFFERING AN ENTHUSIASTIC "WELL DONE" TO THE PILOTS AND CREWS OF VPB 27 AND VPB 2Ø8 WHO BRAVED HEAVY ENEMY FIRE TO STRIKE AT THE WELL DEFENDED JAP CONVOY LAST NIGHT X THE ADMIRATION OF ALL HANDS FOR THE VALOR OF THE ACT IS EXCEEDED ONLY BY THEIR GRATITUDE FOR THE SAFE RETURN OF ALL WHO PARTICIPATED X CONFOUNDING THE SILK PURSE-SOW'S EAR PRINCIPLE, THEY MANUFACTURED EXCELLENT STRIKERS OUT OF ASP PLANES X IN THEIR HANDS, PBM'S MADE HISTORY LAST NIGHT XXX

Authenticated: Signature name and rank.

Attacking ship convoys with heavy firepower was not standard operation for Navy patrol bombers. I couldn't help thinking of the Army pilots in Europe who flew every mission through heavy flak and fighter aircraft, and the toll it took on the men and their planes. They flew en masse every other night; we had one mission like that. I felt grateful and reborn.

Since my return home from the war, the date of that flight has remained a highlight of my service. For the last sixty years, Elaine and I have always celebrated by going out to dinner on April 27 to a Japanese restaurant.

24
Meeting Elliot Maltzman

PBM Martin Mariner refueling from the fantail of a tanker

It took a week for C'est La Guerre to be repaired and waterproofed aboard Pine Island. There was no definite report on what we had achieved in attacking the Japanese task force because of the distance involved. Vague reports claimed several ships damaged, and perhaps we received credit for sinking half a ship. We enjoyed the respite from flying by writing letters, playing wardroom games, reading, making conversation, and receiving mail from home.

I usually wrote long letters, cleared by our squadron communications officer, Bob Ogram, with his initials on a CENSOR stamp before allowing them to proceed home. Elaine's letters were written daily between class and working in the family store. I would receive a pack of mail with some things of interest on the home front, and a closing (sometimes with a lipstick kiss imprint in the corner): "I hope you are well, I miss you, I love you. Elaine."

Elaine's brother Harry was working on restricted scientific programs for the Navy in Washington, D.C. Her brother Ernie was a doctor with the Air Force in San Francisco, and I felt equal to both as a Navy pilot and the ensign brother-in-law in a family of officers.

I did learn that my best friend, Bud Plone, was still instructing in Atlanta and had married a Dorsey High School girl named Jackie Hester. In addition to the home connection and the physical attraction, Jackie had given him a subscription to *Time* magazine for his birthday, so intellectually Bud felt they were born to be together.

My mail also revealed that our best man and lady, George and Betty Woodford, were still in Boca Raton, with administrative flight duties that kept them comfortably at home. Al Nadler was still a frustrated carrier pilot, assigned as a flight instructor. Les Silver was now in officers' training school. Rudy Saltzer, another high school pal, was an ensign on a ship carrying freshwater to every outpost in the Pacific that needed it.

I had noticed in my log book that I had been designated a second pilot as of May 12, 1945. I was surprised because I already thought I was one. The big stamp came later, July 19, when I qualified as a first pilot, a PPC, ready for a crew of my own when I returned home.

Back in the routine, we alternated day and night flights, still hunting submarines the enemy couldn't produce. We managed to chase and beach a Japanese powerboat, contacted unknown aircraft in flight, and scoured the coast of China and Korea for enemy shipping. Our biggest challenge was taking off and landing in a forever relentless sea. This description would be defied by J. B. Watsabaugh, the PPC of Easy 15. His challenge was a routine night flight on June 21. His plane was attacked and shot down by a P-61 Army night fighter. With one engine shot out and the forward bunkroom in flames, he made an open sea landing in the dark of night. The crew scrambled into life rafts as their plane sank and were, fortunately, rescued the following morning with no injuries.

Otherwise, life continued at Kerama from one day to the next. The kamikazes continued only for their "one way one day." Daily attacks were constant, and the radar picket ships, mostly destroyers, stationed between Okinawa and Japan, were hardest hit. They were there to warn the collection of ships at Kerama of the impending attacks. Those suicide planes that managed to get through were mostly shot down, but still, a few caused damage and tragedy. One hit a hospital ship near us, exploding on the deck, killing forty and injuring many more. By the end of the Battle of Okinawa, 1,900 suicide planes had sunk 28 American ships and damaged 225 more.

The shipboard routine was broken when once again the pilots and crews of the Shelikof were called together on the ship's fantail. Captain Chase was there with McQuire and Kendrick, standing before a table laden with small, uniform boxes. He nodded a greeting to each group as they arrived and stood at attention, shoulder to

Receiving the DFC aboard the USS Shelikof *left to right:* Lt.(jg) Richard Kendrick, Lt. William McQuire Jr., Captain Norwood L. Chase II, and Lt.(jg) Irvin S. Cooper, Kerama Retto, Okinawa, June 1945

shoulder. The captain called, "At ease," and all hands relaxed as he started by congratulating the men assembled. He then cited a list of actions and accomplishments that Squadron 27 had achieved. Each pilot and crew member was called individually, and a Distinguished Flying Cross medal was removed from its box and pinned on the squadron member's uniform. The medals were awarded to those crews that had made twenty contacts or exchanged fire or sunk ships or trawlers in combat with the enemy. Again, I thought of our Army Air Force counterparts and what they had done to achieve such recognition. For them, it was more than just flying twenty missions over Europe; it was surviving them.

As much as I was honored to receive such an award, I was also promoted to Lt.(jg) and received, along with Amos, who already had that rank, the first pilot accreditation. On our next tour of duty we would be PPCs, each with a crew of our own.

Back to our chore, our first flight in C'est La Guerre with all repairs cleared was an all-night mission with nothing to show. As we entered the Kerama seadrome, Joe had me land between long, rolling swells and taxi between the moored ships and planes. The sky turned night to day; we found our buoy to tie up and waited for the launch to take us to our ship. Joe turned to me and said, "Coop, good landing. Once we're off, take your watch crew and get gassed."

In a matter-of-fact manner, Joe gave me directions where to go. After sitting eight hours in the copilot seat, splitting time between handheld controls and automatic pilot, I had been asked to assume the plane commander's duties. Joe and Amos and six of the crew took the launch to the Shelikof for a hot breakfast and a turn in the sack.

I had Bale and Bradford man the waist hatches of the plane with our canvas sea anchors to control the direction of the plane on each side if needed. Stover monitored the controls at the engineer's panel, as I slipped into the first pilot's seat. I quickly reviewed the starting procedure and turned on the twin engines to an idling mode. Bale released us from the buoy, and we eased out into the sound. I know my crew accepted their assignments as routine, but for me, moving the Mariner into the open waters alone was a satisfaction that I could only enjoy within myself. I had brought the plane in on an emergency action and made numerous landings and takeoffs with Joe in the copilot's seat. But having the ability, and being given the responsibility and privilege, to control this massive naval aircraft, totally on my own, was exhilarating.

By now the morning sun had risen and beamed glorious rays of sunshine over Kerama Retto. I was at the controls of the U.S. Navy's mighty Mariner, reflecting on my first solo flight in the Cessna at Lone Pine. If you get up into the air on your own, no one can get you down but yourself. And here I was, maneuvering this half-million-dollar aircraft through scores of ships and aircraft at buoys, knowing that the only way back would be through the skills the Navy had taught me. It was a repeat of my solo flight, except the stakes and expectations were much higher. My ego craved for someone to watch me, like the child who wants his mother to watch him splash in the swimming pool.

I moved each throttle as needed, and the engines responded with the help of my rudders to maintain a direct line to my goal. If I needed to tighten a turn as the rolling swells maintained an inconsistency of direction, I called out for the port (left) sea anchor to be dropped. As soon as Bale caught the current, he called back, "Aye, aye, Sir, port sea anchor set."

As the plane responded to the drag, it sharpened its turn, and the nose turned ahead in alignment with my path. I called out, "Trip the port sea anchor."

Bale turned the loop parallel to the plane and released the blockage of water. With no resistance on either side, the aircraft floated smoothly ahead, facing the fantail of the fueling ship. I was sitting smugly, royally above the water, proudly guiding my Mariner toward the fuel line buoy. Bale hooked the plane's cable to the buoy, and I killed the engines as he gave me a thumbs-up that we were secure. A tow cable hitched to the ship's winch set the fueling crew into action. They carefully pulled the line, bringing the aircraft closer to the gas hose. Bradford, on top of the wing, unlocked the gas cap and set the hose nozzle into the tank. When assured the connection was secure, I motioned the crew on the ship to start fueling.

A young ensign on the fantail was directing the crewmen to proceed in a cautious and concerned manner. Aware of the fire potential, he confirmed the connection before giving orders to proceed. As I watched the organized way in which the high-octane gas was pumped into our plane, a sudden jolt startled my recognition process. I leaned out of the cockpit, squinting with disbelief, and yelled out, "Elliot?"

The young naval officer stopped. He looked up at me with eyes of curiosity. "Elliot," I called again, shouting my name, "Irv Cooper."

"Oh, my God," he blurted out with a statement that needed no answer. "What are you doing here?"

Elliot Maltzman lived within three blocks of my home in West Adams. We were in the same class at Dorsey High School. He graduated from U.C.L.A. and entered the Navy officers' training program when I entered the Naval Air Corps. Here we were, in the middle of a war, 10,000 miles from home, thrust together in a most unlikely situation. With Elliot directing the refueling on the fantail of the ship and me, sitting in the cockpit of the plane, communication was difficult. There was too much commotion and space between us. Elliot signaled a possibility to meet after the refueling.

There was a recreation and trash island that was part of the Kerama lagoon. "I've got to take a detail there in about an hour. Can you meet me?" he shouted. I told him I'd try, as we filled our tanks with 2,000 gallons of high-grade aviation fuel, ready for our next twelve- to fourteen-hour patrol.

With the gas hose removed and the cables released, I started the engines. I rotated the props, and with the help of Bradford and Bale on the sea anchors, this time using the starboard (right) aid, maneuvered the plane back between the carriers and cruisers, the supply ships and destroyers, and the ships of varied specialties. Our command had combined all these intensely individual pieces, on a geographical scale, in a coordinated effort to defeat our common enemy. And here we stood, on the brink of ending this war. I found myself, as the momentary lone plane commander, wishing I could finish this tour of duty and command a crew of my own into whatever mission the Navy required me to do.

We secured our plane at our buoy and launched to the Shelikof. Bradford, Bale, and Stover went off to breakfast. I grabbed a quick bite and then sought a boat to the refuse island. I was informed that all the launches were in use but that, for some reason, I could use the captain's gig to ferry me. The captain's mode of transportation was a smaller boat with a custom cover, a personalized motor, and a personal seaman to control it. In this bit of luxury, I was transported to the island where the sailor could wait and relax and then transport me back to the ship.

In addition to running the gas crew, Elliot alternated with the garbage detail, directing a working crew to take the ship's trash to the island and have it burned in a designated area. In the meantime, we were able to unwind and tell each other our adventures getting to this point. I told him I had married Elaine, whom he knew quite well. He was very close to Elaine's brother Ernie, and his family had shopped in the family delicatessen ever since he could remember. We exchanged stories about classmates. I told him about Bud and me going through training together, and that Bud ended up as a flight instructor in Atlanta and George Woodford was an Army pilot and flight administrator in Boca Raton. I told him George had married his high school sweetheart, Betty Sommers, and that they were the best man and lady at our wedding. He knew my friend Jerry Foreman was shot down flying a P-38 and that he was the first Dorsey alumni to be killed in action.

We expressed delight and pleasure in meeting here in Kerama Retto. We said goodbye, and Elliot went back to his disposal crew and I returned to my ship in the captain's gig.

When the war was over, Elliot and I moved to a West Los Angeles area called Cheviot Hills. Our homes were about four blocks apart, and we would run into each other at Overland Avenue

Elementary School functions, which our children attended. After that, we seemed to bump into each other at various social functions every two, three, or five-plus years, without the convenience of a captain's gig.

THE SECRETARY OF THE NAVY
WASHINGTON

The President of the United States takes pleasure in presenting the DISTINGUISHED FLYING CROSS to

LIEUTENANT, JUNIOR GRADE, IRVIN SHIELL COOPER
UNITED STATES NAVAL RESERVE

for service as set forth in the following

CITATION:

"For heroism and extraordinary achievement in aerial flight during operations against enemy Japanese forces in the Western Pacific Area, from January 5 to June 14, 1945. Participating in twenty missions during this period, Lieutenant, Junior Grade, Cooper contributed materially to the success of his squadron. His gallant devotion to duty was in keeping with the highest traditions of the United States Naval Service."

For the President,

James Forrestal

Secretary of the Navy

25

Flying with Otho and Bill

Simon Bolivar Buckner Jr., Commanding General of the Tenth Army. Killed June 18, 1945, Okinawa

The bloodiest Pacific battle was over. The Marine and Army units had secured Okinawa, the largest island in the Ryukyu chain, on July 2, 1945. Varied numbers described the tremendous losses of American, Japanese, and Okinawan lives. When the Marine and Army units first landed on April 1 with a force of 60,000 men, under the direction of Lt. General Simon Buckner, there were 130,000 Japanese troops with 450,000 civilians, many drafted for labor as well as combat. The Japanese fought from hillsides and caves and lost 107,000 men, with 7,400 taken prisoner. Thousands more were incinerated by flame throwers in caves and tunnels.

Japan's great hope came from the "die before surrender" indoctrination and the utilization of the kamikaze as its ultimate weapon. In this final operation, 7,300 Americans were killed and 32,000 wounded. The Navy toll was 36 ships lost and 368 damaged. Lt. General Buckner was a frontline warrior. While observing his Marine troops in battle, he was hit by a Japanese 47-millimeter antitank shell and killed. The name of the harbor at Chimu Wan, Okinawa, was changed to Buckner Bay. On July 14, the Shelikof and the other tenders were ordered to move the twenty-five miles from Kerama Retto and lay anchor in the newly named Buckner Bay.

By virtue of accumulating 200 hours of flying time, the Mariners' twin Pratt & Whitney engines were due for a complete overhaul. Every five days, our squadron rotated a different plane and its crew to Saipan. In the short time since we had left, Saipan had progressed from a combat island battlefield to a recreational, supply, and maintenance center. While the engines were being refurbished, the pilots and crew had the five days to relax, swim, play sports, and enjoy beer-drinking nightlife in the Officers' or Enlisted Men's Club on the island. Aside from a general physical checkup per man, the rest was all sun and fun. Excitement charged through our crew. Our time had come!

After breakfast aboard the Shelikof, we took the launch to our plane and loaded our personal gear, including our colorful, dormant swimsuits and Hawaiian shirts. Amos, who had the plane watch with his three crewmen, had readied the plane for takeoff and set the flight plan. Once in the air, he would take a nap while Joe and I flew the plane to Saipan and our anticipated R & R.

We took off on a high, choppy sea and leveled off at 4,000 feet. The sky was clear and beautiful with a few scattered clouds softening the horizon. After nine and one-half hours of mostly uneventful automatic pilot, we came into view of our vacation in Saipan. We took the controls manually and eased into a casual glide mode. With no need for radio silence, we were given instructions to land and taxi to an open concrete ramp. We circled Tanapag Harbor, lined up our descent, and leveled our wings into the wind for landing. We skimmed along the crest of the water and settled in perfect cohesion with the small, rolling swells. With the engines idling, taxiing clear of the ships in the harbor, we opened the bow hatch, cut our engines, and sailed to tie up at the launch, landing about thirty feet from the ramp. Smitty snarled the loop and hooked the plane's cable to the waiting buoy. Two shirtless sailors in cutoff denims were waist high in the water. They connected a steel cable to the hull and attached the two temporary wheels to each side of the plane. The cable dragged along the concrete ramp to a yellow Caterpillar tractor at the top of the concourse. The sailors signaled the tractor to pull us up the ramp. As we moved up the slope, from the cockpit I saw Otho Edwards from our ship, standing on the right of the tractor with several members of his crew. Their plane was sitting on the concourse behind them. I was curiously surprised they were still there and not on their way back to Kerama Retto. As the tractor pulled us to the top of the ramp, safety blocks were wedged into the wheels. Bradford had opened the side hatch

Lt.(jg) Otho Edwards, front center, with his crew, Easy 17

and dropped the cable ladder down to the deck. While some of the crew secured the inside of the plane, Joe and Amos and I climbed down to the concrete and were met by Otho and his two copilots, Bill Holligan and James Bistodeau. Before we could question their presence, Otho greeted us with something like, "Gentlemen, we have a problem."

It seems that while their plane engines were being repaired, Otho and his crew were given a general physical checkup. James had failed his eye test and was examined for glasses. A NATS (Naval Air Transport Service) plane had taken his prescription to Guam where they would have glasses made and hopefully returned to Saipan in time for him to fly back with his crew. Since the plane had not returned in time, that meant that someone, Amos or I, as copilots, would have to take his place. James would return with our crew, while one of us flew with his. That meant one of us would lose our R & R and have to fly back with Otho and Bill.

Joe pulled a coin out of his pocket, looking at Amos and me, and said, "Call!"

He flipped the coin in the air as Amos called out, "Heads!"

The coin landed on its edge and took a circular roll, falling flat with George Washington's head staring up at me.

"Okay," Joe said, looking at me, in a somewhat sympathetic tone. "I guess you'll have to go back."

Lt.(jg) James Bistodeau: Lt.(jg) Otho Edwards, PPC; Ens. Bill Holligan

I believe my immediate response was, "Shit! There goes my R & R." I shook hands with Joe and Amos and said goodbye to my crew. My duffle bag was already on the ground, with my Hawaiian bathing suit and shirt, still unused. One of Otho's crew carried my bag to his plane as I climbed aboard to fly back to Kerama Retto. I knew Otho casually aboard ship but was very friendly with Bill. He and I had spent considerable time between flights talking and playing acey deucey. James had always seemed overly cocky to me, and I never had any social rapport with him. Otho and his crew had flown successfully with us on the April 27th raid up the Yellow Sea. We shared a common bond.

As I stepped into the plane heading for the flight cabin, Bill greeted me warmly and Otho asked if I would like to fly the first shift back. He motioned toward the left-hand seat as he climbed into the copilot seat on the right. I strapped myself in as the chocks were removed from the wheels and the tractor slowly lowered us down the concrete ramp. As the hull settled in the water, the same crew removed the temporary wheels and headed out of the surf and back to their quarters. I checked the takeoff manifest list, tested the controls, and kicked the rudders away as we drifted free from the ramp. With our cable inside and the hatch secured, I called each station, and each crewman responded with a brisk "Aye, aye, Sir." As a new pilot aboard, I sensed their more formal response.

Otho nodded a "Let's go," and I pushed the twin throttles forward, taxiing with caution by the assorted ships at anchor, and headed toward the open seadrome. Bill had laid out our course to Kerama Retto as I turned into the wind and a setting sun and took off. I climbed slowly and set our tabs at 4,000 feet. Otho was very professional and apparently wanted to check my ability to follow procedures and standards. Halfway to Kerama, he let me know he was pleased with my control and was confident we had a good team for the missions to come. Naturally, I was pleased that he told me. Bill took my seat at the controls, and I took his seat at the navigation table. Bill landed in the dark with only one bounce, well after 3:00 a.m. We waited for a launch to take us to the Shelikof. The galley was closed, so we all turned in for much-needed sleep.

The following day was a normal day aboard ship, with a kamikaze alert and a rush to battle stations. The pilots sat in the Ready Room, waiting it out. I endured some friendly needling from Otho and Bill, as they exaggerated the wonderful time I was missing on Saipan. They said the tents with the wooden floors had all been replaced with new Quonset huts and coral pathways. To make up for the recreational time I was losing, they assured me they would make me as miserable as possible. I did have a good bonding relationship and a good feeling for my own security with a good working crew.

The next night, we were scheduled for our first all-night patrol off the coast of China. Midway through the flight we contacted a suspicious target on our radar. We exchanged unknown radar blips and dove to 500 feet above the ocean to protect our underside from possible attack by enemy aircraft. We played cat and mouse in the middle of the night, with our gunners manning their stations. Just as suddenly, the mouse disappeared, and we searched the coast at low altitude. We landed at dawn and had a day's rest before our next scheduled flight, twelve hours to another unknown confrontation.

It was an interesting experience to fly with a different crew. They treated me with professional respect, testing my mood and manner of authority. My own crew was far more relaxed by comparison, having spent so many seemingly endless hours confined and reacting together on long flights and plane watches. I received more "Aye, aye, sirs" than the informal "Yes, sir" or "Okay, sir" that I received from my own crew. With each outing, our relationship became smoother and more trusting. Flying with Otho and Bill was a real pleasure. It took a little time for the crew to adjust to a new copilot, but after the second mission together, I felt a mutual respect and a good comfort level after such a short time.

My crew had still not returned from Saipan when we were assigned a fourth night search and antisub flight off the coast of Formosa (now known as Taiwan). As I got into my flight suit, I thought surely this would be my last flight with Otho, Bill, and their crew. I went up to the aft deck of the Shelikof and joined the crew waiting for the launch to take us to our plane. I checked my gear, my .38 Smith & Wesson, my hunting knife, the mini toothbrush, and the fishing line and hooks I carried in my flight suit pockets. Automatically, my hand tapped my chest pocket to make sure Elaine's picture was there. I adjusted my limp Mae West as the launch pulled alongside the ship. Bill and I were standing together, waiting for the launch to disembark its passengers so we could board and get to our plane. I was surprised when the first person topside was Joe Eglies, followed by Amos, James Bistodeau, and the rest of my crew. They looked loose, tanned, and relaxed and greeted me warmly after their days of leisure at Saipan.

After exchanging handshakes and pats on the shoulder, I was about to go down the ladder when I caught James by his arm. "Hey,

Jim," I said, "you may as well go with your crew tonight so I can get back with mine."

Jim seemed annoyed. "Hell," he said, "I flew all day today and you want me to fly again tonight?"

Normally, I figured myself as pretty easygoing. In this case, I stood up for what I thought was right. "Hey, one of us will have to fly two hops in a row regardless. If I go with your crew tonight, I'll have to fly with my crew tomorrow. I think you should go with your crew now and let me get back to mine."

I reminded him that while he had taken my R & R, I had to fly two consecutive flights in a row coming back to Kerama. There was a reluctant submission in his response. I noticed his glasses for the first time as he grumbled an "Okay" and shoved his duffle bag at me. "Put it on my bunk."

I shook hands with Otho and Bill and thanked them for their hospitality. I nodded farewell to the crew I was just getting to know. As they went down the ladder, Otho gave me a thumbs-up gesture, "See you when we get back," and disappeared into the launch. I swapped more greetings with my crew as they went to clean up and head for dinner and chow. Still in my flight gear, I stood on the deck and watched Otho, Bill, and James climb into their plane with the rest of their crew and prepare for takeoff. The sun was beginning to set as they taxied to the open seadrome. Another plane from our squadron, stationed aboard the Onslow, moved to the left of Otho's wing. The two planes revved their engines, churning the water high over their twin tails. They plowed through the water, broke the suction, and lifted gracefully into the air. As I watched them flying wing to wing in a loose formation, I wondered who would have made the takeoff had I been aboard. Soon they disappeared into a low-settling overcast, heading for their mission to Formosa.

I never saw them again.

26

Missing in Action

Searching for two lost planes

It was early the following morning. Amos came in from plane watch and met Joe and me in the wardroom for breakfast. We each picked up our designated napkin rings and removed the clean linen cloth twisted evenly inside. I spread my napkin's corners equally on my lap. I couldn't help thinking of the Marines and soldiers mushed in wet foxholes, with sweat-saturated uniforms, fighting mosquitoes and a deadly enemy, opening their packaged rations just a few miles inland from where our tenders swayed gently in the bay. Our ship's purpose was to provide quarters with showers and kitchens for the flying personnel assigned to face the same enemy in the sky. I was thinking how blessed I was when Richard Kendrick, our squadron information officer, entered the wardroom. Before we could start breakfast, he poured himself a cup of coffee from the open pot, and spoke.

"We lost two planes last night," and paused. "Otho Edwards and Bernie Gallagher, a replacement crew from the Onslow. There has been no communication and they have not returned. They are now officially listed as missing in action."

He turned to the three of us and said, "Your mission today has been changed. You and one other plane will head for Formosa on a search-and-rescue assignment."

My log book recorded the date, August 7,1945. "My God," I thought. "I was supposed to be on that flight." I reflected quickly on the conversation I had with James and how I had insisted that he take his patrol so that I would not have to fly two flights in a row in his place.

We hurried our breakfast and met the crew on deck. We explained the day's mission as the launch pulled alongside. The crews were very close since they shared living space aboard ship. There was concern, anxiety, and a desire to find their friends, hopefully safe in the life rafts carried by the PBMs. We launched to our plane.

After our routine procedure check, we plowed through heavy swells and barely lifted off the top of a crest with just enough airspeed to keep from mushing down, and set our heading toward Formosa. It was a clear morning sky, and still no signals had been received. With radar and high-powered binoculars, we made low-level passes along the island coast. We crisscrossed patterns, scouring the area hundreds of miles to sea. We spotted what we thought was a large shank of metal just under the surface of the water. As we dove low to verify, our "find" turned out to be a whale that lazily rolled deeper into the depths of the ocean.

For two seaplanes as large as the PBM to disappear with no trace of a wing, a tail, a wing float, or some interior floating gear was unreal. There had to be a remnant, some sign of its demise, that we could use to fathom its final action. We chased the slightest blip on our radar or deceptive reflection on the open sea. Light turned to dark, and our fuel tanks indicated time to return to our sea base, discouraged and disappointed.

Reporting back aboard ship, we learned that the two planes had left Buckner Bay at 1800 hours on an antishipping sweep off Formosa. At 2000 hours, they reported they had successfully attacked and beached three enemy motor torpedo boats and were continuing their assigned mission. No further word was heard from the two planes after that.

We continued our searches with nothing to report, and on the 10th of August I was called to see Captain Chase on the Onslow. I was saluted aboard ship and taken to his cabin. Captain Chase, as usual, looked his authoritative self, clean shaven, with an aura of leadership that always seemed to glow from his presence. It gave you no fear, but a feeling of respect when he addressed you.

"Cooper," he looked directly at me as he spoke. "You were on the last flight with Otho before he was lost?"

It was a statement, asked as a question.

"Yes, Sir," I responded.

"Otho has a brother here on the island, near Naha. I want you to go ashore and inform him that his brother is missing, but we haven't given up hope. There will be a Jeep, with instructions, for you to drive to his base. You will contact Bill Edwards, a crewman on PB4Y2's, stationed at the airstrip near Naha. Assure him we are continuing our search for survivors, and we haven't given up hope."

I answered with a quiet, "Yes, Sir," left his cabin, returned to the Shelikof, and checked and followed my instructions.

Okinawa had been a bloody battleground with a cost of 50,000 casualties. Allies, Marines, Army, and Navy personnel lost their lives in taking Japan's last line of resistance. Japan lost over 100,000 troops, plus civilian lives, in the three-month battle for the island. I couldn't help but compare my efforts with those battling in the mud and rain with face-to-face confrontation, in mosquito-ridden forests, with packaged food and lack of freshwater. I lived aboard ship, enjoying a daily shower and hot meals. Our responsibilities were dangerous, but impersonal. Flying twelve to fourteen hours of alternating day and night flights, attacking ships and shore installations, searching for submarines, rescuing downed pilots in open seas, and engaging Japanese aircraft was nothing like the contribution of the infantry soldier. Going ashore and seeing the conditions under which our forces lived, and prevailed, filled me with awe. It wasn't guilt, but an overwhelming respect. According to instructions, I was met at the dock by a Navy yeoman, now part of America's occupying forces, who provided me with a Jeep and simple instructions to the air base at Naha. I followed a dirt road past a very large expanse that I assumed was part of an extended airfield. It was divided by a lengthy chain-link fence. On one side a heavy-duty Caterpillar was grading the ground and smoothing the surface. On the other side of the fence, some 500 Okinawans, with long poles stretched across their backs, balanced wreath baskets on each end. Other laborers hand-picked rocks and debris and filled the baskets as they shuffled uniformly across the plain. I wished I had a camera with a wide enough lens to photograph the mass of human labor on one side of the fence, working at an equal pace with the one-man operator of a powerful grading machine on the other.

I admired the military administration that had wisely put the survivors to work for the food, medical attention, and temporary housing they provided. These were the survivors who had been told to commit suicide rather than be raped, murdered, and have their children eaten by the American invaders. These natives grieved for the families who were told suicide was preferable to living under the impending atrocities. This was also an agricultural land whose people were taken over and ruled by a forceful foreign invader.

I found Otho's brother as directed. He was an enlisted gunner on the Privateer, a four-engine land-based attack bomber assigned to the Navy. The plane was originally a Consolidated B-24 Liberator, but was adapted for naval services as the Privateer. Bill Edwards's surprise in meeting me was offset by the shock of my message. I explained to him that his brother Otho had not returned from a flight, and that since I was the last to fly with him, I was asked to deliver this message. I stressed that a continuous search was ongoing and that we hadn't given up hope. During this whole encounter, I couldn't shake that "movie feeling," that I was acting a part completely foreign to my being. I had never been prepared to console another individual under such circumstances.

The day before Otho's loss, Bill had been on a two-plane mission off the Korean Strait, strafing a secluded Japanese destroyer. Their wing plane had been shot up in the attack, and as he watched, the plane dived headfirst into the sea with a crew of twelve and completely disappeared. He was amazed at the quickness and the lack of debris that remained at the site. I felt the shock he was suffering from the loss of his buddies and now facing the thought of his brother suffering the same fate.

At this time, I was subjected to another personal shock. I inquired about my friend Milt Gibson and his whereabouts flying Privateers. I was told that he had been killed. I learned that his plane had attacked a ship at such a low level that the bottom of his plane had been ripped open by the mast of their target. At that elevation they couldn't recover and the plane and crew were lost. I remembered Milt's words clearly, how his PPC was going to get him killed; and he did. I thought about his wife, Jolene, and what a shock the news would be for Elaine. Back aboard the Shelikof, our squadron, as well as surface ships, maintained continuous searches. Each flight became more pressing than the one before. My eyes and the crew's strained through our binoculars, continually combing the sea with negative results. Eleven days later, a PBM wing float was seen and photographed in waters where the planes could have gone down. The loss of Otho Edwards, Bill Holligan, James Bistodeau, and their crew, as well as the pilots and crew of their companion plane, was final.

One of the theories as to what happened was that the two PBMs had possibly spotted a Japanese sub. They may have flown a low-level crossover attack from either side, a maneuver our squadron had practiced in Hilo, Hawaii. In the dusk, or dark, diving from opposite sides, carrying 500-pound depth charges, the planes could have collided over the target. The head-on collision could have caused such an explosion as to leave no evidence or fine debris floating on the surface of the water.

Had I been on that flight, I would have been the one lost. James Bistodeau would have been sitting in my seat, peering through my binoculars, and thinking my thoughts. Many times, in later years, I could see James clambering down the ladder and Otho giving me the thumbs-up gesture. I often reflect on my life, finishing my education, building a home, raising my family, living the joys of life, and think of Otho and his crew buried in the waters off Formosa. Had I been with them, what would James be thinking now? Maybe his reflections would be the same, with one exception. He couldn't imagine my thoughts of my not seeing Elaine again.

27

The Shandong Peninsula

U.S. naval ships gathering at Ulithi for the invasion of Japan

With the capitulation of Germany and the war in Europe at an end, the success of American naval power provided the bases that enabled the transfer of the B-29s to the Pacific War. From the Philippines and the tiny island of Tinian, off Saipan, the long-range bombers carried their havoc and destruction to the Japanese homeland on a daily basis. On the atoll at Ulithi, hundreds of American ships were in the process of gathering for the attack and invasion of Japan: battleships for the coastal bombing; carriers with planes to cover the invasion; landing craft with supply ships carrying tanks, transportation, and heavy armory; hospital ships; supply vessels carrying fuel, food, equipment, clean drinking water, and every type of equipment necessary for a sustained invasion; ships with thousands of men waiting to participate, learning to control their seasickness until setting their feet on a soil even more hostile.

In contrast to this armada for the planned invasion, every Japanese man, woman, and child who had survived the bombing destruction of their cities and towns was instructed to use guns, if available, knives, rakes, hammers, farm tools, or any means to attack and kill the American invader and to give their life rather than surrender. The last basis of military defense was placed in the effectiveness of the kamikaze attack. From a humane point of view, the American bombing and fire attacks on Tokyo and other major cities and manufacturing areas may have appeared overly harsh. But then what can you say about Pearl Harbor?

We had trained to the point of being highly proficient antisubmarine specialists, arriving at this time of battle to protect our ships from being attacked in the proposed invasion of Japan. Our predecessors in air and sea really beat us to the job. Logging hundreds of hours chasing and hunting the Japanese, our forces inflicted heavy losses on the Japanese submarines that had attacked many of our ships. The impact of these losses and the lack of available fuel left the Japanese with little means to present any threat to the American forces. Our flights were relegated to reconnaissance, attacking and sinking small vessels, shore encampments, and rescuing pilots in open seas, anywhere, anytime.

From the coasts of Korea, China, and Japan itself, there were small areas of resistance. One of our planes returned from one such enclave called Shandong Peninsula, a historical Chinese land occupied by the Japanese. There was a series of inlets, one particular cove with a palisades coast set back like a small harbor behind a large island rock rising some forty or fifty feet out at the entry of the bay. As our plane patrolled the area, a large motor launch roared out from behind the rock, heading toward the inlet shore. Our plane banked hard and dived after the getaway boat. As its bow gunner took aim, several cannon explosions from the hillside blew several holes in the Mariner, fortunately not injuring any of its crew. The pilot whipped the plane back and pulled around the island rock and away from the shore battery.

After a debriefing on their tender, a notice was delivered to all patrols in our squadron not to be lured by the target boat at Shandong. Had the guns in the palisades waited, they could have caught the Mariner closer and probably knocked the plane down.

Our squadron was made up of eighteen flight crews. Each crew was led by a plane commander on at least his second tour. His copilots and crew were selected by a process of first come, first serve, or by thoughtful integration of which combination would best serve the needs at hand. I had started out in the captain's crew with Evan Hushbeck as PPC, flown with Watsabaugh, and ended up with Joe Eglies. It seemed to me that each crew sort of took up the personality of its leader. I knew one group of swaggarts, another group that could hardly finish a flight before rushing for a beer. Introverted, extroverted, each crew had its own personality, but all together we had a common bond.

Joe Eglies was from New Jersey and had his training as a copilot in South America before being given his command at Harvey's Point. He was quiet, professional, with a dry sense of humor, and a damn good pilot. Amos Krum, our other copilot, was from the Midwest, a nonstop chain smoker except when "The smoking lamp is out" was in force. He was better on radio and navigation than I, but had a quiet demeanor and a dry sense of humor. Whatever the makeup, we all got along well, and treated each other respectfully by choice, and not by designated rank.

Our next flight was a reconnaissance patrol that would take us along the Shandong Peninsula. After a pretty rough takeoff from Buckner Bay, we rose to a beautiful August sunrise, cruising along the coast at about 500 feet off the water, with clear visibility of the shoreline to spot for any boats or encampments hiding in one of the inlets. I was flying copilot with Joe, when somewhere around four hours after our takeoff, Amos announced we were coming toward the Shandong range. His navigation was right on, because suddenly along the open coast, this lone island rock: jutting into the sky as a protector of the cove, stood guard at the circular bay behind it. Again, my mind saw a movie set before me, the rock, the bay, the rocky coast peacefully rising at the end of the shore. As if a director yelled, "Action," a powerboat in a blaze of blue smoke pulled away from the back side of the rock as we approached the area.

Joe's hand abruptly left the wheel and pushed the twin throttles full forward, saying "Let's get 'em," and nosed the aircraft directly aft of the launch. The move caught the nose gunner by surprise, Amos caught himself pulling away from the navigation table, and a black puff of smoke appeared off our right wing, followed by the sound of a cannon's roar.

Instinctively, I pulled back on the yolk and kicked the left rudder, catching Joe off guard. "Joe, what the hell are you doing?" I yelled.

"Our orders were to stay away. You've got twelve guys and a half-million-dollar plane against a $300 motorboat!"

I had missed the adrenaline charge that suddenly made Joe attack the boat. He muttered a fast "Okay" and finished pulling away from the launch as another wild cannon shot filled the air. For that moment, I wondered, why did I compare the cost of our plane against the value of our target? Years later, I thought, was that a Jewish thing?

Joe said something about making a quick pass and hitting the launch and getting out without any intention of following the boat. That was the only time I ever saw Joe lose his cool, probably brought about by the countless hours of boring surveillance and inaction.

We landed back at Buckner, Amos had the honors, and we then boarded the Shelikof with nothing to report.

28

Japan Surrenders

Atom Bomb

Possible resistance from the Shandong Peninsula kept our planes in daily surveillance. Most night flights had been curtailed, and the mission for our coming schedule was to participate in the planned invasion of Japan. Our role would be to cover the landings, lend support, and conduct Dumbo searches for downed pilots as needed. On the sixth day of August, we heard that a B-29 had dropped an atom bomb, whatever that was, on the city of Hiroshima. It completely wiped out an area of four and one-half square miles and an estimated 200,000 lives. It was supposed to end the war without having American troops invade Japanese soil. The devastation was of unprecedented magnitude, but the Japanese still refused to surrender even amid warnings that greater destruction would follow. With that news, we anticipated the war coming to an end. We waited with curiosity and enthusiasm, but still no announcement. The following day, we took to the skies for a routine patrol back to Shandong, returning with nothing to report.

Between flights, life aboard ship was relaxed. There were no kamikaze alarms, and speculation and discussion exceeded the usual board games and letter writing. Everyone sought information on the atom bomb and the resulting effect of a new word in our dialogue, "radiation." The radioman aboard ship became a central figure, as he was the first to transmit the news as it happened. President Truman had called for Japan's surrender but was met with nothing but determined defiance. Three days later, on the ninth day of August, we heard about a second bomb that was dropped on the city of Nagasaki. Since the order of the plane watch was still in effect, I had to spend that night aboard our plane, along with Bradford, Stover, and Bale. Normally, we were not allowed to use our aircraft radio, but because of the current developments, I took exception to the rule.

C'est La Guerre was bobbing easily in the Buckner Bay water as I was lounging in the first pilot's seat, earphones on, fiddling with the radio. I was trying to find out what was happening and convey it to

Nagasaki, August 10, 1945, from C'est La Guerre

my anxious crew. My reception went dead as the booming of a large explosion muffled the radio sound. More sound explosions and gunfire seemingly rocked the plane as flares and lights and tracers filled the sky. Between the endless blasts, an excited voice pierced through the noise of my earphones, "The war is over!"

From the cockpit, I could see the flares light up Buckner Bay, and the splash of bullets could be seen hitting the water. Whatever was shot up knew its way down. I don't recall which I yelled, "Jesus," or "Holy Cow," or even "Shit." My thought was that I was sitting here with my crew who had been through so much together, as helpless ducks, waiting for a stray celebratory bullet to come through our plane and hit any one of us in the head. We had some metal helmets stacked in a corner behind the navigator's table. I stuck one on my head and yelled to my crew to get covered. Some authority recognized the danger, and a "Cease Fire!" was frantically screeched over the air. You could hear the voices of happy crewmen yelling from one ship to the next. "The war is over!" The bullets stopped dropping from the sky.

The following morning, the launch came alongside the plane. To our surprise, it was loaded with sacks and boxes of toiletries, chocolate bars, cigarettes, and food packages. We helped unload the boat and placed the supplies in the center of the plane for our scheduled day's flight. The launch took us back to the ship where we had breakfast, and I checked our mission with Joe and Amos. Our main goal, the day after the second atomic bomb was dropped, was changed to fly to an area called Fukuoka, along the northern shores of the Ryukyu Islands to an interior inlet of Japan. We were headed for a prisoner-of-war camp that held mostly Australian and Canadian captives, and were to drop the much-needed supplies in the compound by small parachutes that we attached to the packages.

Amos and I would alternate takeoffs and landings. Joe would take his turn at the navigation table, and Amos and I would fly

Dropping relief supplies to Australian and Canadian prisoners

together, alternating in the first pilot's seat. Joe gave us ample experience as future PPCs, as we each logged equal time in the cockpit. This was my takeoff day, and the day's agenda, this time accompanied by a sense of flight without fear, was devoted to headings and sightseeing.

Following the coast of Japan on a clear, sunny day was a revelation of beauty. It seemed that every piece of land, from flat plains to mountainsides to the many tiny islands rising off the coast, was cultivated from base to pinnacle, totally green with trees or crops, peaceful and beautiful. As I drank in the scenery, I became enthralled with the idea of someday flying this route with Elaine by my side, to share this view I so totally enjoyed. Somehow, I never gave thought to how I would get a plane with 2,000 gallons of gas not supplied by the U.S. Navy.

Amos leaned between Joe and me with an aerial map in his hand. We would be going right past Nagasaki on the way to Fukuoka. Joe got the message, and Amos gave us the heading, and that's where we went. All we could see was the vast greenery of the mountains below us. As we cleared the top of a crest, there were seemingly twin valleys adjacent to each other. As we flew over the one on our left, it looked like it had been scooped out of the earth, a dust bowl with nothing but the outlines of streets and curbs and a random concrete structure scattered in nondescript fashion. The other side of the valley carried the same untouched green landscape we saw as we circled the rim of what had paralleled Nagasaki.

The contrast was so defined that the thought of radiation came to mind. I had my right hand on the yolk and used my left hand to cover my crotch to protect myself from the possible effects of radiation penetrating from the ground below. Our concern was that its invisible rays could curtail our future procreation. I saw a few isolated people wandering on the empty, dust-covered streets. Joe lowered the plane to fly past a six-story concrete building whose interior was completely gutted black. With our aerial exposure to radiation, we pulled up and headed away from the site of destruction caused by America's second atom bomb. Al Bradford, from the open side hatches of the plane, took some quick photos of the result.

Next stop, Fukuoka. We found the camp. The prisoners, apparently unattended, were out waving at the Navy insignia on our American plane. We dropped low enough for our small open chutes to land as close as possible to the empty field next to a barracks building. As we circled the camp, those able-bodied men removed their shirts and laid them out to spell "Thank You" on the ground. Of all the flights and fruitless missions, this was a day of great satisfaction for pilots and crew.

Japan's record on prisoner-of-war camps was brutal. Later, in war crimes trials, it was revealed that forty percent of those who were captured did not survive. You worked, or you died. Whereas the Nazis were merciless to civilians, only a small percentage of their prisoners were randomly killed. In Japan, medical attention for prisoners was mostly nonexistent. Survivors later testified that a few sympathetic doctors did what they could with limited supplies. Most of the guards were uneducated and beat and starved prisoners, even killing the weak, shooting and beheading at random. We later learned that the few Red Cross packages that managed to get through were shared by the prisoners, and in many cases were the only thing that sustained lives. Aboard ship, we were unaware of the general brutality practiced in those camps. The pilots would often joke, confusing their knowledge of Chinese restaurants back home with what they thought was Japanese, that if one pilot was captured, he was given a bowl of rice a day. If a second pilot was captured, they would add a fish head, and with three pilots you got an egg roll.

Back aboard the Shelikof, the word was that arrangements for an armistice were in the works. Had it not been for Japan's emperor, Hirohito, the Japanese generals and admirals would not have surrendered. I couldn't imagine the resulting death toll had the invasion fleet from Ulithi and other Pacific strongholds stormed Japanese shores. Whatever losses the Americans would have sustained, the Japanese indoctrination of death rather than submission could easily have led to the loss of millions of lives.

We flew a total of four day flights in the following week and a half: two more missions to Shandong, a reconnaissance flight around Formosa, and a one-day flight to Shanghai to patrol the mouth of the Yangtze River. It was here, a few months earlier, that Lt. Bob Scott in Easy 3 was severely injured by a bullet in his neck after being attacked by Japanese fighters called Oscars. Guy Eby, his copilot, took command of the plane and became the PPC when Bob was sent home. After Scott's experience, we had gone through the same attack.We had exchanged gunfire with the fighters and dived low over the water and escaped without injury. Our theory was the Japanese did not have enough fuel to pursue.

Our squadron was selected to transfer from our tenders to a Japanese seaplane base in Sasebo. Each crew had the option to stay with VPB 27 or elect to return home to the States. New flight crews joined our squadron as replacements to those crews that chose to return. I would have loved to have spent time in Japan, but the thought of going home and seeing Elaine outweighed any other options. Amos and Joe and the rest of our crew opted for home, to leave on the 4th of September with several other crews. At this point, our planes were transferred to our replacements for the move to Japan, and we would fly the older aircraft back to Hawaii. We removed our personal gear from Easy 12 to our homeward craft and prepared to leave at dusk for the ten-and-one-half-hour hop to Saipan. Whatever nostalgic thoughts we carried of leaving our home ship were somewhat tempered when we couldn't get our port (left) engine started. Smitty, our plane captain, set up a hanging catwalk off the engine and hung battery lighting to illuminate the uncooperative Pratt & Whitney engine. Bradford, Bale, and a third crewman, Art Young, had mechanic ratings, and they removed the cowling and discovered a faulty coil that had to be replaced. Following Smitty's instructions, the crew found a replacement coil, which had to be installed before the engine could be started. Balancing on the small catwalk plank with the water rising and falling, great care was taken not to drop their wrenches and tools in the bay below.

We received notice from the ship that a storm of hurricane proportions was predicted to hit the Okinawa coast by morning. If we couldn't get the plane started, we would have to come back aboard ship and wait until it blew over, which could last for a number of days. It was imperative that we make our repairs and take off by midnight, otherwise our flight would be canceled. As the daylight disappeared into the sea, the lights wobbled on their temporary perch, and the water became more choppy and exhibited a proclivity for greater disaster. The rest of our crew could offer nothing to help. In ground school we had seen plastic cutouts of our engine and watched the mechanism turn over and start and develop the thrust that could lift a 56,000-pound aircraft into the sky. That was the extent of our mechanical training. Again I remembered a movie scene, seeing Clark Gable landing his single-engine aircraft in a farmer's field and taking the hair pin from his attractive co-star, fiddling in the engine, and taking off into the wild blue yonder. I was amazed at what Smitty and his crew could do with this 2,000-horsepower Pratt & Whitney engine.

It was dark. The water was rougher. The scaffold swayed. Several other planes had taken off, and when we tried to turn over the engine, nothing. It was past ten in the evening. Smitty kept saying we'll get off before twelve. At 2330 hours we were concerned. None of us wanted to be aboard ship in a hurricane. A warning from the Shelikof cautioned us to prepare to return to the ship. Less than ten minutes before midnight, Smitty had Bradford remove the catwalk. He closed the cowls and stuck his thumb in the air. We turned on the switch. A cough of blue smoke gasped out of the left engine. It started. We turned on the starboard side to match, and both propellers rotated smoothly in unison. We dismantled our lights, released from the buoy, and with everyone at their stations, we bounced in the wind, taxiing to the seadrome for takeoff. We announced a job well done and congratulated Smitty, along with Bradford, Bale, and Young. The water was getting mean, and after a rough bounce on takeoff, we were in the air on our way to Saipan and home.

Saipan felt like old home again. We had the Mariner mechanics check our war-weary engines and two days later flew back to Kwajalein. Once again we crossed the date line, back to Johnston Island, and at last Kaneohe. At this point I was trying to imagine what real milk would taste like and could hardly wait to try. Back on base, the answer: Delicious. Unchanged. Satisfying.

Back in civilization, dinner in the officers' mess required you to wear a black tie with your khaki shirt. It was buffet style, and you filled your tray and sat at long tables in the order in which you were served. I selected a large bowl of soup as one of my courses and noticed a group of Navy nurses several people ahead of me. Since my thoughts were always about Elaine, I realized I hadn't seen a woman in six months. I stalled my position at the buffet, allowing several officers to go ahead of me. I timed my serving so I would sit opposite the ladies at the table. My maneuver succeeded, and as I set my tray down, the nurses looked up and I nodded and casually smiled. As I bent over to take my seat facing the ladies, I was greeted with giggles and laughter. As smug as I felt, I looked down to see my tie floating in my soup. To gracefully ring it out in the napkins provided gave us a topic of conversation and my first exposure to postwar social graces.

We were scheduled to return to the mainland as passengers on an aircraft carrier due in Kaneohe the following week. It would take about five days cruising, and until then our time was free. No flights scheduled. Sun, surf, food, sports, and relaxation was the order of the week. It seemed that each crew received orders to report to different bases all over the country. Joe, Amos, and I would have three weeks' leave upon arriving in the States and then report to a test pilot school at Quonset Point, Rhode Island.

With our anxiety to get home, communication by telegram had a high priority. I wired Elaine my pending schedule and told her to make plans to meet me in San Francisco when the carrier arrived in port. In the Ship's Store, I bought the five combat ribbons I earned to pin on my uniform under my wings. Excited, and still waiting, I was so anxious to go home. I guess you could say I was literally waiting for my ship to come in.

29

Last Flight Home

The Golden Gate Bridge, San Francisco

Anyone want to fly a Mariner back?"

I don't know who called that out from somewhere in the officers' lounge, but I jumped up from my conversation chair and found the voice that delivered the question. I raised my hand and yelled, "Where and when?"

A lieutenant in working khakis had entered from the outside with clipboard in hand. I got to him first, and a couple of curious stragglers joined me at the door. "We've got a war-weary that can head back to Alameda tomorrow night, whoever's interested."

Our carrier was due tomorrow for fuel and supplies and to add several hundred passengers, including us, to those already being transported. The understanding was that a good number would be sleeping on the deck for their five-day cruise to San Francisco. The thought of being home in a day was greater than the curiosity of living aboard a people-crowded carrier for five. The lieutenant took my name and several others and would notify me later that afternoon upon confirming my first-pilot status.

Again, I wired Elaine to stand by and arrange to take the Santa Fe train to San Francisco as soon as I could confirm my departure. Shortly after, I was cleared to fly the plane back the following night with a pickup crew of volunteers. My last telegram asked that we meet at the Palace Hotel. I said my good-byes to Joe and Amos and would meet them in Rhode Island. I said my farewells and thanked the rest of my crew, who lived in the East, Midwest, and South.

Elaine, the photo carried in my breast pocket

My worldly goods filled a large-size Navy duffel bag, which I carried to the seaplane ramp. There the veteran PBM, going home to be studied for wartime fatigue, awaited. I met the pickup crew and two copilots, all from scattered squadrons, as anxious to get home as I. We loaded our gear, and I told them this was probably our last flight in the "Ancient Mariner."

As the designated PPC, I thoroughly checked all the takeoff procedures and confirmed each person's role. I made sure the crew knew where the life rafts were stored and that nothing was missing that they were usually responsible for. With affirmations, and relaxed "Aye, aye, Sirs," we were all in agreement to go. I signaled the tractor for departure. He eased us down the ramp, and two sailors, waist high in water, removed the temporary wheels as we cast off our rope and started our engines. First one, then the other. With flaps down, I taxied toward the seadrome to take off, checked my breast pocket of my khaki tunic, making sure Elaine's picture was there, and headed the plane into the wind. My copilot set up the radio, and I quickly got a report that we would be accompanied by a slight tailwind condition for the transpacific flight home.

Good news. Kaneohe Tower gave us clearance to take off. We pushed the throttles forward and built up speed on perfectly choppy water, lifting easily to the step and into the air. I realized it had been a long time since we had taken off without a load of bombs, ammunition, or cargo, with a plane carrying nothing but a crew and their personal belongings.

Cruising comfortably at about 120 knots, I reflected on my flying experience. I had really enjoyed flying the OS2U Kingfisher and felt I had a complete mastery of that airplane, whether on wheels or pontoon. The PBM was a partnership craft. It took a crew of coordinated combinations, from the pilots up front to the crewmen in the various stations of the plane. It was a team effort, and the love of that plane was shared by all who flew it. Its efforts and ruggedness gave everyone a feeling of pride; no one could claim it as their own. Thinking of the cannon hole in our C'est La Guerre and how it brought us home with shattered hydraulic lines was enough to warrant anyone's love. I know it certainly did mine. These thoughts were there because these aircraft had done their job. I kept thinking, a world at war is over. The planes and their crews and the people who maintained them could only reflect on the contribution of man and machine that culminated in ending the war. I started to hum "Moonlight in Vermont," where I had never been.

I suppose it was an obvious transition. It was really the love of the plane that brought us home to the ones we loved. I checked my watch and tapped my breast pocket, knowing that after nine months of separation I would be with the one I loved. I also thought of the ones that would never share my anticipation and feelings. Jerry Foreman, Milt Gibson, Otho, Bill, James, and so many others who would never return. I thought of the nameless numbers, like 5,000 Marines and Army soldiers killed on a single island, and the thousands of others in nameless battles on land, aboard ships and aircraft, or killed as prisoners of war, or victims of kamikaze attacks. I knew I was one of the lucky ones, here, flying home to the ones I loved.

The third pilot had set the course, and we flew in a relaxed, compatible ease, each in our own thoughts. As thorough as I thought I was, I asked one of my unknown crew if he could check out the coffee situation. He was able to produce the coffeepot, sans the ingredients to fill it. Now I did feel stupid. Everyone had brought sandwiches and water, which had to hold us until we landed at the end of the flight.

The clouds were thin and wispy, and the stars twinkled sporadically between the openings. With the use of the sextant, we adjusted our headings, reset our autopilot, and cruised steadily homeward. My original flights from Alameda to Hawaii were well over sixteen hours' flying time. I kept thinking of past flights, and savored my memory of the hour and fifteen minutes in the copilot's seat of the four-engine Mars. It was when we returned from ferrying PBMs from Alameda to Hawaii, in November of 1944, and took almost fifteen and a half hours. With our continued tailwind, we would be home in fifteen hours from takeoff. We predicted an ETA at close to 0900.

Flying eastward, the sky lightened, and the sun rose lazily off the end of the world, with splotches of light bouncing between clouds off the water's edge. Radar indicated we were within 100 miles of our destination. We all had a sense of suspension rather than excitement. This had to be a moment we all dreamed of, and the constant, solid rhythm of the twin Pratt & Whitneys affirmed our sense of security in the plane that brought us safely through the months of search, battle, and now home. Yes, I think all of us, in our own private way, loved our Mariner and the fulfillment of our mission.

The copilot looked at me, poked his finger forward of the windshield, and as if to acknowledge his action, raised his hand mike and announced, "Land ahoy."

There it was, a thin, brown line drawn across the edge of the ocean. Flat at first and then small rises and falls as we flew closer. We shut down the autopilot and took manual control. Some of the crew had climbed into the nose turret and top turret behind empty machine guns to get a better view. We were all rewarded as the California coastline came into sight. Alameda Tower contacted us, giving us an adjusted change in heading. As the coastline grew closer, the mountain range separated, and probably one of the most memorable sights appeared in the form of a gradual span over a mile and one-half wide from one point to the other: the Golden Gate Bridge came into view. I dropped our elevation to about 1,500 feet as we passed Nob Hill and its buildings and saw cars scurrying in all directions. I banked to the right, past Alcatraz Island, and entered the bay. This was my moment:

Cockpit of the PBM Martin Mariner, Pima, Arizona, Air Museum

"Alameda Tower, Peter, Bogey, Mike, requesting permission to land in Alameda Seadrome. Over."

"Peter, Bogey, Mike, cleared to land in south seadrome. Taxi to concrete ramp. Over."

"Alameda Tower, Peter, Bogey, Mike, thank you. Confirmed. Over."

The seadrome, marked by the mile-long string of buoys with the Golden Gate Bridge now well behind us, glistened in the morning sunlight. We lowered the plane and leveled off with the nose slightly

PBM at typical concrete ramp

raised. Just as the hull was about to touch the water, I gave a short burst of the throttle and eased the hull slightly above the touchdown rather than dropping with a jolt as the lift lost its vacuum and greased the touch of plane to water. I cut back the engines, and we skimmed along to a smooth ending and leisurely turned toward Alameda's concrete landing.

Our plane was pulled up the ramp, chocks set under the wheels, and a ladder dropped out of the hatch. The flight took fourteen hours and forty-five minutes, and outside of getting out of the seat to stretch, I sat the length of the flight. The two copilots shared their flying time as well as navigating our way back. I thanked them and the crew, whose names were exchanged in our greeting and forgotten in our departure. I checked the aircraft and took one last look in the cockpit, and I noticed my Navy binoculars resting on the navigation table. Years later I regretted not taking them when I saw them for sale in surplus stores.

I took my bag, checked out at flight control, and waited until an official brown folder with duplicate copies of orders was delivered to me in my name. I took a quick look and decided to go through them after I called the Palace Hotel from a pay phone. Excitedly, I waited. I asked for a Mrs. Cooper. How do you record your feelings hearing the voice you thought about during the long months of separation? From her end, she was happily pleased that I was safely home, and from mine, that she was here in San Francisco waiting for me. I took a Navy jump bus to public transportation. San Francisco being what it was, it seemed like all the trains and buses somehow ended up on Market Street. In my case the streetcar went right by the Palace Hotel, where I got off. I entered the hotel, unaware of its worn elegance, and headed toward the elevator and to the fourth floor. The door opened, and we were together.

Whether I took a shower after the long flight is not clear. Whether we ended up in bed together is quite vivid. Elaine got dressed in a gray suit and patterned blouse, with a chic gray coat, smartly fulfilling the picture of my imagination. I wore my Navy green uniform, with gold wings on my left side pocket and the Air Medal and Distinguished Flying Cross ribbons tucked beneath. We entered the beautiful high-ceiling dining room for our first peacetime meal together and discussed our next step. My official envelope of orders gave me three weeks' leave, and then I was to report to Quonset Point, Rhode Island, to meet with Joe and Amos, for whatever program the Navy had planned for us. I was also notified I would be upgraded to full lieutenant with a modest increase in pay. I was a few months short of three years of service to be eligible for release. However, as a holder of the Distinguished Flying Cross, I could request separation from the Service at any time. If I chose to leave, I had three invitations to fly commercially with Pan American, Alaska, and Northwest Airlines.

September 26, 1945, walking in San Francisco

As we sat and talked, neither of us remembered what we ate. We just savored being together, enjoying eye contact, and planning our future. We discussed where we might choose to live. I thought of Wyoming or Montana, where I had never been, to really start our life together in a faraway place, in freedom, without bonds or friends, to embark on a completely new venture. Elaine thought it romantic but not realistic. We both had families. We both loved

ENS I.S. COOPER 12 MAY 1945
PILOT DATE

IS QUALIFIED AND IS HEREBY
DESIGNATED AS SECOND PILOT
IN PBM TYPE AIRPLANES.

Lt. Comdr. USN
Commanding VPB-27

LT(jg) I.S. COOPER 19 JULY 1945
PILOT DATE

IS QUALIFIED AND IS HEREBY
DESIGNATED AS FIRST PILOT
IN PBM TYPE AIRPLANES.

Lt. Comdr. USN
Commanding VPB-27

Stamped in my log book

Squadron reunion thirty-five years later, San Francisco. Same place, same photographer

the beaches and our California mountains. From a practical point of view, for us to move to Rhode Island with the coming of winter without heavy coats or shoes or proper clothing, and not wanting to make the Navy my career, didn't make sense. We finished dinner and walked the streets of San Francisco. As we passed the Saint Francis Hotel, a street vendor photographer took our picture, hand in hand. Thirty-five years later at a squadron reunion, that same photographer took our picture within a block of the original.

We continued our walk and conversation. By the time we got back to our room, a final determination was reached. Elaine was adamant. Let's go home on leave and use your medal, or whatever it is, to get out of the Navy and go back to college.

My last try. “What about going to the airlines?” I proposed.

“No way. You’ve got to go back to college and get a degree.”

Again, I thought, I have to keep up with her brothers. As far as the airlines, she was equally firm. My God, I thought. She must have seen what the new stewardesses look like. Airlines for me? No way. Elaine wanted me home and in college!

30

Home and the $5,000 Photograph

The $5000 photograph

Public transportation during the war years was total confusion, disappointment, exhilaration, and luck. Elaine's dad had a purveyor that shipped delicatessen meats every week from Chicago by Santa Fe refrigerated rail. He would pick up the order each week from the railway depot, and deliver directly at a precise time to the store. The two men, through the years, became close business friends, sharing their personal stories, happy or sad. His connection with Santa Fe enabled him to supply a pair of seats on the daylight coast train from San Francisco to Los Angeles within two days. When we were notified we had reserved seats home, we were delighted for the extra time to spend in the Bay Area, and the extra time to finalize our post- war plans on our own. We agreed, step one was to resign from the Navy as soon as we got home. Next move, enroll in college, find an apartment, and look forward to our future together. We felt smug, organized, and content. We even looked forward to seeing our family and friends, whom we were told were anxiously waiting our arrival the night we arrived home.

Snuggled against the train window, we fell in rhythm with the click-clack of the wheels rolling across the track. We passed through agricultural fields and breathtaking views of the Pacific Ocean, glistening to the end of its horizons. Whatever thoughts we shared, together or in our own reverie, the dominant flow was the fact that the war was over.

It was close to dusk as the train pulled into Union Station. We got off the train and the activity was the same as if we had never left. Amplified directions stating train arrivals and departures blared overhead, and the same crowds as in all the train stations we had passed through continued forward and back. With me dragging my Navy duffle bag and Elaine towing her overnight case, we hustled our way forward to the large bronze station doors. From there, we headed toward the northwest corner of the parking lot, as prearranged, and found my mom and dad waiting in the family's deep green four door Buick.

After hugs and greetings, we climbed into the backseat of the car, left the station, passing L.A.'s famous Olvera Street, and headed home. There were a number of cars parked in front of Elaine's house, so my dad pulled into our driveway, two doors away. All lights in Elaine's home were illuminated as we carried our gear to the open front door, and entered. Loud clapping and cheers went up as Elaine's folks hugged us while a living room full of friends gathered around us. Mom Foreman, with her proudly worn gold star, grabbed us with tears in her eyes. Bud's mom was there with Les's mom, and neighbors and friends of both our parents, all excited because we were home to stay, with the realization that the war was really over.

Between the chatter and the honey cake with coffee, tea, and wine, we learned that Bud and George were still in Florida, and that Les was on assignment in San Francisco, with everyone speculating how soon they would come home. News of our homecoming traveled fast. In the midst of the chatter and the free-flowing, happy tears, a uniformed Navy pilot wearing the same working green uniform as I pushed into the room from the open door, searching for me.

Coincidentally, home on leave as the war ended, my old friend Al Nadler, starting from our original Lone Pine flight training, jockeyed his way through the crowd and wrapped his arms around me in a firm, masculine hug. We exchanged some quick "What have you been doings?" and gave each other visual overhauls. The would-be carrier pilot who never made it to sea spent the war as a flight instructor in the Midwest. When Al saw my ribbons, the Air Medal and the Distinguished Flying Cross pinned to my chest, pangs of envy and jealousy racked through his soul. Al gave me another hug and, fumbling with his jacket, gleefully pulled out a postcard-sized photograph of me in my flying gear. It was a worn copy of one of the ten photos the Navy had taken when we were cadets prior to completing our flight training. One was kept for the Navy files and the rest we had traded or given to family and friends. Why Al had carried my picture was a question about to be answered.

Al held up my photo, swinging an arch for all in the crowd to see. "This photo," he announced to all cramming to see the image, "was worth $5,000 to me." Before anyone could ask for an explanation, Al started to give one.

"Every night after flight school," he began, "I would go into town and head for a local bar. I would sit down on a stool and take this picture out. I would lean it up against a bar glass, and then look at it sadly. Usually, someone came in alongside and would sit next to me, and curiously ask, 'Who's that?'

"I would shrug my shoulders," and Al performed the ritual for me in front of the now-fascinated crowd, "and say, 'That's my pal Cooper. He just got shot down fighting the war in the Pacific.' Without hesitation, the guy would put his hand on my shoulder and say, 'Let me buy you a drink.'" Al looked at me with pride in his eyes, and tapped his fist on my shoulder, "Let me tell you," he said, "that picture of yours bought me $5,000 worth of drinks."

Laughter followed as Al bowed dramatically from the hips.

The following day brought us back to reality.

31

My Great Generation

There was a tired joke aboard ship that always got a smirk. "I whacked it, I waved it, and finally got an Honorable Discharge." Well, I got mine at a Navy station in Chavez Ravine. After a thorough physical exam, and a packet of official severance papers, I was released from the Navy for active duty in civilian life.

Home was in Elaine's bedroom. Trying to find an apartment in our area was impossible. As excited as I was to be home, Los Angeles seemed drab. No one used their ration coupons for house paint or otherwise upgraded their residences because of the lack of building materials. All life had been geared for the war effort. Everything used was recycled, even empty toothpaste tubes. This was a war in which every American was involved in a myriad of ways. Few households did not have a member of their family involved directly in the war or in the production of war materials. Even the manufacturers and corporations producing planes, tanks, uniforms, and everything related to the war were governed to work at cost with a ten-percent overhead and no profit. The country was at war. And now the war was over.

The colleges ran three trimesters a year during that time. It was my first Friday in my new life as a civilian, and I had to enroll that day because the next semester started on the following Monday. I wore my Navy leather flight jacket with the fur collar and my name and Navy wings imprinted on my chest, and was off to U.C.L.A. early that morning.

When they got to my place in line, I was asked if I had my high school transcripts. I told them no, that I had just gotten out of the Navy and they were at Dorsey High School. To my astonishment, I was told it would take six weeks to get my records even though the school was only five miles away. Veteran status, medals, pleading, nothing helped. Rules were rules and I would have to lose a whole semester waiting.

I returned home and wondered what to do. U.C.L.A., as a California public university, charged $27 per trimester, while the University of Southern California, a private institution, charged $12 per unit. When it struck me that the GI Bill would cover my tuition costs, I headed for U.S.C. that same afternoon. Unfortunately, I received the same response. Dorsey High was still only five miles away, but I was assured it would take six weeks to get my records. However, since U.S.C. was a private college, I was able to plead my case, asking that I get started without losing the semester, and when the six weeks had passed, we could resolve my eligibility at that time. The counselor who heard me out suggested I write an introductory essay to help her evaluate my entrance qualifications, which was standard practice and something all prospective students were required to do. Elaine was required to do the same when she had applied to the school some years earlier. The result of that effort determined whether the applicant would be required to take what they called "dumbbell English" or was qualified to proceed directly to a standard college course. Elaine had passed, and she shared with me the opening lines to her essay:

"A rabbit's foot, a good luck charm, will keep its owner safe from harm. I'm wearing one from force of habit, come to think of it, so did the rabbit."

Taking her cue, I wrote: "My wife goes to U.C.L.A.; I want to go to U.S.C. Few marriages have started on a more perilous foundation."

The counselor read the opening line, smiled, and glanced at the balance of my essay.

"I guess you'll be all right. This is a little unusual, but here is a list of courses for you to get started until we can check your entrance requirements."

I knew I was playing academic catch-up, so I signed up for sixteen units. My brother-in-law Ernie, the doctor, was Phi Beta Kappa at U.C.L.A. Harry, the engineer, was a scholarship student and did his graduate work at U.S.C. And I would now catch up to them as a Trojan at S.C., even though my heart was a Bruin at U.C.L.A. I am one of the few Angelenos who roots for both schools, and proud that Los Angeles has two such wonderful institutions competing against each other. Whom do I root for when they play each other? If one or the other is going to bring a national championship or a Heisman winner to our fair city, then I'll pull for that team. I call it civic pride.

As a married vet, the GI Bill paid me $90 per month subsistence, which required me to supplement my income to get by. Between classes, I became a part-time sporting goods salesman at Sears, Roebuck. Even though I had never gone fishing, I learned to cast and demonstrate the new spinning reel and rod in the store's parking lot, passing myself off as an expert fisherman. I would flick the line with pretty good accuracy, and then spread my hands wide to demonstrate the size trout and bass I had never caught. All, of course, on a grateful minimum salary. Sold quite a few spinning reels and earned my keep.

In the evenings and on weekends, I still wore my Navy jacket in the cool night air to park cars on La Cienega's Restaurant Row. One night at Xavier Cugat's restaurant, an old high school 4-F buddy pulled up in a shiny Cadillac and seemed surprised and embarrassed when I opened his door. I know he felt relieved when I told him I was going to college. My ego was intact. I was going to college and certainly felt no sense of social or financial inferiority. He even tipped me a dollar when the going rate was 25 to 50 cents. I was only making $1 per hour, or was it $1.50? All the tips went to the manager of the parking concession, who could predict with uncanny accuracy the amount of tip each car would give. He was fooled this time and I had no way to palm the difference, even if I dared.

I noticed I had pretty good recall of all that had happened to me starting from my first meeting Elaine on that clear February night in 1942. I had fallen in love, joined the Naval Air Corps with almost two years of training, learned to fly a variety of aircraft, married, gone overseas, and engaged in actual combat. I had come within seconds of not returning home, of losing good friends, and of seeing the devastation of war. Yet suddenly I couldn't remember if I received $1 or $1.50 per hour for parking cars in my post-war life. That's when I realized my memories were truly thanks to the genie from under the Venice pier who had given me three years of recall between 1942 to 1945, and that my time window was now up. And now, sixty-nine years later, I'll have to end this tale on my own, without the help of the genie.

It took four and one-half years to complete my courses at U.S.C. I had the incredible experience of taking classes taught by Dr. Frank Baxter, who truly made Shakespeare's classics become alive and exciting. Dr. Baxter also described his experience of researching Sir Francis Bacon in a restricted London library. He combed through the handwritten pages of one of Bacon's original manuscripts and discovered two fragments of dried tobacco stuck at the bottom of a page. Bacon had been an inveterate pipe smoker, so Dr. Baxter carefully turned each page and salvaged pieces of tobacco, filling almost half of his own pipe. When he stepped out on an open balcony and lit his pipe, a guard immediately asked what he was doing. With a twinkle in his eye, he drew a deep draw and replied, "I'm having a smoke with Sir Francis Bacon." Dr. Baxter retired as a television celebrity, reciting his classes on the air that I had the opportunity to attend in person.

Dr. William Davenport was a rakish professor of English literature. He would break down H. L. Mencken and other modern writers of the time, contrasting old literature to its application in current times. Clara Berenger, a former silent film writer and actress and one of the first faculty members at U.S.C., taught cinema classes based on insight, technique, and invaluable experience. I wrote stories and potential movie scripts, and Mrs. Berenger gave me positive encouragement on plots and effort but was frustrated by my spelling and faulty sentence structure. No computer class can give you the personal relationship you have when being taught in the presence of teachers who are knowledgeable and experienced in their field.

Because I lacked a desire for alcohol, I had sent Elaine most of my Navy paychecks, and we had saved $5,000 by the time I got home. While in school, I bought a lot on the west side of Los Angeles in a neighborhood called Cheviot Hills, for $3,500. My dad, who was a builder, helped me build a house. I had a mortgage and a child, and in order to secure a job after graduation, I switched my major from cinema to education, after my experience as the education officer in my squadron.

Upon my graduation, I was called to the admissions office in a panic. I was informed that I had not met the proper entrance requirements for college and was asked how I managed to get in. With thousands of veterans enrolling in school at that time, I must have gotten lost in the paperwork. My transcripts showed that I was short of science, math, and foreign language credits. Again I pleaded my case. I told them I understood that the entrance requirements were necessary in order to ensure that those applying were capable of doing college work, but since I had proved I could do it my transcripts were a moot issue. I then learned of a petition procedure that I could file to eliminate my missing entry credentials. My petition was granted, and I became a proud graduate of U.S.C.

Elaine and I had three children, Robert, Kitty, and Peggy. I taught five years in elementary and adult education and found the bell ringing for classes very confining. When my best friend, Bud Plone, came home from the Navy and built his own home, we went into business together as general contractors and became qualified architects in a fulfilling, creative life. As a running joke, when we were driving to a job, one of us would announce, "My God, we left the safe open." The other would respond, "Why are you worried, we're both here!" From the time I met Bud in junior high school to our flying career in the Navy to being in a lifelong business partnership, we never had an argument.

Cocooned in my college education, I always wondered about all the other veterans home from the war. How did the young ensigns and lieutenants enter civilian life from their status as young officers, controlling aircraft, tanks, ships, logistics, and the life-and-death decisions they made for their squads and platoons? How did they blend into a peaceful society as salesmen, apprentices, craftsmen, entrepreneurs? The war taught our men to kill. The GI Bill taught our men to live successful lives. To all who wanted, it gave the opportunity to become teachers, engineers, doctors, dentists, accountants, and any profession of their choice, to enter American society as educated, knowledgeable citizens who contributed to the greatness of America. With their education and professional skill, and their ability to pay taxes, they became part of an enriched middle class, acquiring the means to purchase homes, furnishings, cars, and goods and to be a part of a flourishing economy in which all classes of America enjoyed an upgraded standard of living. This new generation thrived, and desired their children to follow them and to complete their college educations and to pursue careers beyond their own. Education was the key, and the GI Bill opened the door to millions who could not have possibly achieved their goals at that time on their own. I was proud to be a part of my great generation. I am distressed at the cost of college and the restrictive loans and hurdles that thwart the present college hopefuls.

Elaine and I are still in our starter home, slightly remodeled with an added pool. The lot on its own, without the house, is now worth over one million dollars. I still like the old days.

I have lived these ninety-plus years with relatively few physical problems and still with the girl whose picture I carried in my flight jacket pocket. Becoming a naval aviator was my proudest achievement. I'm still a strong supporter of the military, but can't understand how our country can send young men and women into undeclared wars. Having a loving family, with mixed religious and ethnic backgrounds, makes me a wealthy man. Getting to this point, I tell all my younger friends not to smoke and to eat wisely, exercise, and take care of yourselves. This way you can get to my age and feel the rewards of growing old. That includes the aches and pains, the need for glasses, checking your prostate, and juggling the confusion of memory. I say, stay healthy, keep your mind sharp, and welcome to the wonders of the "Tarnished Years."

After all this time, I have never forgotten those who never had the chance to live the life I have enjoyed. It was not only my friend Jerry Foreman, shot down in his P-38 over England at age twenty-one. Or Milt Gibson, who predicted his pilot was going to get him killed, and was right. Or the flight I missed by a minute, from which Otho Edwards, Bill Holligan, and James Bistodeau have lain at the bottom of the sea off Formosa since the year of 1945. They represent the thousands I didn't know, who gave their lives for our country.

My fondest recollection? Flying home over the Golden Gate Bridge, banking into the Bay of San Francisco, heading toward the buoys at Alameda. Flaps down, throttling back on the engines, the control tower announcing, "Peter, Bogey, Mike, cleared to land in south seadrome. Over."

"Alameda Tower, Peter, Bogey, Mike, confirmed. Over."

And "Out!"

IF A PBM COULD SPEAK

A longtime gone are the buoys that we once tied up to. Also gone is the thunderous roar of our engines as we skimmed along the top of the water trying to break the suction that bonded us to the surface of the water. We were born in time to participate in that global action known as World War Two. Some of us were chosen to deal death and destruction to the enemy. Others of us were chosen to rescue and save lives. Also, some of us were designated as transports for cargo, mail, etc. Whatever, our chosen task was, we did it well. However, it did not come without a price. Some of our remains are around the globe above and below the oceans surface. Some of us fell by enemy hands, while others of us fell due to the ravishing and unrelenting forces of mother nature. After the war was over, some of us were sold to foreign governments and the rest of us suffered an ignominious fate as we were cut up for our scrap metal. I can still feel the pain as my wings and fuselage were ripped apart and cut into small pieces then fed into the gaping mouth of that hungry furnace to be melted down. The can that holds the beer you are drinking was once a part of one of my wings, and that pot on top of the stove was once a part of my fuselage. I deserved a better fate than that. I had always envisioned that in my retirement I would be languishing in a nice cozy museum where all the people passing by would stop to gaze at my majestic beauty. It didn't turn out that way but I know I will live on for eternity in the hearts and minds of those who loved me.

Peter Askervitch
"Trapper"
December 1944

From *Mainer/Marlin Newsletter,* June 1995, Vol. 12, No. 4